TEACHING AS SCHOLARSHIP

TEACHING AS SCHOLARSHIP
PREPARING STUDENTS FOR PROFESSIONAL PRACTICE IN COMMUNITY SERVICES

Editors:
Jacqui Gingras
Pamela Robinson
Janice Waddell
Linda D. Cooper

WILFRID LAURIER UNIVERSITY PRESS

Wilfrid Laurier University Press acknowledges the support of the Canada Council for the Arts for our publishing program. We acknowledge the financial support of the Government of Canada through the Canada Book Fund for our publishing activities. This work was supported by the Research Support Fund.

Library and Archives Canada Cataloguing in Publication

  Teaching as scholarship : preparing students for professional practice in community services / Jacqui Gingras, Pamela Robinson, Janice Waddell, and Linda D. Cooper, editors.

Includes bibliographical references and index.
Issued in print and electronic formats.
ISBN 978-1-77112-143-9 (paperback).—ISBN 978-1-77112-145-3 (epub).—ISBN 978-1-77112-144-6 (pdf)

  1. College teaching. 2. Effective teaching. 3. Learning. I. Gingras, Jacqui, 1969–, editor II. Robinson, Pamela (Pamela J.), [date], editor III. Waddell, Janice, 1955–, editor IV. Cooper, Linda D., [date], editor

LB2331.T38 2016   378.1'2   C2015-905242-4
                      C2015-905243-2

Cover design by Martyn Schmoll. Cover background image: www.istockphoto.com. Text design by Daiva Villa, Chris Rowat Design.

© 2016 Wilfrid Laurier University Press
Waterloo, Ontario, Canada
www.wlupress.wlu.ca

This book is printed on FSC® certified paper and is certified Ecologo. It contains post-consumer fibre, is processed chlorine free, and is manufactured using biogas energy.
Printed in Canada

Every reasonable effort has been made to acquire permission for copyright material used in this text, and to acknowledge all such indebtedness accurately. Any errors and omissions called to the publisher's attention will be corrected in future printings.

No part of this publication may be reproduced, stored in a retrieval system, or transmitted, in any form or by any means, without the prior written consent of the publisher or a licence from the Canadian Copyright Licensing Agency (Access Copyright). For an Access Copyright licence, visit http://www.accesscopyright.ca or call toll free to 1-800-893-5777.

Contents

INTRODUCTION
Teaching as Scholarship: Preparing Students for Professional Practice in Community Services
Jacqui Gingras, Pamela Robinson, Janice Waddell, and Linda Cooper
1

ONE
Interprofessional Education in a Community Services Context: Lessons Learned
Corinne Hart and Sanne Kaas-Mason
9

TWO
The Writing Skills Initiative
V. Logan Kennedy and Sonya Jancar
23

THREE
Learning the Ethic of Care through Family Narratives
Mehrunnisa Ahmad Ali
43

FOUR
The Audacity of Critical Awakening through Intellectual Partnerships
Annette Bailey, Margareth Zanchetta, Gordon Pon, Divine Velasco, Karline Wilson-Mitchell, and Aafreen Hassan
59

FIVE
My Dinners with Tara and Nancy: Feminist Conversations about Teaching for Professional Practice
Kathryn Church
75

SIX
Drawing Close: Critical Nurturing as Pedagogical Practice
May Friedman and Jennifer Poole
89

SEVEN
Educating for Social Action among Future Health Care Professionals
Jacqui Gingras and Erin Rudolph
107

EIGHT
Narrative Reflective Process: A Creative Experiential Path to Personal Knowing in Teaching–Learning Situations
Jasna K. Schwind
137

NINE
Introducing Art into the Social Work Classroom: Tensions and Possibilities
Samantha Wehbi, Susan Preston, and Ken Moffatt
155

Conclusion
Usha George
177

About the Contributors
183

Index
189

Introduction

Teaching as Scholarship: Preparing Students for Professional Practice in Community Services

Jacqui Gingras, Pamela Robinson, Janice Waddell, and Linda Cooper

The nexus for the topics raised in this book is our shared intellectual passion for teaching and learning and our determination to continually examine our classroom practices to ascertain whether they matter and, if they do, then to whom. Over the past decade our commitment to teaching and learning has not wavered. This book invites colleagues and students to join us as we deepen and expand our passion.

Rita Charon, in an opening keynote address about narrative medicine, remarked: "We cannot rely on zeal alone to convey the importance of narrative in medicine." We feel similarly about our passion for teaching and learning. We cannot rely on our shared passion to convey our commitment to what we believe is a necessary and scholarly endeavour: active engagement in the scholarship of teaching and learning. We have taken strategic steps to build upon our zeal so as to anchor our passion in concrete outcomes.

The contributors to this book are both pre- and tenured members in the Faculty of Community Services (FCS) at Ryerson University. The FCS, whose mandate is to "make a positive impact on the community," is home to nine schools that offer a range of undergraduate and graduate programs in Child and Youth Care, Disability Studies, Early Childhood Studies, Midwifery, Nursing, Nutrition, Occupational and Public Health, Social Work, and Urban and Regional Planning. Clearly, the FCS is a "big tent" with programs teaching students everything from designing cities to delivering babies! Yet all nine schools share the imperative of using theory to inform practice in ways that make a difference—on the ground, in real places, with real people facing real problems—by seizing real opportunities. Finding new ways to bring research and practice down to the community scale for learners is one focus of the book; another relates to taking a new approach to thinking about teaching.

In 2005, a small but intrepid group founded a research centre whose principal focus was the scholarship of teaching and learning (SoTL). The Centre for the Advancement of the Scholarship of Teaching and Learning (CASTL) was initially funded through the Dean's Office of the FCS. The initial funds were used to build a website, to hire a research assistant, and to attend SoTL conferences. Very soon after, the group initiated a partnership with the Carnegie Foundation and for three years worked with it to "build SoTL communities" among an international group of like-minded individuals. One outcome of that partnership was a special issue of the journal *Transformative Dialogues*, in which we wrote specifically about how our relationship with Ryerson University afforded us a "watershed moment" in the growth of our centre (Robinson et al., 2009). Since that time, we have continued to make inroads; our latest accomplishment has been to persuade our university to acknowledge the importance of scholarly teaching in its strategic plan.

To expand on this: CASTL was developed to highlight teaching and learning strategies for our colleagues to reflect upon, critique, adapt, implement, revise, and disseminate. In the context of Ryerson University (a polytechnic that became university in 1993), teaching remained the central "business" of many faculty members even though the impetus to focus on research was strengthening. Our aim was to position SoTL as a means for teaching and research to happen simultaneously; this would elevate SoTL as a legitimate and visible form of inquiry. In our minds and in our everyday practices, we knew that SoTL was a meaningful and evidence-based way to integrate the often clashing endeavours of teaching and research. By advancing teaching *and* learning while at the same time drawing on the principles of rigorous scholarship, mid-career scholars could enliven research programs and solidify Ryerson University's culture as one that achieved excellence in both areas simultaneously.

As academics in professional schools, we all lead busy lives with no end of curious, interesting, and sometimes mandatory requests for our time. From its inception, we the editors and authors of this book have asked ourselves, "Why does this book matter?" Many of this book's authors were part of CASTL's collaboration with the Carnegie Foundation's SoTL initiative. This collaboration brought together educators from across North America to build capacity for taking scholarly approaches to teaching and learning. Now, some eight years later, the momentum for taking scholarly approaches to teaching continues to build across campuses in North America. In this regard, this book is a contribution to a growing body of literature emerging from post-secondary education scholars about their craft of teaching.

Yet there remains, in some less forward-looking institutions, the notion that those who teach well do not do research and that strong researchers don't have time for teaching. This book deliberately pushes back on the notion that engaged teachers are not excellent researchers. Many of its authors and editors hold or have held National Research Council grants to fund their research, and for most of them these research grants have had a community focus. But these grants are not directly related to teaching. The authors gathered in this book are notable because besides being successful in "traditional" research contexts, they have brought the same analytical approach to their teaching. This book, then, illustrates myriad ways to be scholarly when facilitating students' education.

The world is changing, and this book speaks to the ways in which education must adapt to these changes. This book will make it clear that in our changing world, people are changing, and thus the ways in which professionals engage with people and their needs must change as well. New methods of care and practice will lead to more nuanced approaches to meeting people's needs. The multitude of methods used in this book to assess teaching reinforce the collective imperative to innovate in the face of change. This book clearly signals that "one size does not fit all." Homogeneity is not the solution in a quickly changing world.

Choosing a title for a book is a challenging but important task. Here the editorial team opted for a plain language title that clearly signals that educators who teach in professional programs with a community focus will find this book relevant to their teaching *and* their scholarship. From the start, the editors of this book strived to solicit contributions from colleagues who took a scholarly approach to their teaching. Faculty members keen to add new teaching tools to their educators' tool kit will gain much from reading this book, but it takes a deeper approach to the practice of reflecting on teaching. The contributing authors strive to bring the same rigour and assessment deployed in their research to their own assessments of teaching. Creative educators are always keen to share new and creative ways of teaching, and scholarly educators ask questions like "How do we know this new approach is working?," "What improvements would we make when we do it next time?," and "Who else has facilitated a similar approach?" At the FCS, faculty members are encouraged to bring the same reflection to their teaching as to their research. In taking a scholarly approach to their teaching, the book's authors deploy different but rigorous methods in different contexts; here in their contributions, they share scholarly reflections about how to take the ongoing practice of teaching to higher or deeper levels. Each chapter in this book speaks to the need to connect theory with community practice, but this scale of impact could easily be replaced with "everyday life," thus expanding the community of educators who could learn from the reflections here. Consistently, as well, the authors reflect on how they engage their students in the process of moving from the abstract to the practical. Those of us who are inclined towards scholarly approaches to teaching have benefited from the previous contributions of others sharing a similar passion. This book adds new voices that raise important questions about teaching.

In planning this book, the editors identified key areas that they hoped the authors would address as well as emerging concepts and practices. Our call for proposals was broad, and as we reviewed abstracts, we carefully noted, and selected for reflexive critique, innovative and creative teaching practices as well as learner-centred approaches (Weimer, 2002). Essential to all of this was our call for prospective contributors to include a practical acknowledgement of how their proposal drew from and contributed to the scholarship of teaching and learning (McKinney, 2007).

After reviews were received from the publisher with a common request to emphasize our conceptualization of teaching scholarship and for this conceptualization to be reflected in each of the chapters to establish a more explicit framing, we invited all the authors to meet in a workshop setting to discuss how to proceed with this request. The discussion was recorded and transcribed and has helped shape how we conceived of our individual and collective work. Bringing the authors together created a space for a lively and passionate discussion about teaching, teaching scholarship, and the wisdom (hotly challenged) of putting forward a singular conceptualization of this phenomenon. One author stated:

> I had three questions, which were: what is the politics of the book, why are these chapters part of that conversation, and what are the tensions between them? We are all haunted by different kinds of dilemmas, and so is the teaching practice.

Another author addressed how to conceptualize teaching in an institution where constraints and contradictions existed:

> I think it's just about having a different conception of teaching than what we've been told is teaching. And, when I say we've been told, I'm talking about those higher-education processes and those neoliberal processes, that define our education or our work as educators as

labour to feed the economy. I think that is partly what we're critiquing, by and large, in our understanding of the role that we're doing here. And, we only enlarge that understanding by looking at the work we're doing, as teaching as actually part of something different, than just I go into the classroom, I teach people to come out and be social workers. It's about enlargement of teaching, it's not about developing something new...I'm thinking, of course, of the context of higher education and how that's changing, and all of those influences. But, it's about naming those debates, and that's a reflexive concept. But, naming those debates, and where we engage with those debates.

Another colleague followed with:

This is a very spirited FCS reflection on the thing that people do across universities, and this is a very FCS book that has emerged from a quirky university in downtown Toronto with a diverse student body with a plurality of faculty members. And, so when asked what is it that binds this volume the traditional academic response would be that it is a theoretical framework of the scholarship of teaching and learning. A more apt response for this book is that it is the collective experience of faculty members working in FCS, a community of practice that is messy, but also very thoughtful and critical.

The outcome of the impassioned discussion of our collective conceptualization of the scholarship of teaching and learning was a commitment to what one author referred to as "troubling the notion of coherence." Rather than striving to create coherence, the editors and authors have compiled a volume with the real intention of honouring the spirit of the debate. This book serves as a rallying cry to get out of the armchair and into the fray. It is a compilation of active and ongoing reflections about scholarly teaching. The threads of resistance and rebellion add depth to the critical reflections on the scholarship of teaching and learning. Its authors are not educational bystanders; they relay situations in which the professional becomes more actively connected to the delivery of the care and new intellectual partnerships between students and faculty blur previously formal distinctions between the two. The new roles that faculty members take when delivering innovative approaches to community-services-related learning sometimes lead to awkward and difficult situations that need to be considered and addressed. The frontiers here are not neat, formulaic, or easy to navigate, yet the findings signal the importance of forging ahead with scholarly reflection. This book provides space for an important conversation about post-secondary education.

The nine chapters are organized according to what they offer and reflect in terms of their contributions to SoTL. The first section privileges "narrative" and the second "pedagogy and curriculum"; the third describes specific initiatives underpinned by SoTL. Throughout each chapter it is interesting to note that the educators/authors use language that conveys a deep belief that they are doing something different and important. Bailey and colleagues write about audacity, and Friedman and Poole share their "radical act." This book's authors are seeking to reposition how universities think about and deliver impactful education. Yet they also delineate the challenges of taking these approaches in terms of emotional, intellectual, time, and capital investments. These messages need to reach members of tenure and promotion committees and people in positions of administrative leadership. To reap the benefits of scholarly approaches to teaching at the level of communities, faculty members are taking risks and making investments. This is not a book about the educational paths most easily, efficiently, or inexpensively taken, Rather, it offers important insights for those assessing the progress of new faculty members and those making strategic decisions about the directions universities might take.

Increasingly, pre-tenure faculty are being asked to keep teaching dossiers as part of their submissions for tenure and promotion. In some universities, the offices of teaching and learning provide supports for dossier development; in others, the teaching dossier is a submission that faculty members are left to fumble through on their own with the help of "how to" sites on the Internet. This book, chapter by chapter and as a whole, is a touchstone for pre-tenure faculty members striving to develop scholarly approaches to their teaching. The metaphor of the choir applies to this book: here you have different people "singing together" a choral piece advocating for scholarly and impactful approaches to teaching. Each chapter, or section of the choir, has a different role and a different way of contributing, but the sum of the whole is a composition that hangs together. Yet those of us who have served on tenure and promotion committees know that individual faculty members position their work in myriad ways. This book resists calls to harmonize approaches to the scholarship of teaching and learning. For pre-tenure faculty members working on teaching dossiers, this book could prove instructive because of the range of voices it combines to reflect upon scholarly approaches to teaching.

A guiding question for all the contributors was "How is an educator going to use this chapter?" Faculty who teach in fields with a professional and/or community focus will find this book directly relevant to their work. But this book also speaks to wider and more specific audiences. In Canada, universities do not hold a monopoly on education that seeks to impact communities. Many people in community colleges and other community settings train students and collaborate with universities. In this book, the authors engage in ethical debates related to framing education that can have a real impact. These reflections bear consideration outside universities as places of learning. We hope the conversations here will inspire other educators to be scholarly in their assessments of teaching. The disciplinary content might be different, but the reflections and perspectives are relevant to any context. Your feedback will determine our success.

We have also endeavoured to contribute practical suggestions for putting the ideas arising from each chapter into action in real classrooms. Adapt and implement the ideas to suit your particular context, and share with others the outcomes of that process. The sharing through informal and formal avenues is crucial as we continue to weave together the results of our impassioned and reflexive inquiry in the name of superb scholarly teaching across disciplines and professions. Our students expect nothing less.

Acknowledgements

We acknowledge the ongoing support of Dr. Usha George, Dean of the Faculty of Community Services, who understood and championed our idea for this book from the beginning and then added her wisdom to the volume by contributing a final thematic chapter. Judy Britnell was instrumental in the review process and kept the project moving forward amid busy academic schedules. Our CASTL associates contributed their perspectives on the proposed book's theme and continued to maintain the energy of our centre during the book's production. Finally, we thank the contributors and the publisher for their enthusiastic commitment to this book.

References

McKinney, K. (2007). *Enhancing learning through the scholarship of teaching and learning.* Bolton, MA: Anker.

Robinson, P., Gingras, J., Cooper, L., Waddell, J., & Davidge, E. (2009). SoTL's watershed moment: A critical turning point for Ryerson University. *Transformative Dialogues: Teaching and Learning Journal*, 3(1). [Available: http://kwantlen.ca/TD/TD.3.1/TD.3.1.6_Ryerson_SoTLs_Watershed_Moment.pdf]

Weimer, M. (2002). *Learner-centered teaching: Five key changes to practice.* New York: John Wiley and Sons.

1

Interprofessional Education in a Community Services Context: Lessons Learned

Corinne Hart and Sanne Kaas-Mason

Introduction

Over the past decade, notions of interprofessional collaborative practice and care have become increasingly embedded into the discourse of a range of health and social service professions. Within this, interprofessional education (IPE) has been identified as a key strategy for supporting the development of practitioners who have the skills and competencies to engage in the type of collaborative teamwork that is at the heart of interprofessional practice. While some of the focus has been on shifting the practice of existing health care professionals, much attention has been placed on the education of pre-licensure students. Indeed, there is a common assumption within the health professions that pre-licensure students who have structured opportunities to "learn with, from and about" other professions (CAIPE, 2002) will develop the requisite competencies for interprofessional collaborative practice.

While there is a robust literature related to the substance of interprofessional education, there has been only minimal focus on the pedagogy that underlies IPE. Other than reference to competency frameworks, there is little in the literature that either examines the underlying educational approaches to interprofessional education or discusses and debates how pedagogical decisions can inform the development of IPE. Yet if interprofessional education is to be a legitimate scholarly endeavour, rather than merely a strategy for shifting the dynamics of practice, it must move beyond its current focus on competencies, toward a more critical discussion of its pedagogical underpinnings.

This chapter contributes to the scholarly discussion around interprofessional education. Drawing on the experiences of Ryerson University, it describes and discusses how the principles of critical pedagogy were used to develop and support *RU Interprofessional*, the IPE initiative at Ryerson University. In doing so, this chapter illustrates how a critical pedagogical approach can support internal consistency between the strategies and activities of interprofessional education and the structures and values of the context in which it is located. In doing so, it supports arguments for shifting the discourse of interprofessional education to incorporate a pedagogical model that more overtly includes critical reflection and analysis of the social, political, and historical factors that inform both professional and interprofessional practice.

Background – IPE as a Teaching Strategy for Interprofessional Practice

Over the past decade there has been a tremendous drive to increase access to interprofessional education both inside and outside the academy. Underlying this is the assumption that integrating interprofessional education into undergraduate programs, when students are still developing their own professional identities and values, will support a shift from traditional models of care whereby each profession remains entrenched, its own professional lens, toward practice frameworks that allow for more fluid boundaries across professional perspectives (Abrams, 2012; Gilbert, 2010; Hinderer & Joyner, 2014; Sakai et al., 2012; Willison, 2008). In Canada, this belief was the impetus, in 2007, for Health Canada to fund the Accreditation of Interprofessional Health Education (AIPHE) initiative, to ensure that standards for interprofessional education are integrated into the accreditation programs for the professions of physiotherapy, occupational therapy, pharmacy, social work, nursing, and medicine (Health Canada, 2009). In Ontario, the potential for IPE to enable a shift in health care practice led HealthForceOntario and the Ministry of Training, Colleges, and Universities to fund six universities with medical and allied health professional schools in 2006–7 and then two years later to extend this funding to additional universities and colleges with health- and social-service-related programs. Ryerson University was in the second round of funding. In keeping with its strong history of interdisciplinary teaching and learning, the funding was tied to the Faculty of Community Services (FCS).

Tying the funding to the FCS created a unique context for delivering interprofessional education. Like many broad-based faculties in other academic institutions, the FCS is not a single entity but rather an umbrella group that includes the Schools of Nursing, Midwifery, Nutrition, Early Childhood Studies, Child and Youth Care, Social Work, Disability Studies, Urban and Regional Planning, and Occupational and Public Health. As such, the FCS not only prepares students to practise in health care settings where interprofessional practice and care is part of the institutional discourse, but also is home to disciplines that do not self-identify as traditional professions, let alone health professions. Within this, a number of the schools are grounded in an anti-oppression framework that challenges both traditional notions of "professional" and the power dynamics that so often occur in health care practice and policy, and many of the schools incorporate principles of critical theories into their curricula. Additionally, Ryerson—the FCS in particular—has deep roots in interdisciplinary education, which on the surface has many similarities with IPE, in that both focus on teaching and learning across professional boundaries. IPE at Ryerson would have to reflect this unique context.

As FCS is steeped in a critical lens, it was obvious that we could not simply import IPE into our setting without understanding its assumptions and exploring how and where it could fit into our institutional context. There was little (at least at the time) that problematized the assumptions of IPE in general or its value as an educational approach. Rather, it seemed to be taken for granted that IPE was an integral strategy for developing interprofessional practice and should therefore be part of pre-licensure health profession education. As such, most of the literature was descriptive, centring on discussing various curriculum- and practice-based interprofessional activities and programs (Cullen, Fraser, & Symonds, 2003; Gordon & Ward, 2005; Ladden et al., 2006), the importance of competency development for interprofessional practice (Barr, 1998; D'Amour et al., 2004; Thistlethwaite & Nisbet, 2007), appreciation for other professions (Cooke et al., 2003), issues of professional identity (Adams et al., 2006), and challenges of integrating IPE into professional curricula (Barrett, 2003; Davidson et al., 2008). Additionally, and especially relevant for the FCS, the IPE discourse was to this point in time focused primarily on the education and practice of health care professions such as medicine, nursing, and occupational and physical therapy. It had not yet been broadly extended into education in disciplines whose history, dynamics, philosophy of practice, and practice environments differed substantively from those of traditional health care practitioners. We therefore felt that to integrate interprofessional education into our context, it was important for us to consider where within the FCS it fit. As we began to consider our options, using critical pedagogy as an overarching guide made intuitive sense.

A Critical Approach to IPE Curriculum Development

Critical pedagogy draws from the work of Paulo Freire, who saw critical education as a primary tool to address social inequalities by exposing ways in which ideology constructs and maintains dominant discourse (Giroux, 2011; Kincheloe, 2008). Central to his work is the idea of *conscientization*, or the raising of critical consciousness as a primary step toward transformative action (Freire, 1973). A critical pedagogy similarly focuses on encouraging learners to deconstruct the ways in which information, language, and taken-for-granted wisdom are shaped by the social, cultural, political, and historical context in which they occur. In the health field, critical pedagogy has been used successfully in the area of health education (Matthews, 2014). As such, a critical pedagogical approach was relevant to our context, for it is grounded in the values of collaboration, social justice, and equity—which are central to the FCS—besides making relations of power explicit. Critical pedagogy also encourages engagement in praxis: the "reflection and action upon the world in order to transform it" (Freire, 1970, p. 38) that underpins the practice of many FCS schools.

A critical approach includes multiple perspectives and voices. As a primary step, we therefore created a steering committee with representation from both the FCS schools and the School of Continuing Studies, where the current interdisciplinary courses are located. This committee included people who were already interested in and supportive of IPE, those who were uncomfortable with the idea, and several who were still unsure of the value of interprofessional education. To ensure that we acknowledged and drew on existing expertise, the steering committee also included faculty members who had been integral to the implementation and delivery of interdisciplinary teaching and learning over the past two decades. This group was tasked with guiding the direction that interprofessional education at Ryerson would take.

A basic premise of the *conscientization* inherent in critical pedagogy is that change cannot happen without knowledge (consciousness) about factors in the environment that support, constrain, and challenge the ability to move forward. Thus, we needed to understand our historical, social, and political environment and know where the supports and tensions might lie. So we began with an environmental scan of our internal and external environments. Within Ryerson this included extensive interviews with the directors and chairs of each of the FCS schools and with most of those faculty members who had been instrumental in the development and delivery of interdisciplinary teaching and learning over the past two decades. The external scan involved an Internet search and analysis of interprofessional education activities in other academic institutions and formal and informal discussions with a wide range of people involved in IPE in Toronto and across the province.

While the external scan was valuable for showing various academic models for interprofessional education and for creating a presence in the IPE community, it was the internal scan that more directly supported the contextual development of interprofessional education at Ryerson, for it made overt both institutional and social factors that could challenge and support our work. Structurally, the scan showed that even with the full support of the FCS, the way that workloads were distributed and tenure and promotion assessed, as well as the curriculum model in use at Ryerson, constrained both the ease with which faculty could teach across disciplines and the opportunities for students to take courses outside their own school. The scan also foreshadowed some of the less tangible challenges we would face as it brought to the fore a number of philosophical and organizational questions related to IPE more broadly.

The process of doing the environmental scan cannot be overemphasized. It provided us with essential knowledge about institutional supports and barriers and indicated where we would find immediate and potential allies and detractors; it also uncovered tensions inherent in interprofessional education and practice that in 2008 had not received much attention in the literature. We knew these tensions had to be unpacked and addressed before we could feel confident that what we were doing was academically sound and philosophically congruent. The process and outcome of the scan pushed us to think critically about interprofessional education, challenge some of its assumptions, and reflectively and deliberately create interprofessional education that fit the values and structures of our own environment. In doing so, it also highlighted the value of a critical pedagogical approach to IPE more broadly.

What's in a Name: Unpacking the 'Professional' in 'Interprofessional'

As we found ourselves consistently trying to explain what we meant by interprofessional education and how this was different from the "interdisciplinary" teaching and learning that already existed, we quickly discovered that words matter. Indeed, while the idea of collaboration resonated with everyone we spoke to, the word "interprofessional" did not. For some faculty, the "professional" part of "interprofessional" was in many ways antithetical to how they saw themselves and their practice, so they were uncomfortable with the idea of IPE. A critical first step, therefore, was to unpack and explicate what we were talking about.

We began by deconstructing the words "profession" and "professional" as the central underpinnings of the term "interprofessional." While the online Oxford dictionary (2014) describes a professional as "a person engaged in a specified activity...as a main paid occupation rather than as a pastime," this is a simplistic view. Indeed, the notion of professional is imbued with historical, social, and political implications that on the surface seem incongruous with the assumptions of interprofessional education and practice. Even a cursory review of the sociology of the professions shows professions to be inherently exclusionary and non-collaborative, for specialized knowledge, autonomy, authority, and privilege (Freidson, 1970; Hodson & Sullivan, 2012)—the hallmarks of a profession—necessarily separate those who belong from those who do not. Exclusion and siloing have been especially apparent in the medical and health care professions, where power dynamics have historically been at the centre of relationships between medicine and other health professions. Drawing on Weberian notions of social closure (Weber, 1968), writers such as Freidson (1970) and Witz (1992) have described how the health professions assert and maintain professional power and legitimacy by applying strategies of professional closure to demarcate their territory and to set boundaries around their knowledge and skill.

For schools steeped in a framework of anti-oppression, in which a fundamental value is to challenge dominant power relationships, the idea of "profession" was inherently problematic. A number of faculty members expressed concern that since the assumptions of both a profession and a professional implicitly perpetuate traditional power dynamics, the term inter*professional*ism inevitably implies a top-down, non-collaborative, expert-driven approach. Questions were raised about who would (and could) be part of interprofessional education and whether IPE could include disciplines that do not belong to a regulated profession or that define themselves outside a conventional professional lens. Equally important were concerns about the place of the client in an interprofessional context: a focus on the notions of "profession" and "interprofessional" seemed to take the client out of the mix. More broadly, concerns were raised about the congruence between the assumptions of a profession and the values of collaboration that are so integral to all FCS Schools; indeed, there was unease around whether the "professional" in interprofessional could truly be reconciled with a collaborative approach.

It is relevant to note that this unease was not without substance. While at the time, there was little in the literature to confirm or challenge these concerns, more recent literature suggests that even the discourse of interprofessional education, with its focus on shared leadership and collaborative practice, has not been able to mitigate issues of power and dominance across professional relationships. Kuper and Whitehead (2012), for example, have argued that rather than helping to level power dynamics, IPE may instead perpetuate traditional notions of physician dominance, while Lake, Colquhoun, and Lee (2009) illustrate how nurses' discursive language in an online IPE program created and maintained their professional dominance. Salhani and Coulter (2009) similarly describe how, in practice, nurses use myriad forms of power to gain control over their own work and increase and protect their professional jurisdiction.

Besides philosophical concerns with the idea of professional, there was the more practical need to differentiate between interprofessional and "interdisciplinary." This was not simply a matter of semantics, for how these were defined could have financial and resource implications for both IPE and the existing interdisciplinary program. It was crucial that we articulate what we meant by interprofessional education right from the start, so that it would not become, or be perceived to be, an exercise in either "reinventing the interdisciplinary wheel" with a different name or attempting to usurp an existing program.

A final concern related to the integrity of promoting interprofessional education as the *sine qua non* for interprofessional practice without evidence of its enduring impact. The relatively recent integration of interprofessional education into professional education meant that research had not yet tracked the long-term impact of pre-licensure interprofessional education on either individual or collaborative team practice. Indeed, despite the increasing popularity of IPE, the literature has identified difficulties moving from education to professional practice (Baxter & Brumfitt, 2008; Caldwell & Atwall, 2003). We needed to assure ourselves that interprofessional discourse was not merely a rhetorical device that deflected entrenched power dynamics and that put the onus on individual practitioners to "play together in the sandbox," but rather signified a true commitment to systemic change. This was especially important, for we did not want to inadvertently disempower students by promoting an approach that would not be reproducible or sustainable in practice. While we could provide internal supports and commitment, we could not guarantee that these would exist outside the Ryerson context.

The process of unpacking the concept of interprofessionalism and identifying its inherent tensions was pivotal to developing a clearer vision for our interprofessional initiative and its individual strategies and activities. Raising our own consciousness by gaining insight into where the frictions lay allowed us to understand when to be pragmatic and when to challenge the status quo. As a consequence of this process, we decided that while we could extend notions of interprofessional education through the substance of our activities and strategies, it was also important that our framework be recognizable as interprofessional education. Being part of the broader IPE community would provide legitimacy and a seat at the provincial interprofessional table. Aligning with accepted principles of IPE would also support our students, many of whom would be working in settings where interprofessional practice was embedded in the institutional philosophy and goals.

Integrating a Critical Lens into a Competency-Based Framework

We decided to use the CAIPE (2002) definition—"Two or more professions learning with, from and about each other to improve collaboration and the quality of care"—to describe interprofessional education at Ryerson. However, to better reflect the Ryerson context, and to acknowledge that not all schools provided "care," we extended the definition to include "quality of *service* and/or care." To further locate our initiative in a recognizable interprofessional context, we drew on the competency framework then being developed by the Canadian Interprofessional Health Collaborative (CIHC) as the overarching structure for *RU Interprofessional*. Although we had reservations about the congruence of a competency framework with a critical approach, upon examining this framework in the context of the FCS mission and vision, we were able to see how it aligned with FCS values. Indeed, the six competency domains outlined in the document (interprofessional communication; patient/client/family/community-centred service/care; role clarification; team functioning; collaborative leadership; and interprofessional conflict resolution) and the CIHC's acknowledgement that interprofessional competencies involve "the ability to integrate the knowledge, skills, attitudes and values shaping judgments" (CIHC, 2010) supported the key principles as well as critical thinking, both of which are fundamental to ethical, collaborative practice. Equally important, the CIHC framework acknowledged that IPE on its own would not create a sustainable shift in practice but rather "interprofessional collaborative practice requires a consistent culture between learning and practice" (CIHC, 2010, p. 9). The recognition that education did not occur in a vacuum enabled us to reconcile using the framework as part of a critical pedagogical approach.

RU Interprofessional was ultimately underpinned by a conventional definition and competency framework. However, the route to arriving at that point needs to be noted carefully. In the end, what was most important was not the framework we chose but rather the process we followed to arrive at it. A critical pedagogical approach deliberately guided us to carefully consider the potential of each decision we made for creating an IPE framework that mirrored our values. Somewhat unexpected was the impact of "real life" interprofessional experience for the steering committee. Reflecting on our own process of working together reassured us that the interprofessional competencies of communication, conflict management, and collaborative decision-making were indeed important. It also provided insight into the types of interpersonal and interprofessional factors that can both challenge and support collaboration across disciplines. In this way, our own experience became part of the information we took forward in developing the specific strategies and activities of *RU Interprofessional*.

Beyond Competencies: Using Critical Pedagogy to Underpin IPE

The Oxford dictionary (2014) defines competence as "the ability to do something successfully or efficiently." The purpose of a competency framework is to identify the cognitive, affective, and/or psychomotor knowledge, skills, and behaviours that are necessary for success in a profession and to articulate the criteria for meeting these (Whiddett & Hollyforde, 1999). Competency frameworks have been integral to educational programs for a wide range of professions and are especially common in the health professions, where they are often used to define the benchmarks of safe practice (Balmer, 2012; Englander, Cameron, & Ballard, 2013; Gruppen, Mangrulkar, & Kolars 2012; Hendry, Lauder, & Roxburgh, 2007). The CIHC National Competency Framework moves beyond a uniprofessional lens to identify joint competencies for interprofessional practice.

Notwithstanding the value of a competency framework for safe practice, a critical approach extends the discussion by pushing learners to recognize that factors beyond knowledge, skill, and behaviour influence and indeed shape practice. Thus instead of attributing interprofessional conflict to poor communication, and focusing on strengthening competencies related to communication, a critical approach leads learners to first consider how external factors such as the stress of staffing shortages, processes that limit participation, and the legacy of traditional hierarchical relationships might be contributing to conflict. A critical approach also encourages learners to think beyond behaviour by explicitly integrating issues of power into interprofessional education.

Embedding a critical approach began with our name. Marketing theory states that a name is an important branding tool as it offers a public expression of what a project is and how it wants to be known (Hillenbrand et al., 2013). As an added benefit, a unique name would differentiate IPE from the existing interdisciplinary teaching and learning and help separate the two. We ultimately decided that *RU Interprofessional: Collaborating for Healthy Communities (RU IP)* best described our initiative. *RU*, the commonly used acronym for Ryerson University, located us clearly in the Ryerson context. Incorporating *Collaborating for Healthy Communities* into the name was intended to emphasize our values of collaboration, health, and the community focus shared by all FCS Schools.

While the name was important, it would only be window dressing if we did not then enact our values in our strategies and activities. It was here, at the point of engagement with IPE, that a critical pedagogy could have the greatest impact. To this end, all of the curricular components of *RU Interprofessional* were created to support the development of interprofessional competencies and encourage students to reflect on the influence of social, structural, and historical factors on interprofessional practice.

For example, a two-part online simulation was developed. It is both a strategy for teaching the interprofessional competencies of role definition, communication, conflict management, and interprofessional leadership and a means of guiding students to identify and consider power and power relationships. In the first segment, which focuses on the overt and covert power dynamics influencing an interprofessional committee tasked with developing a revitalization process, students are directed to think about how factors such as interprofessional mix, facilitation style, verbal and non-verbal communication, and even seating arrangements affect how power is created and enacted. The second segment includes community members in the planning process and leads learners to similarly examine how an interprofessional team can inadvertently further marginalize an already vulnerable individual. Issues of power are also openly incorporated into the student workshops that support *RU IP* year-long interprofessional placements. In these workshops, students talk about the power relationships and dynamics among their various professions and identify how these might affect how they communicate with and trust one another. They subsequently examine interpersonal, interprofessional, and organizational factors that contribute to conflict and then identify and explore the tensions between the theory of interprofessional practice and the realities they experience. Throughout the workshops and in practice settings, students are encouraged to critically reflect on how interactions among the external environment (structures, processes, and policies in their placement), their own professional lens, and practice requirements and interprofessional power dynamics support and challenge collaboration across professions. These principles are further extended into a series of IPE workshops, which address topics such as "walkable communities," communicable diseases, and caring for a child and family with cancer. All of the workshops are designed to explore each topic from multiple perspectives and to include discussion on how factors such as power, ethics, and professional expertise can affect collaboration. In this way, the principles of critical pedagogy help students learn to think beyond the individual and to appreciate the complex nature of interprofessional practice.

Where Do We Go from Here?

As interprofessional education and practice are increasingly entrenched as the norm in both academic and practice environments, it is vital that we deepen the scholarship of the discourse. In particular, we need to more purposefully question the assumptions of IPE and examine and debate the pedagogical underpinnings of our interprofessional learning strategies and activities. This chapter contributes to this discussion through its discussion of critical pedagogy.

A critical pedagogical approach is relevant to IPE for a number of reasons. At its most basic, it can be useful as roadmap for developing interprofessional education that fits closely to the values and structures of the institutional setting in which it will be delivered. Our experience suggests that engaging with the notion of *conscientization* can provide the impetus for purposefully uncovering and addressing those factors that might either obstruct or expedite the uptake of IPE. Thus, without comprehending the constraints affecting interdisciplinary teaching and learning, we might have simply re-created these challenges in developing IPE. Similarly, identifying faculty unease allowed us to problematize notions of IPE and then use our new understanding to inform our next steps.

More important, however, is the potential for critical pedagogy to enable and support sustainable, systemic change. There is a growing literature that suggests that despite the best intentions of interprofessional education, issues of power, politics, and institutional factors continue to challenge interprofessional collaborative practice (Baker et al., 2011; McNeil, Mitchell, & Parker, 2013; Miller & Kontos, 2013; Nugus etal., 2010, Zborowsky et al., 2010). When we open the dialogue beyond the individual to include current and historical structures, processes, and relationships, the consciousness raising inherent in critical pedagogy can move IPE forward in a way that a competency framework alone cannot.

This can occur in a number of ways. First, by reminding us that there are factors outside the individual that influence how well the lessons of IPE translate into sustainable behaviour, critical pedagogy may help alleviate some of the tensions that continue to affect interprofessional teams. A focus on competencies suggests that the individual alone is primarily responsible for his or her behaviour within a team. By encouraging a systemic analysis for uncovering the root of interprofessional tensions, critical pedagogy may take some of the onus off the individual and in doing so make practitioners more willing to explore tensions. Common sense suggests that it easier to address something once you know what it is.

A critical pedagogy can also support sustainable change by moving knowledge toward action. Students who learn the importance of and skills for critical analysis, and who recognize that what appears on the surface may not be the problem itself but the outward expression of deeper systemic issues, may be more likely to ask hard questions, challenge assumptions, and seek the type of change that gets at the root of interprofessional tensions. While there is obvious value in developing competencies at the individual level, for IPE to truly become the *sine qua non* of interprofessional practice, it needs to extend its lens; indeed, the long history of interprofessional dynamics cannot be changed without a critical broadening of the interprofessional discourse. Without this, interprofessional education will remain an individual, interpersonal response to systemic tensions and challenges in practice.

References

Abrams, S. E. (2012). The case for interprofessional education. *Public Health Nursing 29*(5), 385–387. doi:10.1111/j.1525-1446.2012.01049.x

Adams, K., Hean, S., Sturgis, P., & Macleod Clark, J. (2006). Investigating the factors influencing professional identity of first year health and social care students. *Learning in Health and Social Care, 5*(2), 55–68. doi 10.1111/j.1473-6861.2006.00119.x

Baker, L., Egan-Lee, E., Martinmianakis, M. A., & Reeves, S. (2011). Relationships of power: Implications for interprofessional education. *Journal of Interprofessional Care* (March 2011), *25*(2), 98–104. doi: 10.3109/13561820.2010.505350

Balmer, J. (2012). Transforming continuing education across the health professions. *Journal of Continuing Education in Nursing, 43*(8), 340–341.

Barr, H. (1998). Competent to collaborate: Towards a competency-based model for interprofessional education. *Journal of Interprofessional Care, 12*, 181–187.

Barrett, G. (2003). Integrating interprofessional education into 10 health and social care programmes. *Journal of Interprofessional Care, 17*(3), 293–301.

Baxter, S. K., & Brumfitt, S. M. (2008). Professional differences in interprofessional working. *Journal of Interprofessional Care, 22*(3), 239–251.

Caldwell, K., & Atwall, A. (2003). The problems of interprofessional healthcare practice in hospitals. *British Journal of Nursing, 12*(20), 1212–1218.

Canadian Interprofessional Health Collaborative. (2010). *A national interprofessional competency framework*. [Available: http://www.cihc.ca/files/CIHC_IPCompetencies_Feb1210.pdf]

Centre for Advancement in Interprofessional Education. (2002). *Defining IPE*. [Available: http://www.caipe.org.uk/resources/defining-ipe]

Competence. (n.d.). In Oxford online dictionary [Available: http://www.oxforddictionaries.com/definition/english/competence]

Cooke, S., Chew-Graham, C., Boggis, C., & Wakefield, A. (2003). "I never realized that doctors were into feelings too": Changing student perceptions through interprofessional education. *Learning in Health and Social Care, 2*(3), 137–146.

Cullen, L., Fraser, D., & Symonds, I. (2003). Strategies for interprofessional team objective structured clinical examination for midwifery and medical students. *Nurse Education Today, 23*(6), 427–433. doi: 10.1016/S0260-6917(03)00049-2

D'Amour, D., Beaulieau, M. D., San Martín Rodríguez, L., & Ferrada-Videla, M. (2004). Chapter 3: *Key elements of collaborative practice & frameworks: Conceptual basis for interdisciplinary practice.* In I. Oandasan, D. D'Amour, M. Zwarenstein, et al. (Eds.), *Interdisciplinary education for collaborative, patient-centred practice*: Research & findings report. Ottawa, ON: Health Canada.

Davidson, M., Smith, R. A., Dodd, K., Smith, J., & O'loughlan, M. (2008). Interprofessional pre-qualification education: A systematic review. *Australian Health Review, 32*(1), 111–120.

Englander, R., Cameron, T., & Ballard, A. (2013). Toward a common taxonomy of competency domain for the health professions and competencies for physicians. *More Academic Medicine, 88*(8), 1088–1094.

Freidson. E. (1970). *Profession of medicine: A study of the sociology of applied knowledge.* Chicago, IL: University of Chicago Press.

Freire, P. (1970). *Pedagogy of the oppressed.* New York, NY: Herder and Herder.

Freire, P. (1973) *Education for critical consciousness.* New York, NY: Seabury Press.

Gilbert, J. (2010). The status of interprofessional education in Canada. *Journal of Allied Health. Suppl. Special issue on interprofessional education and care, 39*(3), 216–223.

Giroux, H. (2011). *On critical pedagogy.* New York, NY: Continuum International Publishing Group.

Gordon, F., & Ward, K. (2005). Making it real: Interprofessional teaching strategies in practice. *Journal of Integrated Care, 13*(5), 42–47.

Gruppen, L. D, Mangrulkar, R. S., and Kolars, J. C. (2012). The promise of competency-based education in the health professions for improving global health. *Human resources for health, 10*(43). doi:10.1186/1478-4491-10-43

Health Canada. (2009). Accreditation of Interprofessional Health Education (AIPHE): Principles and practices for integrating interprofessional accreditation into the accreditation standards for six health professions in Canada. [Available: http://www.cihc.ca/files/complementary/AIPHE_PrinciplesandPracticesGuide_2009.pdf]

Hendry, C., Lauder, W., & Roxburgh, M. (2007). The dissemination and uptake of competency frameworks. *Journal of Research in Nursing, 12*(6), 689–700.

Hillenbrand, P., Alcauter, S., Cervantes, J., & Barrios, F. (2013). Better branding: Brand names can influence consumer choice. *Journal of Product & Brand Management, 22*(4), 300–308.

Hinderer, K. A., & Joyner, R. L. (2014). An interprofessional approach to undergraduate critical care education. *Journal of Nursing Education, suppl. 53*(3), S46–S50.

Hodson, R., and Sullivan, T. A. (2012). *The social organization of work.* Belmont, CA: Wadsworth Publishing Co.

Kincheloe, J. L. (2008). *Knowledge and critical pedagogy: An introduction.* New York, NY: Springer Publishing.

Kuper, A., & Whitehead, C. (2012). The paradox of interprofessional education: IPE as a mechanism of maintaining physician power? *Journal of Interprofessional Care, 26*(5), 347–349. doi: 10.3109/13561820.2012.689382

Ladden, M. D., Bednash, G., Stevens, D. P., & Moore. G. T. (2006). Educating interprofessional learners for quality, safety and systems. *Journal of Interprofessional Care, 20*(5), 497–505.

Lake, J. C. F., Colquhoun, D., & Lee, K. W. (2013). A glimpse into nursing discursive behaviour in interprofessional online learning. *Journal of Nursing Education and Practice, 3*(3), 67–79. doi:10.5430/jnep.v3n3p67

Matthews, C. (2014). Critical pedagogy in health education. *Health Education Journal, 73*(5), 600–609.

McNeil, K. A., Mitchell, R. J., & Parker, V. (2013). Interprofessional practice and professional identity threat. *Health Sociology Review, 22*(3), 291–306.

Miller, K. L., & Kontos, P. (2013). The intraprofessional and interprofessional relations of neurorehabilitation nurses: A negotiated order perspective. *Journal of Advanced Nursing, 69*(8), 1797–1807.

Nugus, P., Greenfield, D., Westbrook, J., Travaglia, J., & Braithwaite, J. (2010). How and where clinicians exercise power: Interprofessional relations in health care. *Social Science & Medicine, 71*(5), 898–909.

Profession (n.d.). In Oxford online dictionary [Available: http://www.oxford dictionaries.com/definition/english/professional]

Sakai, D. H., Marshall, S., Kasuya, R., Wong, L., Deutsch, M., Guerriero, M., ... Omori, J. (2012). Interprofessional education: Future nurses and physicians learning together. *Hawaii Journal of Medicine and Public Health, 71*(6), 166–171.

Salhani, D., & Coulter, I. (2009). The politics of interprofessional working and the struggle for professional autonomy in nursing. *Social Science & Medicine, 68*(7), 1221–1228.

Thistlewaite, J., and Nisbet, G. (2007). Interprofessional education: What's the point and where it's at. *Clinical Teacher, 4*, 67–72.

Weber, M. (1968). *Economy and society.* New York, NY: Bedminster Press.

Whiddett, S., & Hollyforde, S. (1999). *The competencies handbook.* London: Institute of Personnel and Development.

Willison, K. D. (2008). Advancing integrative medicine through interprofessional education. *Health Sociology Review, 17*(4), 342–352.

Witz, A. (1992). *Professions and patriarchy.* London: Routledge.

Zborowsky, T., Bunker-Hellmich, L., Morelli, A., & O'Neill, M. (2010). Centralized vs. decentralized nursing stations: Effects on nurses' functional use of space and work environment. *HERD: Health Environments Research and Design Journal, 3*(4), 19–42.

2

The Writing Skills Initiative

V. Logan Kennedy and Sonya Jancar

Undergraduate students are increasingly being criticized for their poor written work during their academic curriculum and upon graduation. Deficits in writing have been reported by academics and students alike. At the most basic level, writing is the primary means by which students successfully communicate knowledge and understanding throughout their academic careers (National Commission on Writing, 2003). However, the development of writing skills has not been situated historically within academic programs and curricula in higher education. Given the mounting concerns about writing proficiency, the lack of which impedes academic and professional success, how might we move beyond viewing writing skill development as the sole responsibility of students and bring writing into focus within classrooms (Rolfe, 1997; Whitehead, 2002)? And how does instruction in writing skills for students in post-secondary institutions relate to the scholarship of teaching?

The National Commission on Writing (2003) contends that academic institutions need to take immediate action if writing is to be re-established as a priority in higher education. Yet identifying feasible approaches to developing writing skill is a struggle, given that the undergraduate curriculum is reportedly already overextended. Furthermore, inculcating that skill across programs has been perceived as a daunting task (Light, 2003; Vardi, 2009). From technical report writing to engaging in reflective practice, undergraduate students are required not just to develop their writing skills but to do so within the broader expectations of their discipline.

The scholarship of teaching and learning assigns academic leaders and faculty tasks that entail teaching beyond the curriculum. One such task is writing skill development. Inquiring into and understanding the diverse learning needs of undergraduate students is paramount. This chapter describes the implementation of a writing skill development initiative within Ryerson's Faculty of Community Services (FCS) and evaluates this initiative.

Student Writing

Characteristics of the Problem

More attention is now being paid to the current weak state of student writing. Some have begun to explore the root cause(s) of the problem. Many blame students for being ill prepared to meet the expectations placed on them when they begin higher education (Brown et al., 2008; Harklau, Losey, & Siegal, 1999; Leamnson, 1999; National Commission on Writing, 2003). The various challenges undergraduate students face with writing range from spelling and grammar, to coherent and logical presentation of arguments, to adhering to new citation styles (Brown et al., 2008; National Commission on Writing, 2003). First-year writing often falls below the standards established in higher education, and often these shortcomings continue beyond the first year (National Commission on Writing, 2003).

Another possible explanation for poor writing skills is lack of familiarity with the subject matter and lack of preparedness for class; both can impede active engagement in learning (Vardi, 2009). This lack of engagement is sometimes reflected in students' difficulty in conveying their thoughts and in incorporating critical analysis into their writing. Finally, educators who instruct undergraduate students have noted that undergraduate students may struggle to adjust to writing in the context of the discipline being studied (Vardi, 2009).

It is likely that these explanations overlap in ways that create writing problems that students, educators, and administrators must address. The first step towards a resolution is to consider formal writing skill development within the curricular framework of undergraduate education (Grauerholz, 1999; Huang, 2010; McLeod et al., 2009). Since the 1980s, scholars have been arguing that teaching writing should be an integral part of university courses (Cadwallader & Scarboro, 1982). The key question is this: How can we bridge the focus on course content with writing skill development without compromising disciplinary learning? To focus on the development of writing skills would be to treat those skills as distinct from mastery of course content. It is essential, instead, for institutional initiatives to value the disciplinary context of students' writing needs (Light, 2003; Vardi, 2009). The task with the project described in this chapter was to explore writing across the curriculum and not to isolate the development of skill in it from disciplinary learning (Kuh et al., 2005). By bridging disciplinary learning with writing skill development, this initiative set out to prepare students for their professional careers, which were felt to be highly reliant on skilful writing.

The Obstacles

In proposing any initiative that would draw on classroom time, an inherent obstacle is the availability of resources. Workloads and competing demands are already a challenge for faculty and instructors, such that prioritizing writing skill development is simply impossible. Faculty are finding themselves increasingly stretched between the demands of teaching and those of research and scholarship (Jacob & Winslow, 2004). Heavy workloads and competing demands may appear to be obstacles in addressing the writing skills development of undergraduate students, for students will not improve their writing without feedback. However, the literature identifies several alternative sources of writing support for students. Current approaches that are being touted as feasible and effective include the creation of opportunities for feedback on written assignments before submission for evaluation, the use of peer review and peer editing within the classroom, and the development of concurrent skills such as critical thinking and critical reading (Vardi, 2009). Vardi is particularly informative about the importance of an effective feedback mechanism in order for students to develop their writing skills, suggesting that feedback is imperative to improve student writing, regardless of who provides it. This shift from expecting instructors to address student writing deficits, to considering alternative approaches, may be exactly what is needed in order to tackle the issue of student writing. If institutions want student writing to become a priority, substantive solutions that do not draw on already overextended resources will have strong staying power and a greater likelihood of positive impact on student writing skills.

The Missing Information

Glaringly absent from the literature on implementation has been a discussion of the diversity of faculties and academic programs. Research suggests that improving student writing skills has been a focus of business-related academic curricula and of the humanities, but not of community or social service programs (Brown et al., 2008; Fallahi et al., 2006; McLeod et al., 2009). Examples of strategies exist for students preparing for careers in business and humanities, but there is an ongoing shortage of information regarding new approaches for students in other disciplines.

Faculty of Community Services Response

The National Survey of Student Engagement

The National Survey of Student Engagement (NSSE) was introduced in 1998 to institutions interested in gathering information on the quality of student education experiences (Trustees of Indiana University, 2013). The NSSE focuses on the activities in which students are engaged as part of their university education. It asks questions about the volume and the number of drafts of written assignments. Ryerson University's 2006 NSSE data brought the issue of writing skills to the attention of the FCS. The Faculty leadership team became aware of the need to establish a focused writing skill development initiative that could be measured through NSSE results in subsequent years. The FCS wanted students' assessment of the university's role in developing writing skills to indicate a commitment to producing students who are holistically prepared for success following graduation.

As the initiative was organized, it was primarily dedicated to addressing one NSSE question regarding institutional contributions to improving the writing skills of students: Question 11.c—University's contribution to development of skills in writing clearly and effectively. The FCS realized that such an intervention could have a positive impact on other issues concurrently. A writing initiative was also believed to have the potential to raise the profile of effective writing skills as a learning outcome distinct from mastery of course content. A writing intervention was not implemented as a remedial action; rather, it was intended to ensure the development of academic writing skills for students at various levels of writing proficiency.

Creating an Initiative
The decision to take action on writing skill development required leadership from the Dean's Office and the structuring of a Faculty-wide approach. The initiative was named the Writing Skills Initiative (WSI) and was first implemented in September 2008. The purpose of the WSI was to (a) improve the writing skills of first-year undergraduate students in the FCS and (b) increase their access to writing support. The WSI was first made available to all first-year, full-time students. It has since been adjusted to be implemented in any year of an undergraduate program.

Integrating the WSI into the FCS programs entailed supporting each school's needs based on feasibility. The WSI was attached to a core course that all full-time students were required to complete. These core (or required) courses varied according to the school but in general had an introductory theoretical focus within the professional discipline of study. Prior to implementation in 2008, the FCS consulted and strategized with the course faculty who were to lead the WSI in their respective programs. Thus, two versions of the initiative exist. In the first, the WSI is fully delivered during class time, with weekly WSI activities provided during approximately one hour of class time. The second version is used by schools that have found it more practical to hold workshops outside of scheduled lecture hours. Similar content is administered in both versions, depending on the disciplinary needs of the school.

Implementation

The WSI framework

The curricular framework for the WSI was developed under the direction of the dean and associate dean of the FCS. The FCS drew on institutional expertise from each of the participating full-time academic programs as well as various teaching and learning resources on campus, including the Ryerson Learning and Teaching Office (LTO), the Ryerson University Writing Centre, and the Ryerson Experiential Learning Centre. The structured framework as it was developed emphasized that weekly writing activities related to course assignments were to be integral components of the initiative. The development team also recommended that mechanisms for engaging students in discussions and providing timely constructive feedback on written work also be addressed. The framework was named "Writing for Success."

The teaching teams have annually undertaken the task of applying the framework of Writing for Success to their WSI activities and uniquely building the initiative into the requirements listed in course outlines. The focus of the framework is not on producing a generic writing intervention but instead on providing a strong foundation upon which programs can develop a successful initiative. Thus, in the WSI there is no standard of practice regarding how WSI activities are structured or delivered. The emphasis, as previously mentioned, is on developing comprehensive and disciplinary writing skills. In order to create the space for this initiative, creative pedagogies were considered; ultimately it was decided to introduce a novel teaching position.

The WSI Teaching Assistant

With a framework in place, the question became how the initiative could be implemented. It was decided that faculty and course instructors could best be supported to implement the "Writing for Success Framework" through the creation of a unique teaching assistant (TA) role. Unlike conventional classroom TAs, who are course content experts, the WSI TAs had to be experts in teaching English writing. As a member of the team, the WSI TA was expected to facilitate weekly small-group activities, to support students through office hours and tutorials, and to assist instructors in providing timely and helpful detailed feedback on written assignments.

WSI TAs developed content tailored to discipline-specific writing needs while focusing on key principles of academic writing, such as critical reading. The content was designed to be responsive to a range of academic writing skills to ensure that all students could benefit from the initiative. By introducing a TA, the WSI was venturing into unfamiliar territory in regard both to hiring and to how best to integrate the writing TAs into the teaching teams. Of course, early efforts met with trepidation and at times resistance. Few faculty and course instructors understood the pedagogical benefits of a *writing* TA who brought no sense of disciplinary content mastery. Professional experiences of writing within the humanities and the arts were not deemed relevant to community services students. So the introduction of WSI TAs required thoughtful navigation as well as faculty training on writing skill development distinct from course content. WSI leaders had to highlight the commitment to develop discipline-specific writing skills, and they had to elucidate why teaching writing in a formal setting is very different from providing basic feedback on writing. In time, faculty and course instructors have largely come to appreciate the expertise of WSI TAs in teaching writing.

How to Find Writing Teaching Assistants
Given the novelty of the WSI TA role, creative efforts were employed to find suitable candidates for the positions. As WSI TAs were to be hired based on their experience in teaching writing to undergraduate students, a broad network had to be used in order to identify eight exceptional candidates. Since inception, the number of TAs who have participated in this program has been less than twenty, given the high rates of retention. TAs have ranged from Ryerson MA and PhD students, to external graduate students, to individuals who have completed doctoral education. These people have contributed to the success of the WSI by strengthening the framework and by providing insight into the unique scholarship of teaching writing to undergraduate students.

Defining the Writing TA Role
Each WSI TA works within an identified program and becomes an integral member of teaching teams by collaborating to conduct activities throughout the semester. Our experience has been that one of the great successes of the WSI TAs has been to expand developmental feedback on written work. Developmental writing feedback—that is, the comments and critiques offered to a student before they submit a written assignment for grading—allows students to learn and develop prior to evaluative feedback (Vardi, 2009). This form of feedback need not be extensive but it must be precise, as well as linked to the student's work, and close attention must

be paid to the mechanics of writing as well as to accurate citations (Vardi, 2009). This form of feedback was almost non-existent prior to the WSI and remains largely unavailable in unrelated courses. The innovation of hiring TAs who that had no content expertise allowed students to work with these resource people specifically on their writing, with no apprehension that content mastery would be inflated. The overall tasks and responsibilities of each WSI TA were at the discretion of the individuals within the teaching team as long as the framework was taken into account (Table 2.1).

TABLE 2.1
Examples of WSI Teaching Assistant Primary Tasks

Task	Description	Timeline
SUMMER		
Orientation	The orientation will be one day and is mandatory for all TAs. Morning: learning strategists Afternoon: logistics, hours, podium access	July
Meet with Course Faculty Lead	At orientation you will be provided with the contract information of the Faculty Lead for your identified school. Within 48 hours of orientation you are required to initiate contact with the Faculty Lead. The WSI Lead TA should be copied on this email.	July/August
Attend TA Planning Sessions	The details of these sessions will be negotiated with the Lead TA and fellow TAs. These sessions are intended for TA team building, skill building, and Fall preparation. Refer to the Summer Contract for the breakdown of available hours. All TAs must be available to attend each session.	August
FALL		
Determine Writing Sample Dates	Identify the written assignments that will be collected as the Writing Samples with the Lead. Identify the due date for the assignments and provide these dates to the Lead TA.	September
Establish Office Hours	Determine days and times you will be available to meet with students.	September
In Class/Course Specific Responsibilities	The majority if the TA tasks will focus on the Class/Course specific strategies that have been established to facilitate the implementation of the WSI.	Ongoing
Professional Development Activities	Two professional development activities will be scheduled in September. Your attendance at these sessions is mandatory.	October/November

Maximizing the Role Potential—Teaching Assistant Preparation and Professional Development

It was identified early on that given the introduction of a new role, resources would need to be committed to the orientation and professional development of new TAs each year. The most urgent concern was ensuring that TAs and teaching teams were equally prepared for the semester, especially as this related to expectations of a specific program. TA orientation was scheduled over two days in late July. During those two days, they were introduced to the history of the WSI and the evolution of the initiative, orientated to the FCS, and trained on the Writing for Success framework. Orientation was facilitated by the FCS support team that was involved in the initial development of the WSI.

Another significant consideration for the orientation was how TAs would address the unique learning styles of adult learners. The integration of multiple teaching styles and intelligences with the flexibility of WSI required close attention to the related skills of reading and speaking. To address the learning needs of diverse students across several disciplines within the Faculty, training was offered on various methodologies ranging from more conventional teaching strategies, including lectures, to one-on-one feedback sessions, interactive participatory writing workshops, seminars on critical reading as a writing skill, and informal writing workshops to practise skills. In all instances, TAs were encouraged to assess the need levels and learning styles of students when developing their approaches to content delivery.

In recent years, the summer WSI TA preparation has grown to include seven to ten hours of collaborative program development. TAs work together to develop and redesign standardized teaching modules on core concepts related to writing. These additional sessions were introduced after a question was raised by TA teaching teams about the effectiveness of having each TA develop his or her own resources each year. Given the primary goal of working directly with students, developing standardized modules allowed for decreased preparation duties throughout the semester, which freed up considerable contract hours to work with students. The WSI program administration has also noticed that TAs become quite familiar with disciplinary content, as a result of the frequency with which TAs have returned to their role. To maximize the benefit of this expertise, TAs are always reassigned to the same school unless a scheduling conflict exists.

Over the course of the WSI, professional development activities for TAs have also expanded. These activities have focused on pedagogical innovation and skill development. Most of the WSI TAs have been aspiring academics building toward careers in higher education. The WSI program administration recognized that there was a reciprocal benefit for TAs and the initiative to invest in professional development activities. Examples of activities that the WSI has facilitated for TAs include instruction skills workshops conducted by the LTO, participatory learning by the Chair of Teaching for FCS, and various pedagogical strategies by the LTO. With so many TAs returning for two and three years, support to enhance their abilities as instructors has been effective in raising the initiative's profile by improving the scholarship of teaching by TAs.

WSI Administration and Evaluation
Any faculty-wide initiative requires high-level central coordination. Embedded in the design of the WSI were the program administration and annual evaluations that would ensure the continued success of the WSI. The FCS believed that the initiative was best coordinated centrally out of the Dean's Office and that a central WSI coordinator could best fill the role of being a liaison between FCS leadership, the teaching teams, and the TAs.

The WSI central coordinator became one key to success for the WSI in the early years of the initiative, when lack of familiarity created confusion and when programs worked diligently to identify a suitable approach for their students. The FCS's goal was to have a central coordinator who was available to support the development of the initiative across the entire Faculty while ensuring that the WSI administration functioned smoothly. The central coordinator worked at arm's length from teaching teams and TAs; this ensured neutrality when challenges arose.

After five years of the WSI, the central coordinator remains a constant in the initiative and has increased in visibility. With an extensive understanding of the origins of the initiative and of the diverse pedagogies used across the FCS, the central coordinator has provided advice regarding the redevelopment and structuring of WSI. Responding to program needs, the central coordinator has played a key role in developing solutions to problems and ensuring that each program remains fully committed to the WSI's success.

Defining the WSI Central Coordinator Role
The WSI central coordinator oversees all activities and functions of the initiative to ensure that objectives are accomplished in accordance with established priorities and time limitations and within the available budget. Factors that have influenced this role have decreased over time as the WSI has become an established teaching method within the FCS. The early days of the WSI saw the central coordinator manage challenges in multiple programs simultaneously, troubleshooting role expectations mid-semester, and reporting to program directors regarding the status and success of the initiative. High levels of student satisfaction with the WSI and TA retention have drastically lowered the amount of time required for problem solving.

Today, the WSI central coordinator focuses on coordination activities and monitors the successful implementation of annual revisions to the WSI among other leadership activities.

Evaluation and Evolution

True to the scholarship of teaching, the WSI regularly engages in rigorous evaluations to examine the strengths and weaknesses of the initiative. Over the first three years of the WSI, evaluative data were collected from multiple stakeholders through questionnaires and focus group sessions. Evaluation of the initiative was based on (1) students' perceptions of their writing abilities and the significance of writing support available to them, (2) faculty members' experiences of integrating the initiative and their perceptions of the beneficial effects for students, and (3) the experiences of TAs across the faculty.

Collecting Quantitative Data—Questionnaires

Formative and summative evaluations were solicited from all students who took part in the WSI each year. This evaluation came in the form of a pre- and post-assessment questionnaire that was designed when the WSI was being created. The questionnaire questioned students on their perception of their personal writing skills, on the importance of writing, and on the FCS's commitment to developing student writing skills. Questionnaires were administered in class in a pre-selected week.

Student participation in the evaluation has varied over time. The percentage of students who have participated in the pre-assessment is strong; on average, 86 percent of students have completed the pre-assessment. The post-assessment data have been more challenging to collect. The average participation in the post-assessment across the first three years of the WSI was 58 percent. The low response rate for the post-assessment is partly attributed to the time of year the WSI tries to collect post-assessment data. As we have tried to collect the data at the end of the semester, when students are busiest, willingness to participate in a voluntary evaluation has been limited. In 2010, we elected to implement a streamlined approach to administering the post-assessment whereby it was administered during an exam review class. As many students attend these sessions, the number of students who participated in the 2010 post-assessment increased to 72 percent of those who completed the pre-assessment compared to an average of 65 percent in the first two years of the WSI.

Results

The results of the pre-assessment questionnaire, across FCS programs, have captured remarkable variances in how first-year students perceived their English-language speaking and reading skills scores, relative to English-language writing skills. There was a strong tendency for students to report either excellent or extremely high speaking skills (42 percent) and reading skills (37 percent). When students were asked about their writing skills, the mean number of students who rated their writing skills as excellent or extremely high was only 15.5 percent. As in previous literature reporting the concerns of undergraduate students related to writing proficiency (Huang, 2010; Light, 2003; Vardi, 2009), the pre-assessment results point to anxieties among first-year students at Ryerson University. The pre-assessment also had students rate the importance of receiving support as they developed their writing skills within their academic program. On average, 68 percent of students rated this as extremely or very important.

In the post-assessment questionnaire, there has been a tendency for students' perceptions of their writing skills to form a normal distribution following participation in the WSI, whereas pre-assessment data have had a negative skew in all three years. This redistribution is thought to suggest that certain students may have overestimated their writing skills in September, while other students' skills may have developed.

Qualitative Data—Focus Group Sessions
Focus groups provided a forum for students, faculty members, and TAs to share their experiences and feedback related to WSI at the end of each year. These sessions were guided by a focus group guide (see Appendix B). Focus groups were facilitated by the WSI central coordinator and were audiotaped and transcribed verbatim for review by FCS leaders. Besides the teaching teams, all students who had access to the WSI were given the opportunity to participate in a focus group. In the first two years of the program, focus group sessions had limited representation from the student body and volunteers were not available from all eight schools. In the third year of the program, representation from all schools was achieved.

Results
Focus group themes have been identified across each of the stakeholder groups. Among the student participants, the qualitative data highlighted the students' tendencies to move from a place of skepticism about the WSI to a high valuation of the initiative. By the end of the semester, students reported feeling that the WSI should be a permanent component of their academic curriculum. The WSI was recognized as having addressed their unique learning needs and styles by offering varied sessions and activities. The notion of practice was often mentioned by students as an advantage of having engaged in the WSI. Faculty participants resorted to similar themes during focus group sessions—they were initially unsure how the WSI would

work, given time constraints, but they came to appreciate the flexible integration. Faculty reported observing a trend among students to be more aware of writing development since the implementation of the WSI. Finally, like the other two groups, the TAs articulated a clear need to maintain the WSI, for they had observed vast improvements in student writing and their commitment to improved writing skills. TAs acknowledged the flexibility of the WSI and their leeway to be flexible in content delivery as a key strength of the initiative.

Evolution and Scholarship
The scholarship regarding the WSI has been informed largely by the evaluation data and by criticisms offered by the core participants. The WSI as a model of teaching is a unique hybrid of the three forms of scholarship—teaching, research, and service—and the four functions of scholarship—discovery, application, integration of knowledge, and integration of education (Hyman et al., 2001–2). WSI as a teaching methodology imparts to students skills that are essential for success. In the evaluation of the WSI each year, emerging data are used to inform change and to respond to student needs (Martin, 2007). Examples of these changes have ranged from limiting the marking responsibilities of WSI TAs, to developing standardized resources for TAs, to increasing the number of meetings for stakeholders throughout the year. While none of these changes seem remarkable, the cumulative effect of the WSI's responsiveness to feedback has been the buy-in by faculty, students, and returning TAs. The WSI evolves at the rate the program dictates. It is by no means a static process and will continue to rely on in-depth research to facilitate change and maintain programmatic success. Finally, the scholarship of service has been an integral component of the WSI through the dissemination of the new knowledge (by disseminating findings) as well as ongoing discovery related to writing skills instruction (Hyman et al., 2001–2).

The WSI has used the three forms of scholarship in concert to develop an iterative process of evolution. The integration of the WSI within classrooms marks a significant shift in what constitutes relevant learning for undergraduate students. It also marks the coming together of conventional teaching with what is often thought of as ad hoc support offered to students through extracurricular services on campus, or "outreach" (Hyman et al., 2001–2).

Engaging Students and Enhanced Learning – Keys to Success
The WSI has been adjusted slightly each year to better meet the needs of the students and all stakeholders. In light of the continued success of the WSI and the evaluative data collected between 2008 and 2010, three keys to

the successful engagement of students have been identified. First, extensive support must be available to TAs and faculty members when innovative pedagogies are introduced. TAs have been leaders in identifying opportunities to further engage students in the process of learning writing skills, and the FCS has supported them in this.

Given the diverse needs of students regarding writing skill development, flexibility and adaptability are essential to the success of a writing intervention. Students have found the ability of the WSI to address their specific needs, regardless of their academic program, to be an unusual asset of the initiative. However, flexibility must come with some caution to ensure that the integrity of content and the objectives of the WSI remain consistent regardless of roll-out across schools.

Finally, positioning the initiative for success each year has been a contributing factor to the high level of student engagement in WSI activities. Hiring TAs who possess extensive experience in teaching writing has enabled strong, respectful relationships between students and TAs. The successful implementation and the continued growth and development of the WSI are owed in large part to the exceptional TAs who execute this initiative.

Future Directions

After five years of successful integration, the WSI is now a permanent component of the undergraduate experience within the FCS. While the initiative continues to evolve in response to the changing needs of students, its essential place as an innovative pedagogy to engage students is fully recognized. While no immediate plans are in place for significant changes to the structure of the WSI, two primary future directions for the initiative have been considered. Currently the WSI runs as a single-semester initiative. As writing development is a process, it has been suggested that student benefit may increase if WSI were offered as a full-year initiative or even throughout the four years of a student's undergraduate program. Finally, the FCS has considered working collaboratively with other faculties across Ryerson to help implement a similar initiative for all undergraduate students on campus.

Summary

The FCS Dean's Office believed that the level of student engagement in writing skill development required attention. To support students in their development, the WSI was created as a Faculty-wide initiative. After five years of implementation the WSI remains an innovative approach to support students in advancing their writing skills within a curricular framework.

APPENDIX A

Excerpt from WSI Teaching Assistant Manual: Monthly Activities

Use this section as a resource to guide the WSI activities throughout the year. While there will be some flexibility, this timeline gives a general sense of your total responsibilities and when best to complete a task.

SUMMER
July
1. *Contract signing*
   Once offered the position you will be required to sign the summer and fall contracts. When you schedule an appointment to sign your contract you will require a void cheque and a completed employee information form.
2. *Summer contract begins (6 weeks)*
3. *Mid-July TA orientation (1 day with lunch)*
   The orientation will be one day and is mandatory for all TAs.
   Morning: learning strategists
   Afternoon: logistics, hours, podium access
4. *Meet with Faculty Lead*
   At orientation you will be provided with the contract information of the Faculty Lead for your identified school. Within 48 hours of orientation you are required to initiate contact with the Faculty Lead. The WSI Lead TA should be copied on this email.
5. *Meeting with WSI Lead TA and Faculty Lead*
   This early meeting with the Lead TA and the Faculty Lead in July or August is intended to review the objectives of WSI and chat about tentative plans for implementation.
6. *Attend TA working sessions*
   The details of these sessions will be negotiated with the Lead TA and fellow TAs. These sessions are intended for TA team building, skill building, and Fall preparation. Refer to the Summer Contract for the breakdown of available hours. All TAs must be available to attend each session.
7. *Confer with Faculty Lead to plan for fall implementation of WSI*

August

1. *Attend TA working sessions*
2. *Weekly check-ins from Coordinator*
3. *Meet one-on-one with Coordinator and Lead TA*
   These brief meetings are intended to identify early concerns that are emerging in regards to the Fall. The can be done in person or by phone. While these are most important for new TAs, it is beneficial to meet with all TAs to have a sense of what changes are being implemented across the initiative.
4. *End-of-summer contract-TA lunch (Bangkok Garden)*
5. *Attend end-of-summer Professional Development activity*
   During the TA working sessions a Summer Professional Development activity will be identified. You are required to attend this session.
6. *Continue planning the semester with Faculty Lead*

FALL
September

1. *Determine Writing Sample dates*
   Identify the written assignments that will be collected as the Writing Samples with the Lead. Identify the due date for the assignments and provide these dates to the Lead TA.
2. *Introduce Writing Samples to class and distribute permission forms*
   Introducing the idea of writing samples early on is essential. Please distribute the writing sample permission form in class and collect signed copies from interested students. Return the signed forms to the Lead TA.
3. *Establish office hours*
   Notify WSI Coordinator if you do not have space to conduct office hours.
4. *First monthly meeting*
   The agenda for the meeting will be sent in advance. Please provide comments and agenda items.
5. *New TAs to FCS TA orientation*
6. *Monitor hours*

October

1. *Collect writing samples and provide to Lead TA*
2. *Second monthly meeting*
3. *Professional development activities*
   Two professional development activities will be scheduled in September. Your attendance at these sessions is mandatory.

4. Student work and complete TA activities as established with Faculty Lead
5. Monitor hours

    Please note, you must inform the WSI Lead TA and Coordinator as early as possible if you feel you are working beyond your weekly contract hours. Contract hours cannot be extended and therefore a plan to reduce hours will be required.

November
1. Third monthly meeting
2. Professional development Activity #2

    Two professional development activities will be scheduled in September. Your attendance at these sessions is mandatory.
3. Collect Writing Sample #2

    The Lead TA will send a reminder one week in advance of the assignment due date to remind you of the upcoming collection.
4. Student work and complete TA activities as established with Faculty Lead
5. Monitor hours

    Please note, you must inform the WSI Lead TA and Coordinator as early as possible if you feel you are working beyond your weekly contract hours. Contract hours cannot be extended and therefore a plan to reduce hours will be required.

December/April
1. End-of-semester party and TA Focus Group

APPENDIX B

WSI Focus Group Guide for Student Participants

1. This semester you were introduced to the writing skills initiative (WSI). How did you feel about the initiative?
2. What were your expectations of the WSI?
3. How did the WSI help in developing your writing skills? OR in what way did the WSI contribute to the development of your writing skills?
4. How would you rate the WSI in assisting you in your writing assignments? Excellent, very good, average, or poor?
5. Please identify any strategies that the WSI TA provided that you have used and found helpful.
6. Please describe how you used the information provided to you by your WSI TA in your assignments. If so, please describe how this changed the way you write OR approach assignments.
7. What was your contact with the WSI TA outside of the seminars or workshops? If you did work with the WSI TA, how did the one-on-one assist you to develop your writing skills?
8. How would you describe the support that you experienced related to the development of your writing skills?
9. How has the WSI influenced your confidence in your writing?

Another important skill that is connected to the academic writing process is critical reading.

10. Please describe any changes in the way you read for class and assignments. Please describe any strategies that the WSI TA provided that focused on this step of the academic writing process.
11. What suggestions do you have for the implementation of the writing skills initiative in future years?
12. If you were involved in developing the WSI for future students, what other information would you recommend to improve undergraduate student writing?
13. Should the writing skills initiative be a permanent component of the student experience? If so, why? If no, why not?

References

Brown, C. A., Dickson, R., Humphreys, A. L., McQuillian, V., & Smears, E. (2008). Promoting academic writing/referencing skills: Outcome of an undergraduate e-learning pilot project. *British Journal of Educational Technology, 39*(1), 140–156. doi:10.1111/j.1467-8535.2007.00735.x

Cadwallader, M. L., & Scarboro, C. A. (1982). Teaching writing within a sociology course: A case study in writing across the curriculum. *Teaching Sociology, 9,* 359–382.

Fallahi, C. R., Wood, R. M., Austad, C. S., & Fallahi, H. (2006). A program for improving undergraduate psychology students' basic writing skills. *Teaching of Psychology, 33*(3), 171–175. doi:10.1207/s15328023top3303_3

Grauerholz, L. (1999). Creating and teaching writing intensive courses. *Teaching Sociology, 27*(4), 310–323.

Harklau, L., Losey, K. M., & Siegal, M. (Eds.). (1999). *Generation 1.5 meets college composition: Issues in the teaching of writing to U.S.-educated learners of ESL.* Mahwah, NJ: Lawrence Erlbaum Associates.

Huang, L. (2010). Seeing eye to eye? The academic writing needs of graduate and undergraduate students from students' and instructors' perspectives. *Language Teaching and Research, 14*(4), 517–539. doi:10.1177/1362168810375372.

Hyman, D., Gurgevich, E., Alter, T., Ayers, J., Cash, E., Fahnline, D., Gold, D., Herrmann, R., Jurs, R., Roth, D., Swisher, J., Whittington, M. S., & Wright, H. (2001–2). Beyond Boyer: The UniSCOPE model of scholarship for the 21st century. *Journal of Higher Education Outreach and Engagement, 7*(1–2), 41–65.

Jacob, J. A., & Winslow, S. E. (2004). Overworked faculty: Job stresses and family demands. *Annals of the American Academy of Political and Social Science, 596*(1), 104–129. doi:10.1177/0002716204268185

Kuh, G. D., Kinzie, J., Schuh, J. H., & Whitt, E. J. (2005). *Student success in college: Creating conditions that matter.* San Francisco: Wiley.

Leamnson, R. (1999). *Thinking about teaching and learning: Developing habits of learning with first year college and university students.* Sterling: Stylus Publishing.

Light, R. J. (2003). Writing and students' engagement. *Peer Review, 6*(1), 28–31.

Martin, L. (2007). Defining the scholarship of teaching versus scholarly teaching. *Society for Teaching and Learning in Higher Education: Newsletter.* [Available: http://www.stlhe.ca/wp-content/uploads/2011/06/STLHE-Newsletter-46-2007-Summer.pdf]

McLeod, S. G., Brown, G. C., McDaniels, P. W., & Sledge, L. (2009). Improving writing with a PAL: Harnessing the power of peer assisted learning with the reader's assessment rubrics. *International Journal of Teaching and Learning in Higher Education, 20*(3), 488–502.

National Commission on Writing. (2003). *Report of the national commission on writing in America's schools and colleges.* [Available: http://www.vantagelearning.com/docs/myaccess/neglectedr.pdf]

Rolfe, G. (1997). Writing ourselves: creating knowledge in a postmodern world. *Nurse Education Today, 17*(6), 442–448.

Vardi, I. (2009). The relationship between feedback and change in tertiary student writing in the disciplines. *International Journal of Teaching and Learning in Higher Education, 20*(3), 350–361.

Whitehead, D. (2002). The academic writing experiences of a group of student nurses: A phenomenological study. *Journal of Advanced Nursing, 38*(5), 498–506. doi:10.1046/j.1365-2648.2002.02211.x

3

Learning the Ethic of Care through Family Narratives

Mehrunnisa Ahmad Ali

Introduction

Several schools in the Faculty of Community Services (FCS) at Ryerson University prepare students for public service in the "caring" professions such as social work, early childhood studies, nursing, child and youth care, and midwifery. Learning the "ethic of care," or the sense of moral obligation associated with specific professional roles, is a key component of their curricula. How can we help them conceptualize what this means? What will help them understand what this looks like in different contexts? How can we evoke an affective response from them, one that could lead to a deep and long-term commitment to the ethic of care? In this chapter we argue that for providers of public services, an effective strategy for learning the ethic of care is to systematically listen to the families they serve and to document their narratives, including their encounters with public services. Our premise is that narratives constructed by families represent their priorities, concerns, beliefs, perceptions, resources, and strategies, and that these are important for service providers to know if they are to understand and appropriately meet their needs.

The Context

Public services in Canada, as in many other jurisdictions, are relatively slow to respond to change. Their structures and cultures are based on the world views, assumptions, and lifestyles of the early British and French settlers and their descendants. However, in the past three decades Canada's population has become highly diverse. Immigration, mainly from Asian countries, is adding about 250,000 people to the country's population annually. What do service providers need to know to serve immigrant children and families whose languages and cultures they do not know? Also, income differences between rich and poor have increased rapidly (Broadbent, 2012). What do service providers, who usually belong to the middle class, need to know about children and families who live in poverty? Individuals with disabilities are also becoming a more visible part of our population. An estimated 4.5 percent of children and youth have one or more disabilities (Statistics Canada, 2008). What do service providers need to know in order to meet their obligations to these children and their families?

Many public service institutions aim for a "client-centred" approach to service provision but do not allocate sufficient resources or develop appropriate mechanisms for attending to clients' needs. For example, the need for translators and interpreters is widely acknowledged by hospitals, schools, and child protection agencies in cities like Toronto, but there is a chronic shortage of these services. The political economy of public services is such that the needs of users who fall outside the "mainstream" get neglected, especially in times of shrinking resources. Even when the need for a change in policy or practice is recognized, the process of change is stymied by sectorial divisions, bureaucratic hierarchies, and lack of agreement among multiple stakeholders. Meanwhile, families such as those who are newcomers to Canada live in poverty, or have children with disabilities, and are at risk of neglect.

Theoretical Background

The ethic of care is not a new phenomenon; rather, it is part of a long philosophic and political tradition (Bath, 2011). Its revival in the 1980s is associated with the work of Carol Gilligan (1982), who presented it as a moral orientation distinctive in its emphasis on contextual sensitivity, responsiveness to individuals, and attention to the consequences of decisions. Others who have built on this work (e.g., Held, 2006; Hankivsky, 2004) have highlighted the relational interdependence of all human beings and shifted the discourse to the public sphere, demonstrating how a care ethic can be practised in public institutions. These authors claim that the liberal ethic of justice, which is based on impartiality and objectivity, further marginalizes those who cannot exercise the same options as the majority. Arguing that empathy and benevolence are insufficient conditions for understanding the perspectives of others, Hankivsky suggests that it is vital to invite them to "to speak and be heard, to tell one's life-story, to press one's claims and point of view in one's own voice" (Fraser, cited in Hankivsky, 2004).

A concept closely associated with the ethic of care is that of "client-centred" professional practice. Carl Rogers, a clinical psychologist working in the 1940s at the University of Chicago, first proposed that clients should take the lead in making decisions about their therapy, rather than passively follow "expert" directions. Other terms, such as person-centred and patient-centred approaches, have also been used in various professions, particularly in health care, to signify individualized, contextually sensitive service provision (Slater, 2006). Decisions about services, treatment, and therapy are based on appropriate information given by the service providers as well as on clients' judgments about what will suit them. An extension of this is the family-centred care model (Kyler, 2008), in which the family of the individual is seen as a partner in the decision-making process primarily because it is also responsible for caring for the person. Despite the scholarship in this field, practitioners continue to struggle with the question of how to interpret and implement these ideas in their practice. Some of this difficulty can be attributed to conceptual uncertainty, institutional apathy, fear of loss of power and control, lack of communication skills, and insufficient time and financial resources.

Sevenhuijsen (cited in Bath, 2011) suggests that care entails situated questions in which the care ethicist sees herself as a participant within a caring practice, which requires that those who are being cared for are listened to. Rinaldi (2006) defines listening primarily as "sensitivity to the patterns that connect, to that which connects us to others; abandoning ourselves to the conviction that our understanding and our own being are but small parts of a broader integrated knowledge that holds the universe together" (p. 66).

Contexts in which listening is advocated are often characterized by power differentials between the listener and the listened to. Brooker (2011) points out that in such contexts, "tokenistic" listening simply reinforces differences of power and status. Dahlberg and Moss (2005) call for an ethical stance in listening, which includes "an openness to the difference of the Other" (p. 104). They acknowledge that listening may lead us to question our assumptions, and they recognize the difficulty of facing uncertainty as a result, but they also invite us to consider dissensus as an opening of possibilities rather than as a threat. It is also important to remember that "receptive attention" (Noddings, 2002), which is a hallmark of ethical caring, is based not on the notion of pity but on the sense of moral obligation associated with one's responsibilities as an ethical professional.

One way to practise an ethic of care is to listen with sustained attention to people recounting their narratives of experience. While there is no consensus in the literature on the term "narrative," our use of the term fits well with Hinyard and Kreuter's definition (2007): "A narrative is any cohesive and coherent story with an identifiable beginning, middle, and end that provides information about scene, characters, and conflict; raises unanswered questions or unresolved conflict; and provides resolution" (p. 778).

Narratives, too, are an old and well-established form of communication. Connelly and Clandinin (1990) claim that narratives provide a way of understanding how individuals draw on their personal practical knowledge to understand life's situations. They suggest that our views about our worlds are derived from our personal, historical, and socio-cultural narratives, which structure the way we act in the present and guide our future practices. Similarly, Fiese and Spagnola (2005) claim that "narratives are a reflection of how the individual or family organizes representation of social exchanges, has learned from the past, and anticipates the future" (p. 52).

When people recount personally important events, they give new meanings to them by re-creating their circumstances, struggles, and resolutions. They elaborate their experiences and reflect upon them, which is much more useful than just the factual information (Bochner, 2001).

Although the terms narrative and "story" are sometimes used interchangeably, Fiese and Spagnola (2005) recommend that the subtle distinction between them be maintained. They suggest that the term narrative acknowledges that people selectively choose, elaborate, and interpret information when creating their narratives. This is different from simply recounting a story, which is limited to the content and structure of recalled experience.

Narratives are also a mechanism for creating a dialogue that illuminates diverse perspectives on the same issue (Shields, 2004). They can give greater meanings to our lives, as well as to the ways we perceive the lives of others (Skott, 2001), and they offer us a chance to explore and communicate our beliefs, relationships, and perspectives (Hendry, 2007). Those who listen to others' narratives gain insight into the narrator's understanding of his or her world and experiences in it. Listening to and reflecting on families' narratives affords listeners opportunities to examine their own implicit and unexamined beliefs (Ali, Corson, & Frankel, 2010; Hinyard & Kreuter, 2007). These narratives can help providers in fields such as health, schools, and child care adapt their services to families' needs. More importantly, narratives can help them draw upon families' resources and strengths and see them as potential collaborators rather than needy, uninformed, and disempowered people.

Listening to narratives often leads to change in the relationship between the listener and the speaker. There is a shift from a focus on general information toward the personal and particular, which in turn opens the way for understanding alternative ways of knowing and doing (Clandinin, 2007).

In teaching and learning, the use of narrative as a heuristic device is a very old tradition, one that can be traced to Aristotle's *Poetics* and Augustine's *Confessions* (Connelly & Clandinin, 1990). It has received renewed attention in recent years in higher education, particularly in the fields of teacher education (Connelly & Clandinin, 1990; Doyle & Carter, 2003; Rossiter, 2002) nursing (Diekelmann, 2003; Ironside, 2003), and social work (Balen, Rhodes, & Ward, 2001; Noble, 2001). Some of these scholars claim that narratives help students connect theory and practice, learn to appreciate multiple perspectives, develop tolerance for ambiguity, and interpret contextually embedded, complex, and evolving situations. Others suggest that narratives are engaging, memorable, and believable and that they invite empathic meaning-making and perspective-taking. They encourage students to think through opaque situations rather than look for quick solutions and immediate interventions.

Reissman and Quinney (2005) claim that in the field of social work, narratives facilitate better communication across racial and class boundaries. Assumptions we make on the basis of our own social locations are challenged by the fuller, more complex accounts of the lives of families we do not interact with on a regular basis in our everyday lives. Those who work in child care, education, social welfare, and public health are also likely to find that information the family considers important for meeting their needs is likely to be missed in the brief standardized forms used by most public service institutions.

For students preparing to work in the caring professions, the experience of developing families' narratives can create an "internally persuasive discourse," which can help them build upon, question, or even disrupt the "authoritative discourses" (Bakhtin, 1981) they typically encounter in coursework or placement experiences. They can learn that the principles they read about and discuss in the abstract in their coursework must be interpreted and judiciously applied in particular cases, or modified, or even discarded. Given the opportunity to juxtapose what they empirically learn about families with what they learn in their coursework, they are likely to become well-grounded, thoughtful professionals, oriented toward the ethic of care.

Teachers in higher education use narratives in different ways. Some ask their students to write their autobiographies, or narratives of their experience in the field, or to analyze cases of clients in their professional fields. Carr (1997) refers to stories that individuals tell about themselves, in formal and informal settings, as "first-order narratives," and accounts that researchers construct based on such stories as "second-order narratives." Some scholars (e.g., Rossiter, 2011; Gambrill, 2013) have pointed out that a key issue in moving from first- to second-order narratives is the difficulty of accurately representing and interpreting narrators' meanings, for researchers' and practitioners' personal, professional, and institutional contexts inevitably mediate understandings of others' accounts. Gambrill (2013) and others (e.g., Rossiter, 2011; Gergen & Gergen, 2006) suggest that we need to be highly self-aware and reflexively analyze the information we receive, especially from those whose backgrounds are very different from our own. We also need to acknowledge and to develop tolerance for the uncertainty in our decision-making, especially regarding those about whom we know very little.

Connelly and Clandinin (1990) suggest that the analysis of narratives as texts and the conduct of narrative inquiry are different learning processes, both of which provide valuable insights but also entail risks and dilemmas. In the study described below, while we were aware of the risk of our participants' premature interpretations and overgeneralizations based on their interactions with a small number of families, we also believed that the learning opportunity was worth the risk. We merged the roles of practitioner and researcher because of our stance that research is essential to professional practice. We asked the participants to document the narratives of a few families and to reflect on what they had learned through their inquiry as well as on the content of the narratives. While the participants in this project were already working in a caring profession, with a few minor modifications, the same approach could be just as effective with students preparing to work in similar professions.

Methodology

For our project, we selected two staff members each from nine family support programs. These programs are sometimes referred to as early years programs, family resource centres, neighbourhood houses, and community development programs.

After gaining approval for the study from Ryerson's ethics board, we solicited participation in our project by sending out a general invitation to members of the Ontario Coalition of Family Support Programs, and selected two participants each from an urban, a semi-urban, and a rural location for the first phase of the project. Ryerson's Interpersonal Skills Training Centre (ISTC) helped us run a full-day training workshop for this group—which we called the Ontario Leaders group—using professional actors to simulate families the trainees were likely to encounter. We videorecorded these sessions for later use. The Ontario Leaders then recruited three families, each representing a newcomer family, a family living in poverty, and a family with a child with disability. Working as a team, the two leaders interviewed each family three times, using an interview guide with several open-ended questions. They audio-recorded and transcribed the interviews. They then created second-order narratives for each family and edited them in collaboration with the family. At the same time, they maintained journals documenting their own learning, including insights, confusions, and challenges.

The Ontario Leaders then helped plan and co-lead a two-day workshop for family support program personnel from other provinces in Canada. The national organization, Family Resource Programs, Canada, helped recruit two staff members from programs located in six different Canadian provinces. The video-recordings from the Ontario Leaders' training session, and their own accounts of documenting families' narratives, were used during the workshop. The Canadian Leaders, as we called them, repeated the cycle of documenting families' narratives and recording their own learning experiences.

Toward the end of the project we asked decision-makers in other public services, such as public health centres, school boards, child care centres, and social welfare agencies, to consider the process of documenting families' narratives and to comment on whether it was a worthwhile and feasible practice to follow in their own institutional contexts. Interviews with these individuals were videotaped and recorded on a DVD and made available to readers of the book *Listening to Families: Reframing Services*. This book contains a fuller account of the project and includes the families' narratives.

In the following section we describe what the Ontario and Canadian Leaders said they had learned as a result of their participation in the project. The data we draw upon here are primarily from their journal entries but include some comments recorded during group meetings.

What the Ontarian/Canadian Leaders Learned

Almost all of the participants in the project reported that by documenting families' narratives, they learned much more than they had imagined they could. Their usual interactions with the families consisted of brief conversations with some members of the family, at the site where the family support programs were offered, often in the presence of children or other families. In this context it was only possible to get partial glimpses of who the families were and what they were going through. A family support worker said she was puzzled why Sita, a newcomer from India, didn't really play with her young son during the parent–child drop-in program. What she learned from Sita's narrative was that despite an MBA degree from a well-known university in India, she was working the night shift at Walmart while her husband worked the day shift there. Sita was sleep deprived because she also had to care for her two-year-old and manage household chores during the day.

Several participants in the project were surprised to find out how much they didn't know about the families they served. One person, who had been working in family support programs for twenty years, said she had worked with a mother and her infant in the family resource centre for over a year. But until she had conducted the in-depth interviews and written up the family's narrative, she had not recognized that the mother was suffering from postpartum depression. "I am good at [identifying depression]. I have had training, and I know I am good at this. But I missed all the cues because I had not paid attention to her in this special way."

Another person noted that it was not until she had transcribed the interviews and carefully reconstructed a woman's heavily accented words that she realized that she had not fully understood her in the past and had sometimes responded to her inappropriately.

A typical response to developing a family's narrative was recorded by one participant in her comment to the family: "This process has been an eye-opener for me. You have been coming to our play and parenting sessions many times, but you've never shared this much with me. So, it's like I really didn't know a lot about you and your family at all."

Some families chose to be interviewed in their own homes, which required the family support staff to visit them there. For some of them, the home visit itself was highly informative. One participant wrote in her journal:

> Although we had worked with Naomi before, we had never been inside her home; any attempts made prior to home visit with her were always made in vain. And although we had expected her living conditions to be poor because of her current situation, and in looking at the front of the building, we were shocked at what we saw. Her tiny two-bedroom apartment was cluttered, dirty and stifling hot. The furniture was worn, old, and smelled.

In most cases the family support personnel were both surprised and humbled to learn that families were so keen to create their narratives. Many families told them that in constructing their narratives, they finally felt someone was actually listening to them. In response to the final draft of the narrative, a father said, "Yes, that's us! That's our family. Thank you so much for doing this for us!" Many of the families reported that they had been asked for health information, or about a child's progress in school, but nobody had ever asked for their fuller story as a family. One of the Ontario Leaders reported that a pregnant woman she had started interviewing was so keen to continue being listened to that when she went into labour, she asked her brother to bring the interviewer to the clinic so she could keep talking to her. Unfortunately, the child died soon after birth. Because of the bond that had been created between the two women, the Ontario Leader attended the baby's funeral. When she met the mother, she was asked, "So, are we on for next week?," referring to the meeting they had scheduled.

By listening to the families' narratives, the family support workers became aware of how some "systems" affected the families' lives. Because they themselves had not necessarily encountered similar situations, they simply did not know about some of the families' challenges. A leader from Alberta wrote:

> Mary would need to wait until her husband came to Alberta, before the family could apply for health care coverage. Right now, without the whole family there, they would only let her apply if she was separated or divorced from her husband. I don't understand the rationale for this policy. It seems antiquated and sexist to me. I also brought the application forms for the leisure cards that Mary wanted to apply for, and showed her that she didn't have to have her Alberta Health Care number to apply for these. She then mentioned that her son's school wanted her to register for the fall, and they would not accept his Ontario Health Care number. She's concerned that she will not get the Alberta Health Care in time to register him for school in the fall. I was not able to follow up with the school.

For the leaders, the practice of "receptive attention" (Noddings, 2002) also meant keeping in check their tendency to intervene, or to try to solve problems for the family. One of the leaders wrote: "I found myself converting to a 'helper' on a few occasions. I was able to recognize this and become a listener and interviewer once I noticed this happening."

The opportunity to document their learning also seemed to engender a higher level of reflexivity among the participants. A leader wrote: "I did not explain my reasons for this decision [to select a different family for the project]. As I see this in print I am second-guessing my decision and wonder if I should have explained myself more fully."

However, the privilege of getting to know more about a family than they would normally expect also left them with a sense of greater responsibility and uncertainty about what to do with what they had learned. One of the leaders wrote:

> One interesting offshoot from this activity was a deepened appreciation for the family's way of being. I am wondering about how this

will impact my working relationship with the family. I now have new information that is not related to my job and this information must remain a part of the project data and not my working knowledge with the family at [the program name]. However, my relationship with this family now exists in a different context that I am unable to ignore. I am also not able to use this information to inform my colleagues about the family issues that may be relevant at our program when working with the family. I did not think about this dilemma prior to my interviews.

What the Project Leaders Learned

The breadth and depth of what the Ontarian/Canadian Leaders learned during this project convinced us that despite the risks, this was a worthwhile undertaking. Each pair of leaders had written up the narratives of three families. As participants in a research project, they had been provided with the time and some financial support to do this work, and we did not expect them to continue the work without similar support. However, we had hoped the experience would help them appreciate the importance of learning about the fuller lives of families, to gather and to document this information in a respectful way, and to see it as a part of their professional ethic of care. Statements such as the following in a journal entry were our reward:

> We learned that every family has a story and until you know their background, you can't really understand their behaviours or the reasons for their actions. Since learning more about Jennifer and Shirley, we have changed our approach in working with them. We only wish we had the time to sit down with each and every one of our families to learn their stories and we know this would help us when we design our programs. We are working towards letting listening be the help that families need.

Nevertheless, we also learned a lot about the challenges of developing family narratives. Many of the Ontarian/Canadian Leaders told us they had not anticipated the amount of work required for the project, particularly the time needed for transcribing and summarizing the narratives, and felt overwhelmed. One leader wrote: "Wow what a visit to Toronto. Fun, interesting but how did I get roped into this? This is work!!! I do not need more work!!! I can barely breathe as it is. Am I angry at myself for not investigating more thoroughly?... [and yet] I am intrigued by this project."

Some of them said that writing was something they had not done in years and that they were not confident about their skills. In our role as professors, we routinely assign our students this kind of work and expect them to meet the deadlines we set for them. We had transferred our expectations to those who had been out of school for many years, and to some who may not have attended university at all. Furthermore, while we had asked their employers to reduce their workload for them to participate in the project, none of us had accurately estimated how much time they would need.

As a result of the in-depth interviews (and home visits in some cases), some family support personnel learned much more than what the families were willing to formally document. They fretted about the accuracy and the superficiality of the sanitized narratives they ended up writing. One of the participants wrote:

> After seeing her story in print, [Susan] requested that several pieces be taken out and we were disappointed because it was points that really illustrated how difficult her life is. All references she had made during her interview about her husband's lack of support and how she feels she is the parent who has to deal with everything, she wanted removed. I think in some way she thought her husband might end up reading this narrative and she clearly did not want him portrayed in any negative light. In actuality, her husband is completely unsupportive and absent for most of the time from his family.

We tried to remind the group that the process of developing the narrative is in itself a worthy enterprise, even though it is impossible to fully and accurately represent any family. However, as researchers, we also gained a greater appreciation for the limitations of the recorded and the written word, on which we often depend for our own knowledge claims.

Our primary reason for initiating this project was to figure out what the family support personnel could learn from developing families' narratives. What we didn't fully anticipate were the ethical dilemmas our project participants would encounter in deciding what to do with the information they had generated. Would the process of creating a family's narrative change their relationship with that family? Would the family begin to expect more than the professional relationship they had established? Would it privilege that family in a way that seemed "unfair" to other families they served? Should they share some of that information with colleagues who work with the same family?

Although none of the project participants reported suspicions of abuse in the families they interviewed, and the confidentiality clause in the consent forms was qualified by our legal obligation to report abuse, we wondered about the ethics of unearthing incidents or relationships in a family's past that might cause them pain in the present. As in the incident mentioned above, there was clearly a tension between the researcher's desire to present a coherent narrative about the family and her obligation to the researched, who wanted to protect a family member's image.

Implications for Teaching and Learning in Professional Programs

We don't have answers to the above questions, and we continue to grapple with them. We do, however, know that the first-hand experience of creating families' narratives was a powerful learning experience for the group we worked with.

Preparing students for public services means teaching them theoretical knowledge and procedural skills, but also "habits of the mind." Participants in this study began to receptively listen to the families (Noddings, 2002). They developed stronger relationships with the families, recognized the limits of their own expertise, and questioned their own tendencies. In short, they learned to be more reflexive as part of the practice of the ethic of care (Gambrill, 2013). Students in any professional program could learn these habits of the mind by systematically listening to families, documenting their narratives, and reflecting on what they learned as a result of this experience.

Most students entering the caring professions have to take one or more practicum or "field experience" courses. The experience of developing family narratives could easily be incorporated into the curricula for these courses. Their supervisors in the field could facilitate their access to the families they serve, and their university-based instructors could help them reflect on what they learned about themselves, the families they engaged with, and the institutional practices they observed that were designed to serve the families. Making connections among the families' narratives, their own prior assumptions, and the institutional contexts in which they will work is likely to help them develop a nuanced understanding of the ethic of care in professional practice. Professors in professional programs often use cases, and sometimes simulation exercises, to engage students in appreciating multiple perspectives and analyzing complex situations. While these are relatively easier to organize and take less time, they are designed to elicit immediate student reaction, which could lead to hasty judgments with insufficient information. Furthermore, they lack the immediacy, the authenticity, and the emotional tenor of direct engagement with families. As one of the project participants noted, even if you develop just one family's narrative, the experience provides a framework to think about the many dimensions and complexities of families' lives.

Participants in this project were already providers of public services. Their roles as researchers *and* as practitioners created a model for how research and practice can be combined to develop more thoughtful, more attentive, more reflexive, and more circumspect professionals. This recognition led the participants to question their habitual practices (Balen, Rhodes, & Ward, 2010) and use their research skills to seek new knowledge. This helped to break down the boundary between research and practice (Noble, 2001). They also began to see their practice from the perspective of the families they served, and to notice the structural barriers faced by the families, which they themselves had not encountered. This is a model of ethics of care in public services, which can be adopted by educators who supervise student learning in the field. Given that "vivid images" of practice modelled by field educators profoundly influence students' conceptualization of their own professional roles (Elbaz, 1991), this model could lead to significant change in the next generation of public service providers.

This kind of work can yield important insights but also presents some risks. One of the most important of these relates to the student or novice professional's assumption that by documenting a family's narrative, she has fully understood and accurately represented the family (see Gergen & Gergen, 2006). Another risk is that of generalizing to other families what she has learned about one family because experiential knowledge often trumps knowledge from other sources. However, the benefits of this work, as noted above, outweigh these risks.

Conclusion

While we are convinced that creating families' narratives was a powerful tool for learning an ethic of care for the group we worked with, we continue to examine the cognitive, practical, and ethical dimensions of this work from other perspectives. Three of us from different schools in Ryerson's Faculty of Community Services (Early Childhood Studies, Nursing, and Social Work) have launched a project to study what undergraduate students in our programs can learn about working with immigrant families using this model, and whether their field supervisors and faculty advisers would support its use in field education curricula. We will, no doubt, raise new questions as we continue to explore this option.

References

Ali, M., Corson, P., & Frankel, E. (2010). *Listening to families: Reframing services*. Toronto: Chestnut Publishers.

Balen, R., Rhodes, C., & Ward, L. (2010). The power of stories: Using narrative for interdisciplinary learning in health and social care. *Social Work Education, 29*(4), 416–426.

Bath, C. (2011). Conceptualizing listening to children as an ethic of care in early childhood education and care. *Children and Society*. doi:10.1111/j.1099-0860.2011.00407.x

Bakhtin, M. M. (1981) *The dialogic imagination: Four essays*. M. Holquist (Ed.). C. Emerson and M. Holquist (Trans.). Austin, TX: University of Texas Press.

Bochner, A. P. (2001). Narrative's virtues. *Qualitative Inquiry, 7*(2), 131–157.

Broadbent, E. (2012). *Equality project*. Ottawa: Broadbent Institute.

Brooker, L. (2011). Taking children seriously: An alternative agenda for research. *Early Childhood Research, 9*(2), 137–149.

Carr, D. (1997). Narrative and the real world: An argument for continuity. In L. P. Hinchman & S. K. Hinchman (Eds.), *Memory, identity, community: The idea of narratives in the human sciences* (pp. 7–25). New York, NY: SUNY Press.

Clandinin, D. J. (2007). *Handbook of narrative inquiry: Mapping a methodology*. Thousand Oaks, CA: Sage.

Connelly, M., & Clandinin, D. J. (1990). Stories of experience and narrative inquiry. *Educational Researcher 19*(5), 2–14.

Dahlberg, G., & Moss P. (2005). *Ethics and politics in early childhood education*. London, UK: Routledge Falmer.

Diekelmann, N. (2003). *Teaching the practitioners of care: New pedagogies for the health professions*. Madison, WI: University of Wisconsin Press.

Doyle, W., & Carter, K. (2003) Narrative and learning to teach: Implications for teacher education curriculum. *Journal of Curriculum Studies, 35*(2), 129–137.

Elbaz, F. (1991). Research on teacher knowledge: The evolution of a discourse. *Journal of Curriculum Studies, 23*(1), 1–19.

Fiese, B. H., & Spagnola, M. (2005). Narratives in and about families: An examination of coding schemes and a guide for family researchers. *Journal of Family Psychology, 19*(1), 51.

Gambrill, E. (2013). *Social work practice: A critical thinker's guide*. Oxford, UK: Oxford University Press.

Gergen, M. M., & Gergen, K. J. (2006). Narratives in action. *Narrative Inquiry, 16*, 112–128.

Gilligan, C. (1982). *In a different voice*. Cambridge, MA: Harvard University Press.

Hankivsky, O. (2004). *Social policy and the ethic of care*. Vancouver, BC: UBC Press.

Held, V. (2006). *The ethics of care: Personal, political, and global*. New York, NY: Oxford University Press.

Hendry, P. M. (2007). The future of narrative. *Qualitative Inquiry, 13*(4), 487–498.

Hinyard, L., & Kreuter, M. (2007) Using narrative communication as a tool for health behavior change. *Health Education & Behavior, 34*(5), 777–792.

Ironside, P. (2003). New pedagogies for teaching thinking: The lived experiences of students and teachers enacting narrative pedagogy. *Journal of Nursing Education, 42*(11), 509–516.

Juujarvi, S. (2006). The ethic of care development: A longitudinal study of moral reasoning among practical-nursing, social work and law-enforcement students. *Scandinavian Journal of Psychology, 47,* 193–201.

Kyler, P. (2008). Client-centered and family-centered care: Refinement of the concepts. *Occupational Therapy in Mental Health, 24*(2), 100–120.

Kolb, D. A. (1984). *Experiential Learning.* Englewood Cliffs, NJ: Prentice Hall.

Navarro, S. (2003). Border narratives: The politics of identity and mobilization. *Latin American Politics and Society, 45*(3), 129–139.

Noble, C. (2001). Researching field practice in social work education. *Journal of Social Work Eduction, 1*(3), 347–360.

Noddings, N. (2002). *Educating moral people.* New York, NY: Teachers College Press.

Reissman, C. K., and Quinney, L. (2005). Narrative in social work: A critical review. *Qualitative Social Work, 4*(4), 391–412.

Rinaldi, C. (2006). *In dialogue with Reggio Emilia. Listening, researching and learning.* London, UK: Routledge.

Rossiter, M. (2002). Narratives and stories in adult teaching and learning. *ERIC Digest.* EDO-CE-02-241. Columbus, OH: Center for Education and Training of Adults for Employment.

Slater, L. (2006). Person-centeredness: A concept analysis. *Contemporary Nurse, 23*(1), 135–146.

Skott, C. (2001). Caring narratives and the strategy of presence: Narrative communication in nursing practice and research. *Nursing Science Quarterly, 14*(3), 249–254.

Shields, C. M. (2004) Creating a community of difference. *Educational Leadership, 61*(7), 38–42.

Statistics Canada. (2008). *Participation and activity limitation survey 2006: A profile of Education for children with disabilities in Canada.* Ottawa, ON: Ministry of Industry.

4

The Audacity of Critical Awakening through Intellectual Partnerships

Annette Bailey, Margareth Zanchetta, Gordon Pon, Divine Velasco, Karline Wilson-Mitchell, and Aafreen Hassan

Ode to Critical Development

It is time to develop critically
While using the utmost discretion
And become empowered in the nursing profession.

Through collaboration with your teachers
And discovering role transformations
At last you have finally found your voice
Despite all of your frustrations.

— Sarabeth Silver, BScN, DCSN Alumna

Introduction

Supporting the development of critical thinking among students is a common pedagogical goal across disciplines. Less prevalent is the goal of developing students as critical thinkers for social justice activism using purposeful teaching and learning strategies. The social and moral expediency of linking schools to an education for activism has been widely debated by scholars for the past three decades (Apple, 2011; Giroux & Giroux, 2004; McCarthy et al., 2005). Despite mixed views on the subject, there remains an indubitable consensus that students' ability to engage with, develop, and apply knowledge critically is necessary for professional development and social justice enactment (Furman & Gruenewald, 2004). Achieving these goals requires engagement of students and teachers in a process of awakening beyond critical thinking (McMahon & Portelli, 2004; Winton, 2010), whereby both undertake deliberate efforts in knowledge creation and transformation through collaborative learning processes. This calls for intellectual partnerships (IPs) that are predicated on mutual learning, as well as a co-intentional, dialectal, and democratic process of critical development. Critical pedagogy, because of its liberating potential and respectful view of learners, is foundational to such partnerships. Critical pedagogy compels teachers and students to interrogate their assumptions about the co-creation of knowledge in the teaching and learning environment (Andrews et al., 2001) and to become agents of social justice activism (Furman & Gruenewald, 2004). As such, we believe it is imperative that educational approaches be devised to guide the process of IPs so as to foster students' journeys toward becoming critically engaged citizens.

This chapter focuses on the collaboration of teachers and students in a mutual journey of teaching and learning beyond the classroom in order to advance critical thinking and intellectual development of students in scholarly, research, and creative activities. We suggest that when teachers engage students in purposeful dialogue and actions that facilitate the development of scholarly activities, they acknowledge students' autonomy and mastery in the teaching–learning process and help them realize their inherent power. Students' pursuit of such a level of engagement in education is provoked by their own intentions for academic growth and critical development. Using Freire's (1973) critical pedagogy, we contend that this teacher–student journey can be understood as IP that can facilitate the development of students' critical state of mind and prepare politically engaged scholars. We present testimonies from students' experiences within IPs. We also introduce a visual representation of IP as posited from the lived experiences of Ryerson University educators in nursing, social work, and midwifery.

What Is IP?

We define IP as a deliberate partnership between teachers and students built on the premise of shared learning and responsibility with the primary aim of accomplishing and celebrating mutual desires in scholarly, research, and creative activities. While intellectual engagement is possible in classroom settings, teachers and students further develop partnerships beyond the classroom where students are involved in deeper and more active ways of learning that are committed to social change, self-regulation, and lifelong learning (Donche & Van Petegem, 2011). This intellectual alliance can exceed the boundaries of the conventional student–teacher mentorship relationship. Students and teachers begin IPs on the basis of their own desire for growth and a willingness to invest equally, wholeheartedly, transparently, and passionately in a process that yields mutual success in learning and scholarship. IPs are initiated by students, often after they have become informed about teachers' willingness to support them in extracurricular scholarly activities. This eliminates a process of selection that would reinforce the notion of privilege and elitism among students, as do initiatives based on high grade point average (GPA). Our success with IPs did not depend on students having prior research and writing skills. While a few students initiated IPs with baseline research and writing skills, the majority did not. These skills primarily evolved in the IP process based on the practice of reading, the exchange of ideas with teachers, and the continuous practice of writing–reflecting–writing.

IP celebrates the notion that knowledge cannot be owned, but should be shared between individuals who know and those who want to know (Shor & Freire, 1987). Teacher and student engage in sharing, remaking, and transforming ideas, thus holding their own responsibilities in the teaching–learning process (Donche & Van Petegem, 2011). IPs guide students' experiences as co-partners in an active and discovery-oriented process of knowledge co-creation and construction. This process is dynamic and spurs continuous problem-solving, as well as critical and creative thinking by both teacher and student (Nicholls, 2002). The sharing of voice and power involved in this process fosters passion to learn and propels students' critical state of mind. As engagement and contribution from their critical development are equally valued, students come to value the need for their involvement in prospective learning opportunities (Angel, Duffey, & Belyea, 2000), both within and outside the classroom. Such involvement yields outcomes that include increased confidence, increased scholarly output (e.g., publications), active contribution to classroom learning, improvement in academic achievements, and socially engaged citizens. Outcomes are not always tangible. For some students and teachers, this can be a process of clarification and understanding. Achieving either outcome requires respectful scholarly dialogue and discovery, which may conclude with the creation of a new state of critical awareness, or continuous re-creation of scholarly endeavours. Through this process, students, as autonomous learners, create a distinctive road map for guiding their own education and career path, realizing more active ways of learning and thus holding responsibility for their learning and development (Chan, 2001). A graduate assistant who worked with Dr. Bailey explained what IP means to her:

A metaphor of driving a car can be used to represent IP between students and teachers. The student is the one responsible for driving the car and teachers in collaboration with graduate assistants provide the fuel. If teachers draw out a map for the students to travel, then students will only drive down that path. Being the fuel however, gives the students the knowledge and skills to create their own educational map. (E. Patterson, personal communication, 21 April 2012)

Teachers in this partnership aim to facilitate students' conscious awareness and/or the realization of their own autonomy, power, and mastery in the journey of knowledge construction (Chan, 2001). This achievement can help shift the student's views of the teacher from the evaluator "who grades me" to a new position of "intellectual co-worker and partner." This sets the stage for a mutual partnership in intellectual inquiry and critical development.

Critical Development through IP: Critical Pedagogy, Power, and Empowerment

Empirical support for IPs is presently limited. However, Paulo Freire's ideologies of critical development legitimize the importance of its emergence. Freire (1999) calls for a shift from the dominant discourse of the teacher as the expert and the student as the passive participant, to egalitarianism and empowerment processes that promote critical development of students. Freire's critical pedagogy is a context-specific, action-oriented teaching and learning approach that seeks to help students become critically aware of power structures, oppression, social responsibility, and citizenship (Giroux, 2001). Current teaching approaches emphasize the advantages of critical thinking in exploring and transforming mainstream ideologies (Ten Dam & Volman, 2004). IPs enable students to become politically engaged agents in transforming their lives and the world around them through opportunities that foster awareness of their social positions (Giroux, 2001; Mullaly, 2010). In a collaborative process, these transformations can be maximized and operationalized for scholarly outcomes. These outcomes align favourably with Freire's philosophy. Freire emphasized that teachers should work fearlessly to counteract the dominant social strata in school trends, and subsequently co-develop a student-focused environment that helps reveal students' power and potential for freedom and creativity (Gerhardt, 2000).

Freire (1999) encouraged students and teachers to engage in critical dialogue that illuminates understanding of oppressive realities and reveals their agency in affecting change. He asserted that schools should never be regarded as sites for top-down, one-way transmission of knowledge (from teacher to student), but rather as critical spaces for advancing social justice (Giroux, 2001). Being subjected to the power of discourses in society related to historical and structural factors (Heron, 2005; Pon, Gosine, & Phillips, 2011; Thobani, 2009), students and teachers are not equally positioned. By becoming transformative intellectuals in collaborative scholarly, research, and creative activities, intellectual partners are positioned to confront structural inequalities in university settings that are deeply internalized without aspiration to change (Gruenewald, 2003). IPs are never free of the subjectivities of teacher and student and the omnipresent operation of power. The fluid, contradictory, and multiple nature of subjectivity (Weedon, 1987) can make these learning partnerships complex, and perhaps beyond what logic models of learning can bear (Irving & Moffatt, 2002). Foucault's (1980) post-structuralist notions of power call attention to how pedagogical encounters are always affected by the circulation of power, in all its complexities, contradictions, and contingencies. Certainly, IPs are not neutral, apolitical processes whereby knowledge is merely passed down by the teacher and passively received by the student (Donche & Van Petegem, 2011). The process is political, dynamic, and malleable to foster creativity, inform scholarly insights, and awaken teachers' and students' awareness of their own privilege and/or oppression in the world. With contemporary learners, it is likely that IPs may include conflicting realities, contradictions, divergent truths, recalcitrance, and dissatisfaction with teaching and learning processes (Wong, 2004). However, students' ability to mediate the relationship between power and knowledge is helpful to enhance their critical development.

Like the usual mentee–mentor relationship, IPs emphasize knowledge development and improved professional outcomes (McKinley, Thornby, & Pettrey, 2004). However, further emphasis on partnership, co-creation of knowledge, and joint ownership of scholarly activities moves this relationship beyond the power structure that drives more usual mentorship relationships. The critical dialogue that occurs between teachers and students in IPs can ignite emotional and subjective reflections of historical power relations, oppression, rights, and the politics of self-liberation and empowerment. This process is especially critical for minority students and for students with low academic performance who may lack the social, cultural, and economic capital to consider graduate studies.

Notably, there are students who struggle to occupy their social space in society and who may be timid about engaging in constructive processes with teachers, even though teachers may give them room for that. Social spaces in society are not equally accessible for all. For students from marginalized groups, their claims to space are never outside the interplay of oppression, risk, fear, and courage. IPs recognize that individuals are positioned differently in power relations because of their "situationality" involving race, class, gender, sexual orientation, and ability (Gruenewald, 2003). Yet there is an understanding that even while they are subjected to discourses, individuals are also active agents in the making of who they are and what they do (Heron, 2005). As such, IPs prioritize critical self-reflexivity for both teacher and student (Gruenewald, 2003) in a process that deliberately engages empowering actions. Subsequent co-creation of knowledge can increase students' critical awareness of their skills, and their autonomy as learners, and enlighten them about their own potential as social change agents and co-producers of knowledge (Chan, 2001; Furman & Gruenewald, 2004; Heron, 2005). The co-creation of knowledge, then, signifies a learning alliance between teacher and student that is never outside the power of discourse and the spectre of unequal power relations.

Positioned within the contingent and contradictory nature of critical pedagogy, IPs are shared intentions to construct knowledge through dialogue. This dialectal partnership between teachers and students can lead to students' empowerment and deepen their awareness of structures and systems that shape their lives (Gerhardt, 2000). In turn, they are able to critically analyze and act against injustice resulting from the objective reality of social structures, which are now perceived by students as changeable (Gottesman, 2010). For this outcome to be achieved, students should be invited and supported to recognize and awaken their power in this alliance of knowledge creation, which includes questioning and dialoguing with teachers.

The views, opinions, and thoughts that build IPs sometimes can start in the classroom. For example, in a Ryerson community health nursing class where critical social theory was used to explore health inequities among minority populations, a student was dissatisfied with the teacher's facial expression after a comment made about women having sex with women. Following up with an email to the teacher, she stated: "It is important that nurses be educated and think critically about these issues in order to address the health needs of this community." Recognizing this contribution to mobilizing the student's potential as a critical co-producer of knowledge (Razack, 2002; Sakomoto & Pitner, 2005), the teacher acknowledged the student's comments and invited further dialogue. At the student's request, this interaction resulted in the establishment of a collaborative research project on sexual health behaviours of women who have sex with women. It is through such acknowledgement that students recognize their rights and responsibilities in constructing knowledge, and consciously give themselves permission to transform into critical thinkers.

A Proposed Model of IP

The development of IP can be complex and unpredictable but a rewarding process. To contextualize this partnership between teacher and student, we have constructed a model inspired by Freire's (1973) teaching approach. Because there is no existing literature on IP, the model also reflects the lived experiences shared by educators in Ryerson University's schools of nursing, social work, and midwifery while working with students as critical scholars in IPs. To date, the model has not been empirically appraised.

The main prerequisite to enter into an IP is the students' willingness to be involved in intellectual dialogue with the teacher (Freire, 1973, 2006). By offering opportunities and accepting invitations for IPs with students, teachers willingly agree to share power and to use their knowledge to intentionally support students' educational dreams, plans, and hopes to achieve academic success. Believing in the mobilized potential of students, teachers invest in critically educating students. Invitations may require time for each's mutual discovery of the other as a contributor to a possible partnership. Some partners may bring enthusiasm for a political cause, an unfulfilled curiosity, self-determination to advocate for intellectual

FIGURE 4.1
The Modelling of a Student Becoming a Critical Scholar Through IP

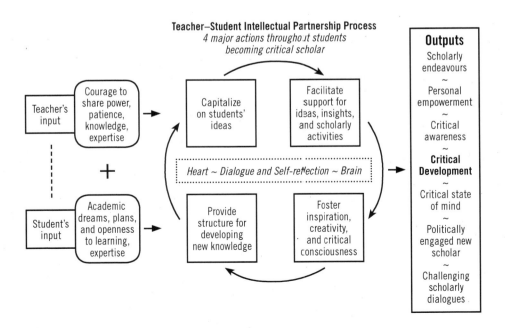

development, or even admiration for the other person's life or professional trajectory. In fact, inspiration, admiration, and respect are seeds for IPs. As stated by a Ryerson nursing student in an IP: "For two years I was in [professor's] class.... I was inspired by [professor's] passion for and commitment to nursing practice, research and education. [Professor] modelled how to question the status quo, seek change and implement the change in practice" (O. Kolisnyk, personal communication, 21 May 2012).

Recognizing that education is a very personal plan, and that students have the freedom to create their own future, teachers work according to the pace, direction, destination, and intellectual aims of students. The above model displays the core of teachers' work as facilitators to nourish a purposeful process of involvement, engagement, and discovery. The teacher's work consists of four leading actions: (1) capitalizing on students' ideas, (2) facilitating support for ideas, insights, and scholarly activities, (3) providing structure for developing new knowledge, and (4) fostering inspiration, creativity, and critical consciousness. Critical development is both a process and an outcome of these actions. However, a purposeful emphasis is placed on the process. The process is particularly important to refine or consolidate learning goals, promote self-discovery, re-create self-concept, and even crystallize social identity. Critical reflection is at the core of the dynamic process involved in IPs. Freire (1973) pointed out that this reflection builds critical awareness skills through an iterative dynamics of action–reflection–action. By acting and doing, students learn to ponder the process of *doing* to produce outcomes, and by reflecting on the process and the outcome, students discover the power of applied strategies. Dr. Pon, a social work professor, shared that in his teaching experience, reflection engages emotional responses to scholarship (heart) and the need for critical self-reflexivity of these emotional responses (brain). These emotional reactions are often linked to both partners' subject locations as well as to their issues of power and privilege. Thus, IP is an opportunity for students to reconstruct their own social reality as learners in the social environment of the school and in society.

Capitalize on Students' Ideas
As intellectual partners in knowledge production, students have a responsibility to contribute to scholarly enterprise such as the development and dissemination of scholarly work. Their ideas are fundamental to collaborative developments and should be deliberately sought, expounded, and integrated. When students' ideas are capitalized on, the benefits of even simple ideas are recognized by the teacher, and opportunities are facilitated to help students expand on their current views of scholarship. Because students learn to respect difference from a secure sense of self and others

(Freire, 2006), their ideas should be acknowledged and clarified through open and non-judgmental dialogue, in a safe, inquiry-based environment. As well, their questions should be regarded as catalysts for creating authentic integrated learning experiences. Critical development of students within IPs involves thinking and questioning as well as searching for answers to questions. Students' questioning of scholarly work in IPs is an indication of the need for clarity, which should be advanced through critical exploration. When a midwifery student questioned Professor Wilson-Mitchell about the birthing experiences of mothers of the African diaspora, she capitalized on the student's queries and ideas for mutual learning and scholarship. This resulted in the co-creation of a joint research study, the dissemination of research findings, and published work.

Facilitate Support for Ideas, Insights, and Scholarly Activities
Freire (2003) argued that teachers can learn a great deal from their students; so teachers must regard students' knowledge as valuable, indeed, as valuable as their own. In doing so, teachers can sustain students' ideas and insights by supporting them to undertake research investigations of interest to them and to share findings at seminars/conferences. Facilitating students' ideas also includes involving them in other scholarly endeavours, such as writing research proposals, critiquing and editing papers, and collaborating on publications. Teachers' genuine and continued interest in students' intellectual growth is crucial to sustaining students' involvement in these activities. Across nursing, social work, and midwifery, we have collectively learned that supporting students' ideas and insights in IP requires teachers to invest trust in their independent efforts, provide space for learning, and exercise patience in witnessing their self-development. One Ryerson nursing student demonstrated the results of such investment:

> Within a two year period I was presenting at national and international conferences. I was surprised to see the impact of this involvement on my regular school work. The resumé I was building with these research projects gave me the confidence to apply to an internship at the World Health Organization. I was accepted for a 3.5 month internship following my graduation and received a grant from Ryerson University to help fund this opportunity. (M. Mohamed, personal communication, 21 May 2012)

Provide Structure for Developing New Knowledge
IPs recognize that students also bring knowledge to the relationship. However, students require an infrastructure to further develop, clarify, and gain new knowledge. Knowledge, according to Freire (2006), "emerges only

through invention and re-invention" (p. 58). Therefore, students need to be a part of an active process of learning that facilitates linkage of knowledge to action. During the process of discovery, this may mean building learning networks within and outside the learning institution and providing linkages to other mentors and resources for learning outside the partnership. Networks can help students elaborate on their thinking while conversing with others (Webb, 2009). This approach can also help students articulate their own talents and academic skills, which may lead to meaningful opportunities for professional collaboration. For example, in the process of discussions with her intellectual partner, an Aboriginal nursing student realized how Freire's ideas were applicable to understanding current health inequities in the lived experiences of Aboriginal people. She created an original conceptual model that was successfully presented in two national nursing conferences, where she was encouraged to contact Canadian authors to have her model integrated as a chapter in a book about Aboriginal health. She co-authored a peer-reviewed manuscript with Dr. Zanchetta and Mrs. James-Henry. The model has inspired her practice as a registered nurse (diabetes educator) in an Aboriginal Health Centre.

Foster Inspiration, Creativity, and Critical Consciousness
Freire (1999) encouraged students and teachers to courageously engage in critical dialogue to illuminate understanding of oppressive realities and their agency in affecting change in the social world. In IP, students benefit when they are offered opportunities to engage in critical dialogue, which enables them to rehearse social criticism and learn how to become comfortable engaging in discussions. Social work education at Ryerson prepares students to address social justice issues such as anti-racism and/or anti-oppression in diverse work settings. Many social work students work in human services agencies. Often, workplace issues arise such as the stereotyping of racialized service users or communities. Social work students or alumni often collaborate with social work professors to deliver professional development workshops to agency staff and managers aimed at strategies for addressing stereotyping and other oppressive issues. Such IPs build students' ideas and initiatives, while helping social work professors to remain current with practice issues. Thus, IPs that prompt students to critically think about topics related to gender, race, sexual orientation, and other subjects of oppression serve as opportunities to make connections to power relations in society. Teachers inspire students' creativity and critical thinking when they foster an open, non-judgmental learning environment that offers them the voice to openly share, analyze, develop, and critique ideas as partners in the teaching-learning process (Mikol, 2005). Students may

then be encouraged to further explore learned content by interpreting and relating new learning to their lived experiences and classroom activities. The focus in fostering creativity and critical thinking is "the process of thinking and questioning what matters—not just the questions and answers" (Mikol, 2005, p. 89). As a Ryerson nursing graduate assistant shared: "The notion of partnership fostered my ability for critical reasoning.... Knowing that a professor saw me as a partner, I began to truly appreciate my own strengths.... As a result, my knowledge, knowledge application, comprehension, and critical reasoning were being developed to complement my graduate studies" (F. Gorospe, personal communication, 12 June 2012).

The outcomes (output) of a successful IP are significant to students' career plans. Students are emerging from IPs able to initiate dialogue or to disagree with authors and to critically analyze what they read or hear. They are able to demonstrate critical and social awareness, they have become more engaged in their classrooms, and they are more motivated toward higher educational pursuits. Many have produced intellectual work that has led to interaction with scholars from different organizations. In IPs, new knowledge may be created. Both the creative process and the created knowledge are worthy outcomes. Former intellectual partners have discussed additional benefits such as superior performance in job interviews, well-developed critical writing skills, and improved confidence. Even students from undeveloped IPs have recognized the benefits of these partnerships. In a post-graduation email to Dr. Zanchetta, one student stated, "I did not have the opportunity to learn more with you.... I did learn to think with you. Thanks for challenging me."

In sum, as members of the FCS, we embrace the teaching philosophy of educating socially engaged leaders and citizens who will be able to share intellectual goods to promote individual and collective empowerment. We are motivated by the opportunity to exercise social justice in education, facilitate societal benefits, and develop human potential. The unison of our teaching philosophies propels our motivation in IPS and characterizes our scholarly outcomes. We view students in IPs as partners in an equitable relationship in which the phenomenon of "othering" has no place. Since critical reflection a hallmark of IPs, we invite readers to reflect upon our audacity in embracing students as intellectual partners in education, and their own responsibility in doing the same.

Implications

The scholarship of teaching and learning embodies the concept of student–teacher relationship. IP is a deliberate approach to advancing relational teaching and learning in university settings by deconstructing the dominant oppressive power structures commonly exhibited in these contexts. Students who participate in IPs are better equipped to influence learning processes. IPs improve social, interpersonal, and problem-solving skills that are suitable beyond the classroom setting (Breslow, 1998; Webb, 2009). They enable students to engage in classroom dialogue because they are comfortable in critical appraisal processes. These skills, along with capabilities in research, presentation, communication, and scholarly writing acquired through IPs, help position students for advanced educational and career opportunities.

The culture of various professions is inviting to graduates who are forward-thinking, socially astute, and confident in their decision-making. The advanced leadership skills gained in IPs can serve them well in leadership positions in professional practice. These students can excel in advocacy roles, especially those that advance the causes of marginalized communities. IPs help students respect differences in perspectives and orientations in practice settings. This better prepares them to take on advanced roles that require effective communication, decision-making, and problem-solving skills, all of which are essential for social citizenry.

Recognizing that IPs can prepare students to critically engage in dialogue with others and advance equity in community health and social services, teachers should continue to foster IPs with students to honour their commitment to social change. The Ryerson community places great value on the engagement of students. Current scholarly programs implemented by Ryerson University outside of classroom settings that support mentorship and engagement with faculty members (e.g., undergraduate research opportunities) are exemplary of the principles of IPs. Efforts should be made to expand such programs and integrate them into undergraduate and graduate curricula. Ultimately, IPs may be the most effective method of engaging professional students whose learning requires continued engagement outside of the classroom. For these students, case studies, classroom discussions, group projects, and social media in the classroom may cease to be engaging or meaningful. Teaching and learning approaches must be situated so as to enhance these students' collaborative and critical reflection skills, and to liberate their voices and actions in the scholarship of discovery.

Is this approach safer or more engaging than others? Could this experience be transferred to other departments in the same university or another? Which gaps and challenges may we expect? We ask all readers to reflect on these questions to find their own answers. We also encourage educators to cultivate and evaluate IPs to see what works in fostering the development of present and future intellectual partners.

Conclusions

In our professional roles, we as teachers have the unique responsibility of enhancing students' personal and professional growth/empowerment while reinforcing the need for a more socially inclusive education. The context of teacher's work allows for dialectical partnership for transforming ideas through intellectual activities even under the chaotic, unpredictable context of learning. In this chapter we have discussed the involvement of IPs in promoting critical awakening among students. Aiming to develop critical learners, teachers in IPs work to transform students' ideas, support scholarship and creativity, provide structure for sharing students' ideas and insights, and inspire and celebrate critical development. Teachers and students share dreams and accomplishments, challenge oppressive versus creative forces, and reframe ideas about education for freedom. To harmonize contradictory and multiple subjectivities in the process, both teachers and students maintain their commitment to self-reflexivity.

Consequently, students are positioned to materialize discourse of power sharing, social change, and transformation as they have experienced in partnerships with their teachers. Thus, we recognize this partnership as an audacious approach toward the birth of socially committed citizens that can comfortably question the meaning of freedom: Why? For what? For whom? We have documented experiences of IPs that resulted in successes such as mastery in the learning process, creation of knowledge, development of teaching tools, and liberation through self-reflection. The participation of Divine and Aafreen (former nursing students and IPs) as co-authors in this chapter is further evidence of the success of IPs. While writing and reflecting on ideas, we welcomed the students' voices to this text, and they became equal collaborators in this academic challenge. The audacity of creating IPs is a manifestation of our enthusiasm, passion, and commitment. More importantly, it is a revelation of our faith in students...faith that remains alive within each of us.

References

Angel, B. F., Duffey, M., & Belyea, M. (2000). An evidence-based project for evaluating strategies to improve knowledge acquisition and critical-thinking performance in nursing students. *Journal of Nursing Education, 39*(5), 219–228.

Andrews, C. A., Ironside, P. M., Nosek, C, Sims, S. L., Swenson, M. M., Yeomans, C.,...Diekelmann, N. (2001). Enacting narrative pedagogy. *Nursing and Health Care Perspective, 22*(5), 252–259.

Apple, M. W. (2011). Democratic education in neoliberal and neoconservative times. *International Studies in Sociology of Education, 21*(1), 21–31.

Breslow, L. (1998). Strategic teaching: Thinking about a handful of variables can make your teaching much more efficient and effective. *MIT Teaching and Learning Laboratory, 11*(3). [Available: http://web.mit.edu/tll/tll- library/teach-talk/teamwork-1.html]

Chan, V. (2001). Readiness for learner autonomy: What do our learners tell us? *Teaching in Higher Education, 6*(4), 505–518.

Donche, V., & Van Petegem, P. (2011). Teacher educators' conceptions of learning to teach and related teaching strategies. *Research Papers in Education, 26*(2), 207–222.

Foucault, M. (1980). Two lectures. In C. Gordon (Ed.), *Power/knowledge: Selected interviews and other writings* (pp. 1972–1977). New York, NY: Pantheon Books.

Freire, P. (1973). *Education for critical consciousness*. New York, NY: Continuum.

Freire, P. (1999). *Educação como prática da liberdade* [Education as a praxis of freedom] (23th ed.). Rio de Janeiro, Brazil: Paz e Terra.

Freire, P. (2003). *Pedagogy of hope: Reliving the Pedagogy of the oppressed*. New York, NY: Continuum.

Freire, P. (2006). *Pedagogy of the oppressed* (30th ed.). New York, NY: Continuum.

Furman, G., & Gruenewald, D. (2004). Expanding the landscape of social justice: A critical ecological analysis. *Educational Administration Quarterly, 40*(1), 47–76.

Gerhardt, H. (2000). Paulo Freire. *UNESCO: International Bureau of Education, 23*(3), 439–458.

Giroux, H. A. (2001). Pedagogy of the depressed: Beyond the new politics of cynicism. *College Literature, 28*(2), 1–32.

Giroux, H. A., & Giroux, S. S. (2004). *Take back higher education: Race, youth, and the crisis of democracy in the post civil-rights era*. New York, NY: Palgrave Macmillan.

Gottesman, I. (2010). Sitting in the waiting room: Paulo Freire and the critical turn in the field of education. *Educational Studies: A Journal of the American Educational Studies Association, 46*(4), 376–399.

Gruenewald, D. A. (2003). The best of both worlds: A critical pedagogy of place. *Educational Researcher, 32*(4), 3–12.

Heron, B. (2005). Self-reflection in critical social work practice: Subjectivity and the possibilities of resistance. *Reflective Practice, 6*(3), 341–351.

Irving, A., & Moffatt, K. (2002). Intoxicated midnight and carnival classrooms: The professor as poet. *Radical Pedagogy, 4*(1). [Available: http://radicalpedagogy.icaap.org]

McCarthy, C., Crichlow, W., Dimitriadis, G., & Dolby, N. (2005). *Race, identity, and representation in education* (2nd ed.). New York: Routledge.

McKinley, M., Thornby, D., & Pettrey, L. (2004). Mentoring matters: Creating, connecting, empowering. *Advance Practice Acute Critical Care, 15*(2), 205–214.

McMahon, B., & Portelli, J. P. (2004). Engagement for what? Beyond popular discourse of student engagement. *Leadership and Policy in Schools, 3*(1), 59–76.

Mikol, C. (2005). Teaching nursing without lecturing: Critical pedagogy as communicative dialogue. *Nursing Education Perspectives, 26*(2), 86–89.

Mullaly, B. (2010). *Challenging oppression and confronting privilege: A critical social work approach*. Toronto, ON: Oxford University Press.

Nicholls, G. (2002). *Developing teaching and learning in higher education*. London & New York: Routledge Falmer.

Pon, G., Gosine, K., & Phillips, D. (2011). Immediate response: Addressing anti-native and anti-black racism in child welfare. *International Journal of Child, Youth, and Family Studies, 3–4*, 385–409.

Razack, N. (2002). *Transforming the field: Critical anti-racist and anti-oppressive perspectives for the human services practicum*. Halifax, NS: Fernwood Publishers.

Sakomoto, I., & Pitner, R. O. (2005). Use of critical consciousness in anti-oppressive social work practice: Disentangling power dynamics at personal and structural levels. *British Journal of Social Work, 35*(4), 435–452.

Shor, I., & Freire, P. (1987). What is dialogical method of teaching? *Journal of Education, 169*(3), 11–31.

Ten Dam, G., & Volman, M. (2004). Critical thinking as a citizenship competence: Teaching strategies. *Learning and Instruction, 14*(4), 359–379.

Thobani, S. (2009). *Exalted subjects: The making of race and nation in Canada*. Toronto, ON: University of Toronto Press.

Webb, N. (2009). A teacher's role in promoting collaborative dialogue in the classroom. *British Journal of Educational Psychology, 79*(1), 1–28.

Weedon, C. (1987). *Feminist practice and poststructuralist theory*. New York, NY: Blackwell.

Winton, S. (2010). Character development and critical democratic education in Ontario, Canada. *Leadership and Policy in Schools, 9*(2), 220–237.

Wong, R. Y. (2004). Knowing through discomfort: A mindfulness-based critical social work pedagogy. *Critical Social Work, 5*(1), 1–10.

5

My Dinners with Tara and Nancy: Feminist Conversations about Teaching for Professional Practice

Kathryn Church

We learn much from understanding the different ways in which learning falters.

— Richard Freeman, 2007

Introduction

This chapter emerges from my practice as a feminist sociologist teaching in one of Canada's largest undergraduate programs in Disability Studies.[1] Formed in 1999 with a handful of students, the school currently hosts several hundred people moving toward bachelor's degree completion on a part-time basis. Most are women, aged twenty to fifty, who are employed in front-line educational settings and service/support agencies across Ontario. Many experience embodied difference—their own or that of someone close to them—as a routine part of daily life. Using online, on-site, and hybrid methods of course delivery, our program expands their skills and upgrades their credentials for job mobility or, increasingly, for graduate-level education.

Disability Studies is a burgeoning interdisciplinary field founded on critical thought and social action. The purpose of our program is to "take the stereotypes, the preconceptions, the pity and paternalism" typically associated with disability and "throw them overboard" (school pamphlet). Courses are designed to "push back against the old ideas that disability is a tragedy and that people with disabilities are broken, helpless or inferior" (school pamphlet).[2] Our students are passionate advocates but they are also continuously learning on the job in ways that implicate them, organizationally, in the exclusions and devaluations our program seeks to undo. Thus, work itself constitutes a curriculum just as potent as anything we have to offer from the site where education officially takes place (Billett, 2008).

Part of my task as an instructor is to contest the views that students bring to class and to resituate them in relation to current theories, practices, and debates in Disability Studies. At the same time, pedagogically, I am deeply invested in what students already know and in starting from their practice to build deeper understandings of what is happening in the disability field. The teaching "troubles" that I encounter stem from this contradiction. How do I value student "work knowledge/s" without being captured by their local and particular realities (Smith, 2005)? How do I respect the fact that, as workers, they are governed by relations beyond their control (Smith, 1987, 2005)? Does what I teach complicate the performance of their jobs in ways that are unmanageable? How do I deepen my capacity to respond to the complexities we are all living, at work and at school (Billet, Fenwick, and Somerville, 2006)?[3]

In Adult Education, there is a well-established body of scholarly literature that validates critical reflection and learning from experience (Paulo Freire, 1986, as a foundational example). However, where the relations between work and learning are concerned, no single line of inquiry or set of findings defines our formal knowledge (Jackson, 2005; Fenwick & Tennant, 2004). Recently, after decades of research, there has been an interesting shift from studies of workplace learning—and concerns about who it serves (Bratton, Mills, Pyrch, & Sawchuk, 2004)—toward studies of learning *at work* (Fenwick, 2001; Billett, 2001; Boud & Garrick, 1999). This emergent scholarship recognizes reflection, participation, and relationship as forms of learning that pervade all work settings (Billett, 2008; Church, Bascia, & Shragge, 2008; Church et al., 2006).

In the pages that follow, I invoke the presence of two Canadian feminists whose scholarship on work and learning I find particularly helpful. The central question for Nancy Jackson is from whose standpoint learning and work are defined: university administrator? employer? manager? worker? or learner? From her roots in the labour and adult literacy movements, she urges us to choose the worker/learner (Jackson, 2001; 2004). She reminds us that we must always situate learning in its social-political context (e.g., Lave & Wenger, 1991; Wertsch, 1985; Rogoff & Lave, 1984), and we must look for the institutional processes that are embedded in work activities. Nancy rallies us to resist any teaching that seeks to rule us.

Tara Fenwick demonstrates that learning happens in unpredictable ways, through disequilibrium and "on the fly." Her vision of *learning in work* encourages a focus on relationships that connect people, experiences, and actions into systems (Fenwick, 2005; 2006). What seem like separate understandings entwine toward a collective knowing; each exchange between us loops outwards, expansively, to change all who are involved. For Tara, all learners are evolving organisms in a sea of change.

Beyond these points of view, Tara and Nancy exist for me as real people—as research colleagues who have actively shaped my understanding with their speaking, listening, questioning, and knowing.[4] My learning from them occurred not through reading or listening to lectures but in the back and forth of conversations that were central to the conviviality of sharing food and drink. In this chapter, I draw from memory and imagination to reconstruct exchanges I enjoyed with each woman over dinner in cities and restaurants where we actually have met. Neither of these occasions transpired in precisely this way, but the dialogues are faithful to Tara and Nancy's published works.

There are several reasons for this narrative style. In part, I am responding to complaints from students about the inaccessibility of most academic writing, about how difficult most texts are to enter, decipher, and retain. By contrast, dialogue is familiar and welcoming: it draws the reader along in ways that permit discovery. The script itself is pedagogy, one that relates directly to debates about how learning happens.

Methodologically, I claim ethnographic ways of writing that place people and human activity—including talk—at the centre of social inquiry: whether teacher or student, researcher or researched (Harding & Norberg, 2005; Naples, 2003; De Vault, 1999; Church, 1995; Diamond, 1992; Fine, 1992; Fonow & Cook, 1991, 2005; Maguire, 1987). In the interpretive tradition, I take writing itself as a form of inquiry—not (just) as a vehicle for rational argument or as a "mopping up activity" at the end of a learning process (Richardson, 2000, p. 923).

Finally, I claim a heritage of feminist challenges to the conventions of masculinist social science (e.g., Finn & Miles, 1982; Smith, 1992; Eichler 2001, 2002). One of my touchstones is Dorothy Smith, who, in forging a sociology from the standpoint of women (for people), insists that we learn how "to address concepts, beliefs, ideology and other categories of thought or mind as people's actual practices in the local settings of their everyday lives" (2004, p. 7). Against the grain of conventional scholarship, Smith's approach is not to split theory and practice (or, for my purposes, theory and story) (Smith, 1999). They go on together such that "theory is itself a practice" (2004, p. 7). This chapter, then, attempts to be the theory in the writing.

Knowledge as Co-emergent — Learning from Tara Fenwick

> *The problem [of training] lies not in underdeveloped critical abilities that should be educated but in a false conceptualization of the learning figure as separable from the conceptual ground.*
> — Tara Fenwick (2001, p. 248)[5]

The scene is Earl's restaurant at the edge of the University of Alberta campus in Edmonton. Having come west for a visit, I am meeting Tara Fenwick for lunch. And I'm a bit anxious. She and I know each other from conferences but I have no idea what it will be like to talk privately. Too late to duck out because suddenly there she is: slender and sophisticated in slacks, a form-fitting mauve leather jacket, and heels. Sighing, she sinks into the booth that I have claimed for us.

"Thanks for meeting me, Tara," I say, clearing my throat. "I know how busy you are."

"Not a problem. I am delighted to escape the office for a while. Let's order before we talk. It's been a long time since breakfast."

Tara selects a fresh berry and spinach salad with grilled chicken and then settles back and waits for me to speak. I give in to an old urge and order a strip of Alberta beef.

"Tara, I hoped you might help me think about teaching students who are already engaged in professional practice. I'm thinking particularly about students in Disability Studies—part-timers who are also full-time workers in the field. Our job is to get them to think critically not just about disability but about the organization of social life. It can cause strain for them in their jobs—or affect their ability to get jobs in the current market. What theoretical debates should I know about in this area?"

"Well, for starters, we need to recognize that massive changes are taking place in the nature of work—and the powerful impact those changes are having on learning [2001a, pp. 3–4]. A global knowledge economy is emerging around us. In Western societies, the stable lifetime employment and company loyalty that many of our parents enjoyed—well, our fathers, anyway—has all but disappeared. Today's jobs demand high productivity but are also insecure, temporary, and contractual. Workers are expected to be responsible, and highly flexible in response to unpredictable organizational change."

"Insecure...temporary...contractual...flexible. Yes, those are all words that describe jobs in the disability field—especially in the community sector. As a School, we are trying to address that—by helping workers get an undergraduate degree that positions them for more stable, better-paying jobs."

"Yes. But that lands you right in the middle of a current debate. There is a tension between the knowledge that universities value—organized around formal disciplines and universal claims—and what learning theorists call 'working knowledge.' The latter, by contrast, is practical and situation specific [2001b, p. 245]. Unfortunately, while you have access to the active and emergent working knowledge/s of your students, you are charged with getting them to produce something else—something more academically recognizable. The plot really thickens!"

"Precisely!" I blurt. "That is my dilemma. I value the working knowledge they bring to class but I know that I have to deliver them elsewhere. *They* want this too, even if the journey is uncomfortable or frightening. Somehow, together, we have to make our way into the realm of theory, for example, or at least learn how to shuttle back and forth between theory and practice."

"Let's focus on that between-ness for a minute. As theorists, our notions of working knowledge have a couple of major flaws. At least, that is what I have argued [2001b, p. 243]. For starters, we tend to view knowledge as a substantive 'thing'—like this cup or [glancing around the room] that barstool...or...a pie. Yes, let's go with the food analogy...since we finally have some!"

The waiter delivers our entrees with a flourish: Tara's restrained greens, my over-the-top strip of flesh. There is a brief pause while we tuck in.

"Theorists presume that learners ingest knowledge as if it were roast beef and apple pie at Sunday dinner," Tara resumes, glancing pointedly at my plate. "And after the learner chews and swallows, knowledge exists inside somehow. Additionally—and I know I'm stretching it here—they assume that each learner 'eats' alone! To put that in academic lingo, learners are viewed as isolated cognitive agents."

Gnawing on the metaphor, I wait for her to go on.

"I find neither of these assumptions very satisfactory," she swallows. "They give me indigestion!"

"Okay," I agree, laughing. "So, where do we go instead?"

"In a sense, that's an open question—perhaps *the* question of the moment. Because of the global reorganization of work, our traditional models of learning are in something of a shambles. For decades, we have concentrated most of our attention on preparing people ahead of time for jobs that were waiting to receive them once they were credentialed. Now we don't know what will be waiting, and we have to adjust to that uncertainty. As educators, we have suddenly recognized that by concentrating on formal education and classrooms, we have ignored the workplace itself as a site of learning. Or perhaps I should say we have ignored the many possible forms of work and workplaces that one person might inhabit and pass through in a lifetime. The latest buzz, then, is about learning *in* work as opposed to learning that prepares *for* work [2001b, p. 246]."

"So, this is the direction of your own research?" I press Tara for more.

"Yes. I am arguing for more attention to knowledge that is embedded in action—attention not just from educators but from sociologists, economists, cultural theorists, and management types, as well. I want us to recognize knowing as a continuous process rather than a thing, and as a quality that is less within people than flowing between them as we participate and communicate with each other [2001b, pp. 247–248]."

"*Between* again," I muse. "The more I teach, the more I feel the betweenness of knowing in the classroom—whether it is a physical or a virtual space. For example, most of my students come from working-class backgrounds—and I connect with them around that experience especially if they have been told they are 'not university material.' I respect the fact that, somehow, they have disregarded that message and come anyway. They have transgressed other people's low expectations to make a modest claim on university as a kind of forbidden space. The fear that someone will find out you are a 'fraud' is one of the hidden messages in the classroom. The only reason I know about it is that it's part of my life too."

"Ah!" nods Tara. "Well, that fraud thing is true of many women of our generation."

"It is. The students and I are co-conspirators in that project. Would you say that our knowledge is co-emergent?"

"What I *have* argued, in one of my papers, is that knowledge, identity, *and* environment are co-emergent, and that learning is continuous invention and exploration [2001b, p. 249]. But let's return to that topic later, over dessert."

She reaches for the menu.

Actors Instead of Instruments – Learning from Nancy Jackson

> *Competent actors in any situation draw upon a range of clues provided by the environment and accumulated through experience over time to address the task at hand.*
> — Nancy Jackson (1994, p. 345)[6]

The scene is a Thai restaurant pungent with spiced noodles and home to a Buddha who spreads peace from a mural on the back wall. Back in Toronto, I have arranged to have dinner with Nancy Jackson. I value her judgment but also her mentorship—a rare relationship in my experience of academic life. She arrives a bit late: a brisk, neat figure in a coral-colored linen jacket that I know to be a prize purchase from a second-hand store in Halifax. Like Tara, Nancy is breathless. We are all breathless, I realize suddenly, bringing to mind other women academics I know.

"I am so sorry!" she exclaims, giving me a fast hug. "I had to nip some forms into the main office before the deadline, and I didn't get a chance to fill them out until late in the day. So it was a last-minute rush."

"Not a problem, truly. I knew that you would get here in your own time."

"Indeed. I wouldn't miss it. Especially since I am starved! Shall we order?"

And so we do: Vegetarian spring rolls to start, Bangkok stir-fry and emerald curry vegetables to follow; a glass of white wine for Nancy and mineral water for me.

"How are you?" Nancy asks, starting to unwind. "And how was the West?"

"Good and good, thank you for asking. The country is beautiful, my parents are well, and I had lunch with Tara Fenwick, which was a pleasure."

"Ah, Tara. I don't get to see enough of her. How is she?"

"In fighting trim, you could say, and very helpful."

"How so? What are you up to now?" Nancy asks, growing alert and a bit stern.

"You always expect the worst of me... or for me!" I laugh. "No worries. I was just asking what her take is on current debates in work and learning. I find her work suggestive; it makes my brain run in interesting directions."

"I've never known you when that wasn't the case! But tell me a bit more."

"Tara posed the postmodern argument about contemporary workplaces: all this business about flexible learning and the 'enterprising self' as core to the economies of late modernity. She reminded me that today's workers are expected to embrace—and embody—the values of the 'new capitalism'—to discipline themselves into high levels of productivity—to be hugely flexible in response to organizational demands under conditions of great uncertainty."

"Hmm, yes," Nancy nods, "and the insidious part is that it doesn't necessarily *feel* oppressive because workers experience these demands as congruent with their own goals."

"Right. It's not just production that's at stake. Managerial definitions of 'excellence' also shape the worker's 'private spaces of self and soul' [Fenwick, 2001, p. 244]. I think I've got that right.... And I recognize the dilemma from my experience with academia: lots of flexibility in terms of managing my time as long as all of my time is spent meeting organizational demand."

"And too many of those demands feel legitimate, am I right?"

It's my turn to nod. Nancy and I have probed this point before; each of us is vulnerable because of how we feel about students.

"Regardless of the motivation, the end result is the same for me: no downtime that isn't penetrated by university demands, and very little personal life."

"Those are major losses, for sure," Nancy nods. "I can read myself into the same picture. Still, you and I have a lot more control over our intellectual 'product' than most other workers. We think and write and speak with an independence that you just don't find elsewhere."

"I agree. But as you often point out," I argue, "that privilege is under attack in the neoliberal university."

"These are long-standing battles," Nancy argues, tucking a rebellious strand of white hair behind one ear, "particularly for those of us situated in radical traditions. It is not new for feminists to be fighting for space in increasingly restrictive environments!"

"I keep forgetting that I'm a radical, sorry!," I laugh, "and that resistance is a form of work. Tara argues that postmodern learning theories underestimate the ability of workers and learners to resist or reshape their job constraints. And she cites the importance of feminist contributions to debates about learning."

"And for her, they would be...?"

"Well, without being comprehensive, one angle is the need to theorize work-knowing as fully embodied in the messiness of actual experience rather than in the tidy systems of the rational mind. The conscious, reflective mind is more limited than much learning theory recognizes."

"Actual experience...now there's a phrase!" Nancy leaps on the term. "What about the actual working practices of front-line workers? Let's pursue that line of argument for a moment, specifically with respect to vocational learning [2000, p. 3]."

"Please do."

"Everyone agrees that the training system in North America is an absolute fossil from the early 1900s. It's a major frustration for educators that no amount of tinkering has fixed the thing. What we need is a restructured vision of 'vocational' that goes well beyond industry's preoccupation with 'productivity' and 'competitiveness.'"

"A call to arms—excellent! Where do we begin?"

"Well, how we teach a work process depends fundamentally on how we conceptualize it [2000, p. 246]. So, to create a new vision for training we need an alternative theoretical framework."

"Just so that I know what I'm up against here, how would you describe the current theoretical framework?"

"The dominant tradition of vocational training is empiricist and behaviourist. Teaching is oriented towards preparing students to perform tasks related directly to work processes operating in the world of actual jobs. And in keeping with a lot of management theory, most non-professional jobs are viewed as a routine set of procedures that are presented to learners as a prescribed set of steps. Learning objectives relate directly to those steps and students are measured against observable criteria."

I feel a bubble of agitation in my gut.

"But what you are describing isn't limited to vocational training! This kind of thing happens in my work life all the time. A lot of the in-house training I take is organized by learning objectives—and they aren't always that grand: something like... 'by the end of the day, you will have met five new people'... that kind of thing."

"The point *I* want to make," Nancy insists, refusing to be sidetracked, "is that no approach to job definition or training that emphasizes the behavioural aspects can or will adequately represent the forms of practical action required to perform most jobs competently in the lived situation [1994, p. 348]."

"So often, organizers proceed as if the people in the room are novices; they miss the expertise that is already there. Is that why I feel that these sessions aren't actually intended for me?"

"That's classic. I mean, what you have to understand is that the function of the meetings you describe, like much of vocational learning, is not to recognize and make use of your expertise. It is to convey the work of the university—or the workplace—from the perspective of those who manage and control it. The meetings may be framed as situations in which—to use your words—you get to 'meet five new people.' In fact, they are often management exercises. What's at stake is labour/management relations. From that point of view, we might have to agree that organizers do their job well instead of poorly as you originally thought."

"Ah! You cut to the heart of it: management cloaked as learning. Why didn't I see that?" I stare sadly at the remains of my rice.

"Well, I am presuming that some of what is communicated is actually useful to you and that your 'work' as a learner in these situations is to sift what you want to keep from what you want to let go."

"True. I acquire a certain amount of 'how to' information that is useful in a sea of trial-and-error learning. Some speakers actually tell us how things work."

"That's management talk. It initiates you into the top-down view of appropriate relations between the university and its students—all guided by appropriate texts, no doubt."

"All on the website," I wink, slyly.

"Let's not go *there!*" Nancy laughs. "Instead, let's loop back to the broader issue of training. You have noticed that the meetings you attend often don't fit either your conceptualization of your work or your subjectivity as a worker. And *that*, I would argue, is the experience of most vocational learners."

"Sometimes I withdraw or quiet myself—and just leave my body sitting there," I mutter.

"But that withdrawal is an act of resistance on your part. You 'vacate' a learning event because it does not recognize and address you as the knowing and acting subject of your own work. In my revolution—come the day!—vocational learning will draw from a combination of radical worker traditions and learner-driven pedagogy to turn that experience of "splitting" inside out. If we position worker-learners in the centre, as the knowing, thinking, sense-making subjects of their own acts, we could revitalize the whole system."

"Actors instead of instruments, Nancy. What a notion."

Conclusion

Situated in the fertile nexus between published works and lively conversation, this chapter is both a scholarly exploration of teaching for professional practice and a pedagogical experiment with text. By conjuring traces of Tara Fenwick and Nancy Jackson in my conceptualization of the issues, I have interrupted the seamless way that thesis, evidence, and argument organize most academic writing. With multiple feminist voices and "phantasmic subjects" (personal correspondence, Tara Fenwick, 14 January 2013), these exchanges have caused me to remember myself as someone who carries traditions of critical inquiry and activist scholarship. At a time when universities are undergoing massive technical and economic transformation, it is vital that students continue to have face-to-face contact and interaction with instructors who embody and reproduce this heritage. The assertion applies especially to students who are on the front lines of an inequitable society. Under such conditions, teaching students how to investigate the dilemmas that arise may be more important than teaching the official canon of expertise (personal communication, Nancy Jackson, 3 February 2013). While it goes against the conventional grain, my dinners with Tara and Nancy have reinforced this position both as historical continuity and as a way of moving forward.

Notes

1 With a nod to the movie *My Dinner with André* (1981), I want to thank the editorial team for the opportunity of their questions in relation to chapter development. I owe a debt of gratitude to Nancy Jackson and Tara Fenwick for being engaged with this writing from the beginning. They do not view themselves as co-authors but they have co-constituted this work through multiple rounds of feedback and strategic advice. It has been a great gift to work with them on this portraiture. Not for the first time, my gratitude to Timothy Diamond for his extensive knowledge of Dorothy Smith's work, his encouragement to be the theory in the writing, and for his dedicated writer's life.
2 I draw here from promotional materials written by Catherine Frazee early in the life of the School ("Ryerson Rocks" and "Ryerson Renegades," roughly 2004).
3 I owe much in this paragraph to Nancy Jackson's feedback on several drafts.
4 Nancy, Tara, and I met through the SSHRC-funded scholarly network on Work and Lifelong Learning organized from Sociology and Equity Studies, Ontario Institute for Studies in Education, University of Toronto (OISE/UT). See www.wall.ca for relevant publications.
5 Tara Fenwick is currently Professor and Director of ProPEL (Professional Practice, Education and Learning) in the Stirling School of Education at the University of Stirling, UK. Formerly, she held positions in Faculties of Education at the University of British Columbia and the University of Alberta.
6 Nancy Jackson retired in 2012 from a position as Associate Professor in the Department of Adult Education and Counselling Psychology at the Ontario Institute for Studies in Education (OISE), University of Toronto. This program, in which she taught for many years, has been moved recently into the Department of Leadership, Higher and Adult Education.

References

Billett, S. (2001). *Learning in the workplace.* Crows Nest, NSW: Allen & Unwin.
Billett, S. (2008). Participation and learning in turbulent times: Negotiations between the community and the personal. In K. Church, N. Bascia, & E. Shragge (Eds.), *Learning through community: Exploring participatory practices.* Amsterdam, Netherlands: Springer.
Billett, S., T. Fenwick, & M. Somerville (Eds.). (2006). *Work, subjectivity and learning: Understanding learning through working life.* Amsterdam, Netherlands: Springer.
Boud, D., & J. Garrick (Eds.). (1999). *Understanding learning at work.* New York, NY: Routledge.
Bratton, J., Mills, J. H., Pyrch, T., & Sawchuk, P. 2004. *Workplace learning: A critical introduction.* Aurora, ON: Garamond.

Church, K. (1995). *Forbidden narratives: Critical autobiography as social science*. Amsterdam, Netherlands: Gordon & Breach. Reprint: New York, NY: Routledge (2004).

Church, K., Bascia, N., & Shragge, E. eds. (2008). *Learning through community: Exploring participatory practices*. Amsterdam, Netherlands: Springer.

Church K., with Frazee, C., Luciani, T., Panitch, M., & Seeley, P. (2006). Dressing corporate subjectivities: Learning what to wear to the bank. In S. Billett, T. Fenwick, & M. Somerville (Eds.), *Work, subjectivity, and Learning: Understanding learning through working life*. Amsterdam, Netherlands: Springer.

De Vault, M. (1999). *Liberating method: Feminism and social research*. Philadelphia, PA: Temple University.

Diamond, T. (1992). *Making gray gold: Narratives of nursing home care*. Chicago, IL: University of Chicago Press.

Eichler, M. (2001). Women pioneers in Canadian sociology: The effects of a politics of gender and a politics of knowledge. *Canadian Journal of Sociology, 26*(3), 375–403.

Eichler, M. (2002). The impact of feminism on Canadian sociology. *American Sociologist*, Spring, 27–41.

Fenwick, T. (2006). Escaping/becoming subjects: Learning to work the boundaries in boundaryless work. In S. Billett, T. Fenwick, & M. Somerville (Eds.), *Work, subjectivity, and Learning: Understanding learning through working life*. (pp. 21–36). Amsterdam, Netherlands: Springer.

Fenwick, T. (2005). *Tidying the territory: Clarifying our terms and purposes in integrating learning and work*. Paper presented to the International Conference on Work and Lifelong Learning, Toronto, June.

Fenwick, T. (2001a). Tides of change: New themes and questions in workplace learning. In T. Fenwick (Ed.), *Socio-cultural Perspectives on Learning through Work*. San Francisco: Jossey-Bass.

Fenwick, T. (2001b). Work knowing "on the fly:" Enterprise cultures and co-emergent epistemology. *Studies in Continuing Education, 23*(2), 244–259.

Fenwick, T., & Tennant, M. (2004). Understanding adult learners. In G. Foley (Ed.), *Dimensions of Adult Learning* (pp. 55–73). Berkshire, UK: Open University Press.

Fine, M. (1992). *Disruptive voices: The possibilities of feminist research*. Ann Arbor, MI: University of Michigan Press.

Finn, G., & Miles, A. (Eds.). (1982). *Feminism in Canada: From pressure to politics*. Montreal, PQ: Black Rose.

Fonow, J., & Cook, M. M. (2005). Feminist methodology: New applications in the academy and public policy. *Signs, 30*(4), 2211–2236.

Fonow, J., & Cook, M. M. (Eds.). (1991). *Beyond methodology: Feminist scholarship as lived research*. Bloomington, IN: Indiana University Press.

Freeman, R. (2007). Epistemological bricolage: How practitioners make sense of learning. *Administration & Society, 39*(4), 476–496.

Freire, P. (1986). *Pedagogy of the oppressed.* New York, NY: Continuum.

Harding, S., & Norberg, K. (2005). New feminist approaches to social science methodologies: An introduction. *Signs, 30*(4), 2009–2015.

Jackson, N. (2005). *What counts as learning? A case study perspective.* Discussion paper for WALL Network meetings, June 19–20, 2005. Toronto.

Jackson, N. (2004). Notes on ethnography as research method. In M. E. Belfiore, T. A. Defoe, S. Folinsbee, J. Hunter, & N. S. Jackson (Eds.), *Reading work: Literacies in the new workplace.* Mahwah, NJ: Lawrence Erlbaum.

Jackson, N. (2001). "Writing up" people at work: Investigations of workplace literacy. *Literacy and Numeracy Studies, 10*(1–2), 5–22.

Jackson, N. (1994). Rethinking vocational learning: The case of clerical skills. In L. Erwin & MacLennan (Eds.), *Sociology of education in Canada: Critical perspectives on theory, research and practice* (pp. 341–351). Toronto: Copp Clark Longman.

Lave, J., & Wenger, E. (1991). *Situated learning: Legitimate peripheral participation.* Cambridge, UK: Cambridge University Press.

Maguire, P. (1987). *Doing participatory research: A feminist approach.* Amherst, MA: Center for International Education, University of Massachusetts.

Naples, N. (2003). *Feminism and method: Ethnography, discourse analysis, and activist research.* New York, NY: Routledge.

Richardson, L. (2000). Writing: A method of inquiry. In N. Denzin & Y. Lincoln (Eds.), *Handbook of qualitative research* (2nd ed.) (pp. 923–948). Thousand Oaks, CA: Sage Publications.

Rogoff, B., & Lave, J. (Eds.). (1984). *Everyday cognition: Its development in social context.* Cambridge, MA: Harvard University Press.

Smith, D. (2005). *Institutional ethnography: A sociology for people.* Walnut Creek, CA: AltaMira Press.

Smith, D. (1999). *Writing the social: Critique, theory, and investigations.* Toronto: University of Toronto Press.

Smith, D. (1992). Whistling women: Reflections on rage and rationality. In W. Carroll, L. Christiansen-Ruffman, R. Currie, & D. Harrison (Eds.), *Fragile truths: 25 years of sociology and anthropology in Canada* (pp. 207–226). Ottawa, ON: Carleton University Press.

Smith, D. (1987). *The everyday world as problematic: A feminist sociology.* Toronto: University of Toronto Press.

Wertsch, J. V. (Ed.). (1985). *Culture, communication and cognition: Vygotskian perspectives.* Cambridge, UK: Cambridge University Press.

6

Drawing Close: Critical Nurturing as Pedagogical Practice

May Friedman and Jennifer Poole

Introduction

In this chapter, we consider the ways that teaching can be considered a form of connection and caregiving and a site of intimacy. We come to this from the lived experiences of our lives as educators and from our remembrances of our lives as students, as well as from our engagement in ongoing learning. Specifically, we have found that we are often surprised by the consonance of our teaching styles and strategies. We often hear from students that they have experienced similar styles in our classes, or that our teaching strategies resonate with students in analogous ways. This awareness of our shared values and beliefs led us toward this collaboration, in which we aim to accomplish what Kreber (2006) has termed "transformative learning through reflection" (p. 90). Ultimately, these are our beginning thoughts, developed in dialogue with each other, on the place of intimacy in our teaching practice and the ways that a reflection on intimacy is especially relevant in the teaching of helping professions. As social work educators we are grappling with ideas of professionalism and the use of self in practice, and these values—the content we share with our students—have informed our ideas of teaching. Our knowledge has sometimes been intellectual and sometimes intuitive, but it has definitely drawn on our lived experiences as teachers, students, practitioners and, of course, many other roles beyond. Consequently, our aim is to trouble the classroom a little, rattle the pedagogy of every day, and argue for something we call nurturing as pedagogy. We aim to share our ideas in this chapter by engaging our intellectual curiosity, but also our emotional reflections on the work we do.

Nurturing may be defined as the act of encouraging, nourishing, and caring for someone or something. The "someone" whom we consider here are the students in our classrooms, who are themselves collaborators in this relationship-building work. The "something" is the caring space we endeavour to create both within and outside those classrooms. We realize this is a somewhat radical act—to speak boldly of drawing close in an age of moving away, to argue for more care and concern when so many of our students are already supposedly "entitled," and to develop relationships at a time when social media, online teaching, and ballooning class sizes are apparently moving us in a completely different direction. By contrast, we see, in this caring pedagogy, a heeding of Boyer's call that "teaching, at its best, means not only transmitting knowledge, but transforming and extending it as well" (quoted in Belcher, Pecukonis, & Knight, 2011, p. 196).

Theoretical Contexts: Beyond the Enlightenment

Before we move into that discussion, however, we want to go back a little, delineate why caring in the classroom has become so entirely outrageous, and theorize about why university educators are not supposed to care and nurture.

In the West, we argue, it began with the Enlightenment. As Jennifer teaches in one of our undergraduate social work theory courses, the Enlightenment was a particular eighteenth-century turning point that began a celebration of all things rational. Out went medievalism and mysticism and in came logic, objectivity, the Cartesian split between mind and body, and the anointing of science as supreme.

On this theoretical foundation, we have built our modernist houses of medicine, psychiatry, government, punishment, and education, to name just a few. These are houses within which all share a veritable worship of reason, linearity, and scientific neutrality as well as "professional" and expert knowledge.

The French philosopher Michel Foucault (1995) argued that this foundation has created a type of docility in us, a tameness, a willingness to obey the rules that privilege disciplinary forms of knowledge and an interest in their perpetuation. Paulo Friere (2007) claims this "worship" has also resulted in what he calls the banking model of education—a process by which knowledge is deposited into passive (and docile) students. Indeed, this kind of knowledge is a "gift" bestowed by those who consider themselves knowledgeable, upon those considered to know nothing. Similarly, existential philosopher Maurice Merleau-Ponty (1989) argues that such a docilizing process has also been a disembodying process, one that renders both teacher and student disconnected not only from each other but from their own embodied ways of knowing and being.

If we add neoliberalism to this mix, with its celebration of cost containment and contracting out, and add in risk discourses, fear of academic misconduct, and managerialism's focus on efficiencies, university educators are now assumed to be individualistic, competitive, "professional," disembodied, and rational individuals who are always responsible, risk averse, knowing, self-motivated, and entirely replaceable. Those educators must publish or perish, get ahead or be left behind. If they must teach, they should be sure to manage their courses, their students and their disciplined selves with deft efficiency, a commitment to best practices, and an excellent knowledge of standards and outcome-based learning (Hutchings, Taylor Huber, & Ciccone, 2011). Indeed, much of the scholarship on teaching emphasizes best practices that focus on efficiency and effectiveness (Kreber, 2006). With respect to social work education specifically, Belcher, Pecukonis, and Knight argue that "the social work academic environment is undergoing an unsettling and historic transformation as it struggles to balance the need for quality teaching with the growing demand for external research funding" (2011, p. 195). However, we two educators want to think, act and teach differently. For Jennifer;

> that shift began over a decade ago. I had long been steeped in critical theory. I had long believed that to be "critical" is not simply a tendency to complain, and I had always held to the sense that being critical involves "detecting and unmasking of beliefs and practices that limit human freedom, justice and democracy" (Usher, 1996, in Glesne, 1999, p. 12). Indeed, during my slow indoctrination into university teaching, a process paved with workshops on discipline, handling difficult students and how to protect one's research time by teaching less, I began to feel distinctly "limited," very much bound by rules that privileged a neoliberal containment culture where contact (and its costs) should be kept to a minimum. What resonated more with me however, was the kind of liberation practices I was reading about in Kathryn Church's autoethnography on mental health in Ontario (Church, 1995) or the centring of relationship and connection I found in the work of Indigenous scholars such as Raven Sinclair and Michael Anthony Hart (2009), Lynn Lavallée [and Poole] (2010) and Cyndy Baskin (2011). These were decolonizing, Indigenizing, critical, justice-centred responses to the neoliberal rules which had bound my pedagogy. Galvanized by this leadership, it felt critical that I attempt to re-imagine those rules going forward.

Personal Contexts: Other Mothering and More

Clearly, some of our reasons for choosing to shift the way we practise are intensely personal and may be borne more from outside the academy than within. We follow Kreber's suggestion that "the most significant forms of learning involve a critical analysis of the processes and conditions by which certain norms we have come to take for granted have evolved" (2006, p. 91). Our professional social work and academic lives have kept pace with other areas of personal growth and have been shaped in response to these "outside" realms. May considers the ways her path toward motherhood has both supported and contradicted her professional growth:

> *I became pregnant for the first time weeks after completing my master's in Social Work and went through my doctorate—and a lot of teaching as a result—while parenting my one, then two, then three small children. As a result, I was learning how to parent and how to negotiate this intense shift in identity, at the same time that I was engaging in other identity shifts, namely into the professional and academic realms. Now a mother of four, I am still navigating these intersections.*
>
> *These shifts were intensely significant for me. Moving into different public and private roles has an impact on everyone, I'm sure, but in my own life, I had grown up without examples of professional or academic success, for the most part. I also became a mother at a younger age than many of my peers and thus had no models for either mothering or scholarly and professional practices. This led to an absolute cyclone of upheaval and adjustment to my sense of self. Perhaps it was the simultaneity of these identity shifts, and the peculiar freedom that comes in the absence of examples of "what one does" that resulted in my cobbling together an amalgam of mothering, teaching, learning and social working that was co-constitutive, that drew from each of these realms and allowed them to inform one another fully.*

Responding to "the importance of the self as a source of reflection and action" (Hutchings, Taylor Huber, & Ciccone, 2011, p. 58), only in hindsight has May become aware of the extent to which her growth as a parent, professional, and educator allowed these roles to become enmeshed with one other but also remain fundamentally contradictory. Some of the contradictions that May experienced drew from the dominant discourses of motherhood. These discourses make clear that mothers are meant to be sacrificial, selfless, kind, warm-hearted, available, and nurturing (Douglas & Michaels, 2004; Hays, 1998; Maushart, 2000). "Good mothers" are meant to serve as vessels of and servants to their children.

Very problematically, the dominant discourse of motherhood, as noted by many feminist motherhood scholars, aims for the erasure of maternal agency by ensuring that children are always the focal point. Significantly, mothers—as opposed to parents—are held to an impossible standard, with other parents (fathers and other caregivers) erased from the totalizing responsibility for children. This is true in expert texts, commercials, editorials, doctor's visits, and many, many sites beyond.[1] Furthermore, as Swanson and Johnston suggest, the expectation of intensive mothering may be especially intense for academic mothers: "Perhaps in reaction to the guilt of preserving an identity outside of motherhood, academic mothers compile intensive mothering expectations on top of already high work expectations" (2003, p. 68).

May's scholarly work aims to challenge and respond to these dominant discourses by showing the ways that myths of good motherhood hold people to impossible standards and keep mothers accountable to and for their children to an outrageous extent. However, in the academy, things were very different.

In stark contrast to the idealized mother, there to catch her children before they fall, anticipating every need and providing endless support, nascent educators are provided with starkly different advice. Educators are meant to provide knowledge and then step away to allow students to take care of themselves (Salter, Pang, & Sharma, 2009). We are meant to avoid becoming enmeshed in our students' lives, especially since "we're not therapists"—even those of us, as social work educators, who may well have provided therapeutic care at some point past or present. We are cautioned against giving up too much of ourselves, being too responsive for fear of being taken advantage of (Singleton-Jackson, Jackson, & Reinhardt, 2010). Pushback from students is viewed as inherently negative and disrespectful (Hara, 2010). In many respects, we are taught to carefully guard against our students, that they are somehow dangerous. Balancing these learnings with the ongoing identity shifts of her parenting role caused May some puzzlement on both intellectual and emotional levels:

> *I found myself in the midst of a severe cognitive dissonance. I was being told that I should subsume myself endlessly to my wonderful but sometimes annoying children, that to do so was natural and obvious. Yet I was being told to avoid my often delightful students, that to engage with their needs would undermine my credibility and would be unprofessional. Neither claim made much sense, frankly, so I decided (more from a need for survival than a strong political instinct) to abandon them both.*

Instead May allowed her parenting and professional roots to merge toward a caring pedagogy. This caring pedagogy allows us to teach with a keen sense of responsibility to and for our students. We do not do their work for them, and we do not call them every night to remind them to do their readings: but we feel entwined with them and engaged with them on a more intimate level than a traditional model of teaching and learning would suggest.

This teaching ideology is informed by feminist work in motherhood studies and by emergent research on maternal pedagogies (O'Reilly, 2004, 2008; Green, 2009; Byrd & Green, 2011) and extends Noddings's work suggesting the imperative to imbue education with caring and happiness (1984, 2003). In the same way that we reject the notion of a maternal role that implies sole and complete responsibility for children, we do not think our students should be solely the responsibility of others. Much feminist maternal scholarship suggests that communality is essential to non-patriarchal parenting structures (e.g., Chandler, 2007; Kinser, 2008; O'Reilly, 2004). Since we wish to parent in a context in which we all work together, as educators we believe we have a responsibility to be a part of the caring networks of our students' lives.

Such an analysis draws on scholarship of motherhood studies that seek to disrupt individual discourses (Chandler, 2007; diQuinzio, 1999; Kinser, 2008). Mielle Chandler, for example, suggests that "the problematic lies not in the equation of motherhood with non-subjectivity but in the privileging of an emancipated individuated subjectivity" (2007, p. 535). In other words, instead of becoming frustrated that motherhood takes away women's autonomy, we must acknowledge that we are all already and always interrelated. This truth resonates for us as social work practitioners and social justice advocates: in looking at our relationships, we find powerful evidence that we are only able to function as components of a vast, dynamic, and interrelated organism. We also hear the ring of truth when we consider our work in the classroom.

In particular, we are intrigued by the ways that as educators we can act as networks of othermothers. Drawing from African and African diasporic mothering traditions, othermothers "look after children to whom they have no blood relations of legal obligation. There is usually a mutual agreement between mothers, aunts, uncles, or fathers who play the role of othermothers in a given community. A woman elder who mothers both adult and children assumes community mothering on the other hand. She assumes leadership roles and she becomes a consultant for her community" (Wane, 2004, p. 230). Wane goes on to make clear that "the only form of remuneration is reciprocity, cohesiveness, and strengthened community ties" (p. 231).

The model of othermothering presupposes that we are all interrelated, in stark contrast to a Western neoliberal paradigm that privileges individuality. Furthermore, othermothering does not seek to reify "natural mothering"—it's not an argument that suggests that women are inherently maternal, since anyone from any gender or relationship to the people being mothered may engage in othermothering. Rather, it disrupts the paradigm that privileges biology and kinship above affection, community, investment, and need.

Interestingly, Patricia Hill Collins presents the notion of othermothers in specific reference to pedagogies, writing that "this community othermother tradition also explains the 'mothering the mind' relationship that can develop between African American women teachers and their Black female and male students. Unlike the traditional mentoring so widely reported in educational literature, this relationship goes far beyond that of providing students with technical skills or a network of academic and professional contacts" (2002, p. 191).

The concept of othermothers and community othermothers is a radical disruption in Western thinking about families and dominant discourses of motherhood (where mothers own their children and are thus owned by them). We want to argue that othermothering may be applied equally radically in the realm of pedagogy. Traditional pedagogies suggest that we value our students' independence, that we aim to bolster their capacity to stand alone. A model that suggests that we act as "othermothers" instead suggests that we must be critically nurturing, rather than distant, that we must implicate ourselves in the web of interrelationships that exist in our classroom, rather than absenting ourselves from these dynamic enterprises.

Even in anti-oppressive circles we are so steeped in our enlightened individualist thought that the idea that we can and should be accountable for one another is radical and potentially frightening. Even the most progressive scholarship in teaching and learning moves toward emancipatory and transformative learning yet avoids a specific focus on intimacy and relationship (Gurm, 2013; Woodhouse, 2010). Yet we see the seeds of this idea elsewhere in our academic and professional lives. Specifically, in the model of anti-oppressive social work that we teach and practise, we routinely call for a focus on relationship, for a commitment to interrelated caring. Perhaps our caring pedagogy is thus an extension of the same compassion, authenticity, and sincere responsibility that we aim to urge our students toward in their practice relationships.

Resisting the Managerial

In addition to ideas around othermothering, we find many lines of pedagogical possibility in the critical theorists we referenced earlier in this chapter. This work could all be collected under the umbrella of what feminist philosophers Margrit Shildrick and Roxanne Mykitiuk (2005) call "post-conventional" thinking. It could also be thought of as post-Enlightenment thinking, an antidote to modernism in its problematizing of reason, rules, categories, and what has come to be counted as "normal," "good," or healthy. Such a barn of bold ideas includes but is not limited to postmodernism, post-structuralism and Foucauldian thought, queer theory, critical disability studies, fat studies, and the scholarship now known as Mad studies.

From Foucault (1995), we find encouragement to be post-disciplinary in our teaching, to deconstruct the learned docility we have all been taught and are teaching and to rearrange the sites of that docility without adhering to what he, citing Bentham, called the panopticon. The panopticon is what we find in classrooms where all the seats are in rows facing forward, as well as on Web tools such as BlackBoard, where only the instructor can see who is logging on and "doing the work" and only the instructor has the power to discipline students through grading.

From Merleau-Ponty (1989) we find encouragement to be what he calls intercorporeal. Rejecting the Cartesian split at the heart of what it is to "act" professional, he argues that as human experience is always embodied, the exclusion of messy, human, embodied emotion is not only false but impossible. As the repressed always returns, so will emotion until we make it "normal" to allow it, and our bodies, into the mix. Merleau-Ponty also argues that any change we make to the self (such as the changes we expect through education, for example) will always also be a change to the body (and vice versa). We feel while we learn, we embody our knowledge, and we embody our knowledge relationships both with students and with our peers. Importantly, this work is never completed, and Merleau-Ponty reminds us that this intercorporeality is always in a state of flux, always under construction.

In the theoretical literature we also find encouragement to problematize false categories and docilizing ways of being. We are called upon to query the border between "being" an educator and being a student, and this means we can allow what we consider a "bothness," a multidirectionality in knowledge production that rattles the rules. It also means we can admit when we do not "know"—indeed, we are encouraged not to pretend we "know" and to queer the supposed normalcy of constructed omniscience.

Equally encouraging for us is Mad studies (LeFrançois, Menzies, & Rheaume, 2013), a burgeoning field of study that argues that madness is difference rather than pathology. In a direct critique of the privileging of reason, Mad studies queries how certain forms of behaviour, mood, and emotion have come to be labelled, categorized, and "proven" as problematic, in need of intervention and disciplinable through punishment, pharmacology, incarceration, rights abuse, and social exclusion. In the realm of science and progress, madness is usually not seen as a gift in these modern times. It is not seen as connected to spirituality or, as Cyndy Baskin (2007) argues, as connected to community and historical health. Instead of a reaction to a set of social, financial, political, or other circumstances, madness has been constructed as an individual, risky, expensive, irresponsible illness.

Indeed, Mad studies argues that to display any kind of emotion, care, feeling, or love in professional spaces is to risk denial, derision, and disciplinary action from employers, managers, and especially our peers (Church, 1995). But if this is the case, we cannot help but wonder, are we really as enlightened as we profess to be?

Indigenizing Practices

The short answer would be no, especially if one is looking at teaching through a lens informed by Indigenous ways of knowing, which is another antidote to the tyranny of neoliberalism in education. For instance, in the practice classroom, Jennifer teaches anti-colonialism. This involves making explicit how Canada is a settler state and how social work scholarship has, often with the best of intentions, completely marginalized Indigenous ways of knowing (Baikie, 2009). It means that Jennifer needs to make clear how settler educators participate in colonization, often without knowing it. From Aboriginal scholar Michael Anthony Hart she has learned that people offering help in this work as teachers should never think of themselves as experts but should focus on speaking from the heart and speaking from their personal experience, using story where they can to build relationship first. Indeed, she has learned that her commitment to closeness and proximity was never new or radical. Indeed, as Hart writes, through an Indigenous lens, nurturing connection has always been the focus: "Nurturing [the] connections leads to health while disconnections lead to dis-ease" (Hart, 2009, p. 36). Settler educators have just been too caught up in individualizing, colonizing ways to notice.

How We Care in the Classroom: From Seminars to Large Lecture Halls

And so, encouraged by all these ways of knowing and by desires to disrupt disciplinary spaces, we want to draw close, to care, and to nurture in all of the spaces in which we teach. But how do we perform caring pedagogy? What are the characteristics of this form of teaching practice?

We begin by letting our students in. We are constantly teaching about the need for use of self, teaching the importance of sincerity and authenticity in social work practice, so we aim for that same authenticity in the classroom. Without being inappropriate, we share our experiences with our students, especially in the places where they have helped us learn. We especially share our own stumbling blocks and mistakes in an effort to disrupt the role of omniscient expert standing at the front of the class. In line with the scholarship on teaching and learning, we are on high alert for "teachable moments" that allow us to "empathetically put [our]selves in the place of the learners who initiate these spontaneous events" (White & Maycock, 2012, p. 322).

We feel as if we create genuine relationships with our students and that they know we truly see them. We concur with Gurm that "good teaching involves participation and interactions with students" (2013, p. 1). We are mindful that there are other structural issues at play in terms of why our students react positively—we're youngish, we're both multiply privileged, supported by our school's commitment to decolonizing practices, and we're both tuned in to popular culture—and so we are hesitant to call on our positive relationships with students as solid evidence that what we're doing works or is safe for all. Furthermore, we acknowledge that some of what we do is "merely" good teaching. On the other hand, the language we hear from our students makes it clear that this idea of critical nurturing *is* distinct from "just good teaching" and *is* working, at least for some of them—they remark on our warmth, they thank us for meeting them where they're at, they are appreciative of the ways we aim to take care of them, rather than simply teaching them.

We aim to be impressed by our students. May suggests that

> *I am a ceaseless cheerleader of my students. I am constantly looking for their strengths and capabilities and, even when they don't do well, am seeking ways to encourage them. I have never been more gratified than when students who have done poorly in my class still give me a hug on the way out. And yes—some students do poorly—because this isn't just a way for me to ensure that I am popular or that my course surveys are excellent—I do everything I can to bolster my students so that I can then be a tougher grader. My reasoning, which I share with my classes, is that I give my students every opportunity to succeed, so I then have high expectations. I will say that, perhaps as a result, I receive remarkably little pushback from my students.*

May also gives students the benefit of the doubt at every turn—they know they are always able to come talk. They also know that they do not need to capitalize on their tears to get an extension—they can simply ask for help and, in almost all cases, be granted that help, independent of their circumstances. This helps avoid that most loathsome of interactions, the 'fake dead grandmother'; it also protects students' need for privacy and different levels of comfort in sharing themselves. This does make receiving their final papers sometimes challenging as they trickle in for what seems like months—but that inconvenience is an appropriate reapportioning of the power of this role—our lives are sometimes a little more inconvenient so that their lives can be a little less intense.

We take very seriously the notion that we must "lift as we climb."[2] We look to Gloria Wade-Gayles, who writes about her own time as a teaching othermother at Spelman College: "I was like a plant from which one takes cuttings. A piece for this one. A piece for that one. A piece for those over there and these over here. Although there were times when I could feel the blade, I did not regret the cuttings. They strengthened my roots" (1996, p. 32).

We need to make clear that while caring pedagogies work to strengthen *our* roots, we do not feel prescriptive about what we do—we do these things first and foremost because they strengthen *us*. We do not nurture our students because we think it's ethical or moral to do so, but rather because we do not know what else to do. May feels herself very precariously figuring out her role as an educator, and newly as a tenure-track professor. By lifting as she climbs, she situates herself, grounds herself, so that the newness and discomfort of this new role are tempered. Jennifer, too, keenly feels her role as tenured "carer," still uncertain in some places and with some people, but always strengthened and nurtured by doing the work in this particular way both within and outside the classroom.

Turning to those classrooms now, many of the nurturing tactics we have divulged above may sound great for smaller classes, but we can hear the obvious question, the elephant in the room: Is it possible to nurture and care in a large class, to cross the great learned disembodied divide between our expert selves and hundreds of students?

The dominant discourse suggests that we cannot, that the sheer number of students we teach must make those connections impossible. We can certainly focus on management, efficiencies in assignments, and even grading perhaps— but really, caring for a large class is not recommended. After all, there is no "box" on our teaching evaluations that speaks to this, no product we can claim for our tenure files. Given the "increased tension between teaching and scholarship" (Belcher, Pecukonis, & Knight, 2011, p. 196) and our adherence to Enlightenment doctrines that problematize connection and emotion in disciplinary spaces, why would we ever want to care?

However, in 2011, Jennifer taught a class of 188 students in a rented movie theatre next to the university. Thinking ahead, she also asked those students to share their thoughts on large classes at the beginning of the semester and again at the end. Speaking to her own concerns and biases at the start, she writes:

> Now anyone who is teaching a large class in such a theatre knows the odds are stacked against you. You know there is good chance the class will be scheduled for 8 am, that the clicker will not work and depending on the planets, the microphone may decide not to cooperate either. Technical and temporal challenges aside, there is also the comfort of the chairs, comfort which frequently enables students to nod off.
> And so I was not particularly optimistic about this large class.

Neither were the students. When asked to fill out a questionnaire early in the term, they said they disliked classes held at 8 a.m. They disliked classes held in theatres. They disliked it when social work, a discipline that teaches people how to relate or draw closer (if only for a little while), was taught in such a large class format. Although they absolutely lauded the theatre's proximity to the subway, they wanted small classes, and they wanted them now. Jennifer gritted her teeth for a difficult experience:

> My heart sunk a little further. But my friends, by the end of the term, I sat looking at their second questionnaires, agog and aghast. I already knew that on any given Monday morning we had a participation rate of at least 85%. I already knew that it had felt good.... But when asked if the class worked, a resounding 97% said yes. When asked why, this is what they told me...
> It worked because, for the first time at Ryerson, the professor took the time to learn my name.
> Because she held office hours for as long as it took to answer our questions.
> Because she not only accommodated my disability, she talked about her own on the first day.
> Because she didn't really use the podium, she clipped on that mike and came visiting, even up to the back rows, where we try to hide. When we were discussing something, she sat with us. When there wasn't enough room in the row, she sat on the steps.
> Because she laughed and cried with us.
> Because she emailed us back.
> Because on that last day, she let us sing.

Because she said we were teaching her more than she was ever going to teach us.

Because I think she actually cares about us...

And that last comment struck me. That caring about students both in and out of the classroom was a surprise, an anomaly. Sitting in my office that day, I had an embodied reaction to this "objective" questionnaire and realized, quite fully and completely, that not only do I care about my students, I realized that caring is my pedagogy. It is at the root of my approach, my office hours, my course outlines, my grading and my tone in the classroom.

In truth, I am made intercorporeal by teaching, I am made less docile, I try to disrupt the panopticon, to cross over structural borders, I am post-conventional, emotional and more than a little Mad. I am transgressive in my queering of normal, depersonalized identity categories, and quite simply, it works.

On ratemyprofessor.com, my students have written that I am a very "hard marker." They also nominated me for a teaching award, which I won in 2010. I want them to feel supported enough to take theoretical risks, to leap a little higher, to wake up and not coast and, it would appear, that they want me to keep showing up and drawing close.

But What about Facebook?

Sometimes despite the positive feedback, there are pitfalls to this approach. When many students are struggling simultaneously, we are nervous about taking on ever larger classes. Very occasionally there is a student who takes advantage of the support, and that stinks (though not enough for us to change what we do in response). Clearly, there must be a catch. There must be a downside to this outrageous caring in the classroom.

Foucault (1990) argued that we must make allowance for the fact that resistance practices, such as caring in the classroom, are both wonderful and problematic, all at the same time. They are problematic because we have been taught to see them as so, to worry, as per dominant discourses on risk, about what reprisal there may be if we care for our students. They are problematic because of what we all know about the perils of inappropriate behaviour between those in what Mad-allied scholars Kalinowski and Risser (2005) call the power up group and those in a power down group. They are problematic because of the perceived threat to expert practices that protect power, excluding others' identities in the process. "I'm not your case worker," we have heard colleagues say. "I'm not their counsellor," we have heard others cry.

Yet the practices of caring are also problematic because of the toll they may take on those who care. First there is the toll it takes to go underground with the care, to keep it quiet in the face of disciplinary education discourses that call for ever more management of students. Such discourses paint students with the same "entitled" threatening brush, suggesting they are not used to being told no.

Then there is the toll of actually saying no. When a student asked if Jennifer could provide therapy, she said no. When students ask to become Facebook friends, she says no, and when they want her cellphone number so that they can text, she says no to that too. In short, she knows that she cares very much for them, but while she is also "disciplining" them, she will not be "friends." It feels more careful this way, but some react negatively unless she states these terms up front on the first day of class.

There is also the fear of student and faculty teaching evaluations, a fear that is less for those with tenure but that could absolutely silence a probationary instructor who wanted to care more. And if we are very honest, we sometimes find it hard to keep up with student emails. We have invited them, we enjoy them, but there are times when we purposely go offline for chunks of time, driving deep into wooded dead zones for peace.

We are also nervous about the ways that we are taken up as mothers and women and nurturing educators, that in suggesting these connections we may—as have other proponents of caring pedagogy—essentialize feminine labour (Noddings, 1984). May suggests that

> *I do fear that this may inadvertently reify motherhood as natural and nurturing—like I'm the chubby mama prof who will hold you close and hear your fears, distinct from the angular man who will merely give you a B. In particular—one of the sweetest and most alarming moments for me was when I taught a course toward the end of my third pregnancy. On the last day of class, three weeks before my due date, when I came lumbering in to review the exam, I found that my students had prepared an impromptu baby shower. I was touched beyond belief—but also unnerved by the extent to which they seemed relieved to have a normative script through which to react to me—I was the expectant mother, rather than the nurturing prof.*
>
> *I worry that the dissonance that may come from blending these two positions—nurturing and pedagogical—may be lost in translation and may simply re-entrench normative motherhood tropes that I'm eager to undermine.*

Yet even in this climate of fear and uncertainty, we feel committed to this pedagogical approach throughout our academic lives, and especially in our teaching of professional practice. We are mindful of Gurm's exhortation that "using the positivistic framework that first you learn knowledge and then you apply it does not work for the practice professions" (2013, p. 4), and we find resonance with this belief in our teaching of social work. Specifically, we see the echoes of our styles in our students' practice lives, in the way they embody compassionate practice and begin to understand themselves as nurturers as well as those being nurtured. While we do not have precise quantifiable ways of trapping our students' growth, we see anecdotal evidence that our caring has made a longer-term impact both in our continued relationships with many students far beyond our classroom contact and in the ways they continually approach their own caring labour with innovation and compassion. If, as Ramsden contends, "the aim of teaching is to make student learning possible" (1992, p. 5), we aim to provide an environment that maximizes our students' capacity to learn and to grow, in the classroom and beyond.

Conclusion

The scholarship of learning and teaching is continuously evolving. We see our approach of a "caring pedagogy" as an extension of existing theoretical terrain. Within the scholarship of learning and teaching, there is a strong analytical thread that is critical of the neoliberal focus on efficiencies (Belcher, Pecukonis, & Knight, 2011; Hutchings, Taylor Huber, & Ciccone, 2011; Gurm, 2013; Kreber 2006). We have aimed to undertake a "premise reflection" (Kreber, 2006; Kreber & Cranton, 2000) whereby we seek to unpack our existing beliefs and values and also the experiences that have led us to place intimacy at the core of our teaching practice. We are heartened to find resonances between our intuitive beliefs and those of the scholarship of teaching and learning. Jelly writes that "it has helped to place students' learning at the center of our work" (2012, p. 125), while Woodhouse suggests a model of "learning-centred teaching" (2010, p. 6). We aim to extend these approaches by suggesting that deep learning is bolstered by deep caring.

In the final analysis, we cannot be certain of the contribution that our caring pedagogy makes to the scholarship of teaching and learning. Indeed, the different theoretical and intuitive models we extend seem to have a mistrust of certainty as their chief commonality. And we ourselves value uncertainty—of our own expertise, about our students' motivations—as a source of extraordinary scholarly and pedagogical growth. Yet in the midst of this, we are nonetheless struck by the potency of the teaching methods we have arrived at down our various paths. In our observations and experiences we find moments of deep "pedagogic resonance." Trigwell and Shale describe pedagogic resonance as: "the bridge between teaching knowledge and the student learning that results from that knowledge. It is pedagogic resonance that is constituted in the individual acts of teaching, and it is the effect of pedagogic resonance that is experienced by students" (quoted in Woodhouse, 2010, p. 6). We feel the power of our relationships as central to our teaching and as vital to the accurate transmission of professional knowledge: in caring, we do not merely make our students (and ourselves) feel good, but we teach them to do good work. We argue that the teaching of helping professions is especially hindered by an adherence to Enlightenment doctrines, and thus especially enriched by the inclusion of theoretical terrain that encourages questioning. In practice, this means we will continue to care deeply, and will continue to view such caring as excellent pedagogy, pedagogy that strengthens our roots, that allows us to continue to lift as we climb.

Notes

1 This view of motherhood is, of course, heavily biased in favour of other sites of normativity: images of good moms are usually white, virtually always middle-class or above, always married, and usually able-bodied and free of mental health challenges. Good moms are no younger than twenty-five and no older than forty; good mothers are also always women, which ignores the range of possible gender positions from which people mother (O'Reilly, 2004, 2008; Green, 2009).
2 Initially the motto of the National Assembly of Colored Women in 1896, the phrase "lifting as we climb" has been taken forward by Angela Davis in several keynotes and writings (1994).

References

Baikie, G. (2009). Indigenizing-centred social work: Theorizing a social work way-of-being. In R. Sinclair, M. A. Hart, & G. Bruyere (Eds.), *Wicihitowin: Aboriginal social work in Canada* (pp. 42–64). Black Point, NS: Fernwood.

Baskin, C. (2011). *Strong helpers' teachings: The value of Indigenous knowledges in the helping professions.* Toronto, ON: Canadian Scholars' Press.

Baskin, C. (2007). Part II: Working together in the circle: Challenges and possibilities within mental health ethics. *Journal of Ethics in Mental Health, 2*(2), 1–4.

Belcher, J., Pecukonis, E., & Knight, C. (2011). Where have all the teachers gone? The selling out of social work education. *Journal of Teaching in Social Work, 31,* 195–209.

Byrd, D. L., & Green, F. J. (2011). *Maternal pedagogies: In and outside the classroom.* Toronto, ON: Demeter Press.

Chandler, M. (2007). Emancipated subjectivities and the subjugation of mothering practices. In A. O'Reilly (Ed.), *Maternal theory: Essential readings* (pp. 529–541). Toronto, ON: Demeter Press.

Church, K. (1995). *Forbidden narratives: Critical autobiography as social science.* Luxembourg City: Gordon & Breach. (Republished 2004 by Routledge.)

Davis, A. (1994). Black women and the academy. *Callaloo, 17*(2), 422–431.

diQuinzio, P. (1999). *The impossibility of motherhood: Feminism, individualism and the problem of mothering.* New York, NY: Routledge.

Douglas, S. J., and Michaels, M. W. (2004). *The mommy myth: The idealization of motherhood and how it has undermined all women.* New York, NY: Free Press.

Foucault, M. (1995). *Discipline and punish: The birth of the prison* (A. Sheridan, Trans.). New York, NY: Vintage.

Foucault, M. (1990). *The history of sexuality: An introduction—Volume 1* (R. Hurley, Trans.). New York, NY: Vintage.

Friere, P. (2007). *Pedagogy of the oppressed.* New York, NY: Continuum.

Glesne, C. (1999). *Becoming qualitative researchers: An introduction* (2nd ed.). Toronto, ON: Longman.

Green, F. J. (2009). *Feminist mothering in theory and practice: 1985–1995: A study in transformative politics.* New York, NY: Edwin Mellen Press.

Gurm, B. (2013). Multiple ways of knowing in teaching and learning. *International Journal for the Scholarship of Teaching and Learning 7*(1), 1–7.

Hara, B. (2010, 22 July). Disruptive student behavior: Meet the thwarters. *Chronicle of Higher Education.* [Available: http://chronicle.com/blogs/profhacker/disruptive-student-behavior-meet-the-thwarters/25708]

Hart, M. A. (2009). Anti-colonial Indigenous social work: Reflections on an Aboriginal approach. In R. Sinclair, M. A. Hart, & G. Bruyere (Eds.). *Wicihitowin: Aboriginal social work in Canada.* (pp. 25–41). Black Point, NS: Fernwood.

Hays, S. (1998). *The cultural contradictions of motherhood.* New Haven, CT: Yale University Press.

Hill Collins, P. (2002). Black feminist thought: Knowledge, consciousness, and the politics of empowerment (2nd ed.). New York, NY: Routledge.

Hutchings, P., Taylor Huber, M., and Ciccone, A. (2011). *Scholarship of teaching and learning reconsidered: Institutional integration and impact.* San Francisco, CA: Jossey-Bass.

Jelly, K. (2012). The scholarship of mentoring and teaching: Mining our practice and sharing our learning. *All About Mentoring, 42,* 125–129.

Kalinowski, C., & Risser, P. (2005). *Identifying and overcoming mentalism.* InforMed Health Publishing & Training. [Available: http://www.newmediaexplorer.org/sepp/Mentalism.pdf]

Kinser, A. (2008). Mothering as relational consciousness. In A. O'Reilly (Ed.), *Feminist mothering* (pp. 123–142). Albany, NY: SUNY Press.

Kreber, C. (2006). Developing the scholarship of teaching through transformative learning. *Journal of Scholarship of Teaching and Learning, 6*(1), 88–109.

Kreber, C., & Cranton, P.A. (2000). Exploring the scholarship of teaching. *Journal of Higher Education, 71*(4), 476–495.

Lavallée, L. F., & Poole, J. M. (2010). Beyond recovery: Colonization, health and healing for Indigenous people in Canada. *International Journal of Mental Health and Addiction, 8*(2), 271–281.

LeFrançois, B., Menzies, R., & Rheaume, G. (Eds.). (2013). *Mad matters: A critical reader in Canadian mad studies.* Toronto: Canadian Scholars' Press.

Maushart, S. (2000). *The mask of motherhood: How becoming a mother changes our lives and why we never talk about it.* New York: Penguin.

Merleau-Ponty. M. (1989). *Phenomenology of Perception.* London: Routledge

Noddings, N. (2003). *Happiness and education.* Cambridge, UK: Cambridge University Press.

Noddings, N. (1984). *Caring: A feminine approach to ethics and moral education.* Berkeley, CA: University of California Press.

O'Reilly, A. (Ed.). (2008). *Feminist mothering.* Albany, NY: SUNY Press.

O'Reilly, A. (Ed.). (2004). *Mother outlaws: Theories and practices of empowered mothering.* Toronto, ON: Women's Press.

Ramsden, P. (1992). *Learning to teach in higher education.* London, UK: Routledge.

Salter, D., Pang, M., & Sharma, P. (2009). Active tasks to change the use of class time within an outcomes based approach to curriculum design. *Journal of University Teaching and Learning Practice, 6*(1), 27–38.

Shildrick, M., & Mykitiuk, R. (Eds.). (2005). *Ethics of the body: Postconventional challenges.* Boston, MA: MIT Press.

Sinclair, R. (2009). Bridging the past and the future: An introduction to Indigenous social work issues. In R. Sinclair, M. A. Hart, & G. Bruyere (Eds.). *Wicihitowin: Aboriginal social work in Canada.* Halifax, NS: Fernwood.

Singleton-Jackson, J. A., Jackson, D. L., & Reinhardt, J. (2010). Students as consumers of knowledge: Are they buying what we're selling? *Innovative Higher Education, 35*(5), 343–358.

Swanson, D. H., and Johnston, D. D. (2003). Mothering in the ivy tower: Interviews with academic mothers. *Journal of the Association for Research on Mothering, 5*(2), 63–75.

Wade-Gayles, G. (1996). *Rooted against the wind: Personal essays.* Boston, MA: Beacon Press.

Wane, N. N. (2004) Reflections on the mutuality of mothering: Women, children and othermothering. In A. O'Reilly (Ed.), *Mother outlaws: Theories and practices of empowered mothering.* 105–116. Toronto, ON: Women's Press.

White, S. R., & Maycock, G. A. (2012). College teaching and synchronicity: Exploring the other side of teachable moments. *Community College Journal of Research and Practice, 36,* 321–329.

Woodhouse, R. A. (2010). Hype or hope: Can the scholarship of teaching and learning fulfill its promise? *International Journal for the Scholarship of Teaching and Learning, 4*(1), 1–8.

7

Educating for Social Action among Future Health Care Professionals

Jacqui Gingras and Erin Rudolph

Introduction

> *Learning has taken place when we observe a change of learning behaviour resulting from what has been experienced.* (Zhou, 2011, p. 73)

Engaging students as co-instructors establishes a learning community in which power is more equitably distributed. This democratic learning space models equitable ways of being-in-relation with future clients, patients, colleagues, and allied community and health care partners. Preparing the curriculum-as-lived (Pinar, Irwin, & Aoki, 2005) has the potential to establish spaces for social equity in health and community care contexts as students move from the academy to health institutions and the community. This chapter describes and contests a course curriculum that was created to equip future health care professionals to take up the call for diminishing health inequities in their practice.

The curriculum was adapted from a model offered by Weimer (2002) that distributes power in the classroom more equitably. In a second-year course (FNF 100: Families and Health), the first class activity allowed students to identify the majority of weekly themes. Students sought out readings to fit these themes, presented and discussed their resources with the class (peer prepping), and were invited to co-construct classroom culture in such a way as to optimize their personal and collective learning experiences. These methods required active engagement by all those involved with the course, including the students, the graduate assistant, and the instructor (faculty member).

Responses to this alternative curriculum were gathered throughout the course via written student feedback, graduate assistant and instructor reflexivities, and formal course evaluations. While students indicated that the course enabled them to understand the importance of becoming an activist, listening to stories, being open to differences, thinking reflexively, avoiding generalizations, and respecting individuals' ideas, opinions, and thoughts, they also pointed out that the unfamiliar terrain represented by the curriculum and their revised roles as decision-makers was sometimes awkward to perform. Students spoke of what they learned as the correlation between racialization, socio-economic status, access to health care, and quality of care and how that correlation might be relevant in their future practice.

Methods of Teaching and Learning

If more faculty encountered the literature, it would not only nourish and sustain the current interest in learning, it would also change practice. (Weimer, 2002, p. 8)

Teaching styles are ways of organizing and presenting learning experiences to, from, and with students. Educational theorists have illustrated the various pedagogical approaches that exist in post-secondary education, which include the means by which power is distributed within the classroom. The teaching method used within the classroom will determine the extent to which students are positioned as recipients or as co-constructors of knowledge in classroom settings. According to Bonner (1999), teaching styles are classified into two general categories: reproductive and productive. In reproductive teaching, students duplicate the teacher's understanding of a topic and turn it into their own understanding. In productive teaching, students direct their own learning and are therefore able to construct their own understandings of how they see the world. The teaching style of the class instructor therefore determines the power distribution within the classroom and sets the tone for the mode of education that will occur within the learning environment.

Mosston's Spectrum is a universal tool, representing a continuum of eleven teaching and learning styles inclusive of both reproductive and productive styles (Simplicio, 2000). The continuum ranges from teacher-centred to student-centred; command is the most teacher-centred, and as the spectrum moves toward learner-initiated, learners are increasingly more involved in decision-making within the classroom (Mosston & Ashworth, 2002). Each teaching style represents a given amount of student initiation and interactivity as well as the power distribution between the student and instructor as illustrated in Figure 7.1.

FIGURE 7.1
Learner initiation and power distribution among learning styles

Teaching Style	Description	Learner Initiated (reproductive vs. productive)	Shared Power (between student and instructor)
		n/a=minimal; I=low; II=moderate; III= high	
Command	Teacher-centred. Teacher delivers knowledge; pupils remain passive.	n/a	n/a
Practice	Pupils carry out tasks as set by the teacher. Teacher may work with groups as the task is completed.	n/a	I
Reciprocal	Pupils work in pairs: a "doer" and "teacher-partner," who evaluates the doers' work. Teacher works with the "teacher partner" to improve their evaluative skills. Pupils learn to judge performance against criteria.	I	I
Self-check	Teacher sets the task; pupils complete it and evaluate their own performance; in collaboration with teacher, they set new targets. Pupils move when they are ready.	II	II
Inclusion	Differentiated tasks are set to ensure all pupils experience success and progress.		
Guided discovery	Teacher sets individualized learning programs for pupils based on their cognitive development.		
Convergent discovery	Teacher has a defined learning outcome in mind but pupils can decide the processes and presentation technique to reach that outcome. Teacher guides as required.	II	II
Divergent discovery	Multiple solutions are possible to a task and pupils devise their own routes, with guidance, and assess the validity of their eventual solution.	II	II
Learner-designed	Pupil designs and carries out program or investigation to answer a particular question; requires knowledge and skills built up in earlier learning experiences.	III	III
Learner-initiated	Pupil provides a question for investigation as well as designing and carrying out the investigation.	III	III

Source: Adapted from Simplicio (2000).

The quality of a student's learning is determined by the objectives and skills to be gained from the course, as well as the compatibility of the student's learning style with the teacher's teaching style (Bonner, 1999; Zhou, 2011). Teaching styles therefore play a pivotal role in the student's learning process. According to Beattie and James (1997), there is agreement that optimal learning stems from opportunities for self-direction, clear relationships between learning, life, and professional experiences, reflection, and action as a result of learning.

Learner-Centred Approach

The impetus to change the curriculum came when one of the authors (JG) was invited to teach the course after the previous instructor was unavailable. The author was also involved in a book club where a small group of School of Nutrition faculty members, a nutrition post-doctoral fellow, and a graduate teaching assistant were reading and discussing Weimer's (2002) work on learner-centred teaching. In that text, Weimer (2002) outlines a participatory curriculum that intrigued the author enough to apply it in the new course.

A learner-centred approach as defined by Weimer (2002) is when students and their learning process are made central to decisions about how to teach the content at hand. Learner-centred education is a philosophy of teaching that focuses on the experiences, backgrounds, talents, interests, capacities, and needs of the students and on the best practices for enhancing motivation, learning, and achievement for all students (McCombs & Whisler, 1997). This approach is theoretically informed by critical social theory (Freire, 1970), cognitive and educational psychology (Ramsden, 1988), feminist scholarship (hooks, 1994), and the scholarship of teaching and learning (Hutchings, Taylor Huber, & Ciccone, 2011; McKinney, 2007). Cory-Wright (2011) indicates that educators need a more learner-centric approach, one that is contemporary and that treats learners as adults, and that assumes they will find their own way and that they will learn for themselves as long as they know what is expected of them in the first place.

Students Building Their Own Course

The course was a second-year health sociology course titled Families and Health. It was subscribed primarily by second-year food and nutrition students but could be taken by any student in the Faculty of Community Services. The course description read:

> This course is a critical examination of the most recent demographic changes in Canadian family life and considers the implications of these changes for health professionals. Based on a social determi-

nants of health framework, the social, political and economic aspects of family structure and functioning are examined and linked to varying degrees of health and illness. Students gain an understanding of the connections between individual, family and community life and their contribution to overall health and well-being.

The objectives of the course were to:
- critically examine the most recent demographic changes in Canadian families
- describe the implications of Canadian demographic changes for health professionals
- apply the social dimensions of health framework to health and illness
- establish connections between individual, family, and community life and articulate the influence of these connections to people's overall health and well-being

On the very first day of the course, students were presented with a real-world problem. After briefly introducing herself, JG announced to the class that besides being students in the class, they were educational consultants employed by a very prestigious firm, *Learning, Inc.* Ryerson University had hired *Learning, Inc.* to develop the most highly regarded Families and Health course in Canada. Ryerson was dedicating an enormous sum of money to the project since it needed the course to be exceptional and ready to go in two hours! The CEO of *Learning, Inc.* had dedicated most of the company's resources to this urgent request (eighty people—coincidently, the exact number of students in the course). These eighty people were divided into twenty teams of four, and each team was provided with a worksheet (Appendix Two) to help students generate and describe two themes to pitch to the other teams. After the forty themes were presented, they would be voted on until only ten themes remained. These ten themes would form the core content of the course (Appendix Three).

After their briefing, the students eagerly set about determining their themes, brainstorming appropriate resources to assist in teaching those themes, and then pitching their themes to the other teams. The most commonly presented resources included journal articles, book chapters, documentaries (National Film Board, CBC), websites, position papers, and Health Canada. Students, working diligently as educational consultants, were encouraged to research, using whatever means were appropriate, to determine the most relevant two themes for such a course, and then to provide associated resources with which to teach others those themes. Some students worked from the library, some worked outside, some in the hallways outside the classroom, and a few students remained in the classroom. All teams were ready to pitch their theme ideas at least fifteen minutes before the one-hour time allotted by the instructor to complete this task.

Five new teams were now formed by combining teams 1 to 4, 5 to 8, 9 to 12, 13 to 16, and 17 to 20. The first round of pitching involved these new teams, each of which had to make decisions about what constituted a "good" theme and which themes could be combined, given their similarities. Each of these five teams also had to elect a spokesperson: an individual who had a good grasp of the four "best" themes in order to pitch them persuasively to the class. Thus, five teams would be presenting four themes each for a total of twenty themes.

Once those twenty themes were described and identified on a white board at the front of the room, the entire class voted on the themes they believed would showcase the most exemplary Families and Health undergraduate course in Canada. The vote was done blindly: after the students briefly described the themes, all students were asked to close their eyes and raise their hand for the themes they preferred (each student was given two votes). In this way, ten weeks of course content was decided along with supporting teaching objects to correspond with weeks three to twelve of the thirteen-week undergraduate course (Appendix Three). The instructor and the graduate assistant together facilitated the process of recording themes, clarifying the meaning of the themes, and counting votes.

Even more important than determining the course themes, the educational consultant role-play—an example of experiential learning—initiated a high degree of student engagement and attachment to the content, given that the students themselves had identified it as content worth learning. As Warren (1998) explains, experiential education is vital to fostering an engaged learning community because it positions the students' experiences, rather than the teacher's, at the centre of knowledge construction. The students' excitement was palpable they left after that first class. One student remarked, "I can't wait to come back next week! This class is going to be great!" Needless to say, these enthusiastic expressions were a first for us as course facilitators.

Besides deciding ten weekly themes, students were able to determine four out of five assignments presented to them as course deliverables (Appendix Three). All students completed the first assignment by virtue of attending the first class and completing the peer prepping activity. All of the activities were adapted or taken verbatim from Weimer (2002).

The final aspect of Families and Health that was collaboratively created was the rubric designed to support ER's evaluation of the student-submitted assignments. While JG drafted the original rubric, the students and graduate assistant were encouraged to give ample and constructive feedback.

Our Roles

Both authors were new to the course and to the development, implementation, and evaluation of a democratic curriculum. This newness provided great stimulation, but also vulnerability with regard to their respective roles in the course. JG's responsibilities were to:
- co-create the course syllabus (with ER)
- prepare and facilitate weekly seminars
- create and sustain an environment conducive to learning
- respond to student queries
- assess student learning in collaboration with students
- administer the course through formal channels (input final grades into RAMSS, etc.)

ER's responsibilities as graduate assistant for the course were to:
- attend graduate assistant orientation workshop
- co-create (with JG) the course syllabus
- attend the first class and subsequent lectures as necessary
- co-create the mid-term questions from the readings, class notes, PowerPoint presentations, and additional, relevant resources posted on Blackboard
- meet weekly with JG
- grade the assignments
- analyze student feedback

The students' responsibilities were to:
- attend class as prepared as possible (which entailed doing the readings, responding to guiding questions, participating in class discussions, writing assignments, and engaging in online fora)
- be respectful of one another, but to contest vigorously one another's ideas
- create a community of learning
- engage in communication with the instructor and graduate assistant as needed
- ask questions when something about the course remained unclear

These roles, especially those related to the participatory aspect of the class, were not outlined in the course syllabus; instead, they were presented and discussed during the second week of the course, after the role-play was executed during the first week. This was intentional—a means to offer the students an appropriate context for the structure of the class. The instructor believed that without the first week's activity to draw upon, it would be difficult for the students to understand the intent in an embodied way, which is the benefit to be gleaned from experiential learning. In retrospect, it would have been better to outline this aspect of the class even briefly in the course syllabus so that students would have this course objective in writing and for them to refer back to from time to time.

Reflexive Statements

JG: I was the instructor of record for the course. It was the first time I had taught a large class at Ryerson University. I was entering my fourth year of a tenure-track position with the School of Nutrition. For the previous three years, I had taught smaller, highly interactive undergraduate seminar classes, team-taught a first-year introductory course with several colleagues, and team-taught as well as individually facilitated a newly developed graduate seminar for our Nutrition Communication graduate program. During the months preceding the Families and Health course, I experienced some apprehension about what new teaching skills would be required of me to facilitate learning among a class of eighty second-year students. I had successfully completed an intensive, three-day instructional skills workshop a year and a half earlier (December 2008) to learn and hone my skills as an instructor in higher education. I had attended a Learning and Teaching Office workshop called The Highly Interactive Classroom, where Dr. Gosha Zwyno presented ideas for maintaining active student participation in large classes. And, as mentioned, I was reading Weimer's (2002) book and discussing the ideas in it with teaching peers.

As Families and Health was a new course (for me), I thought it an appropriate course to test new ideas about which Weimer had piqued my curiosity. I am naturally open to trying new things in the classroom, I believe that knowledge is co-constructed in social contexts (including classrooms), and I value equity and fairness in my relationships with others. I also believed that if I taught the course more than once, I would be able to build on a first attempt to strengthen the learning experiences of students enrolled in the subsequent year. I shared my ideas for the course with my reading group, with a student who had taken the course previously, and with ER. All provided me with constructive feedback that helped me refine my thinking as the course's start date approached. I expected for both ER and I to present our experience with the course at an upcoming Health Equity conference. It was imperative that the results from our scholarly efforts be shared and debated with peers in order to improve the course and enhance our own teaching abilities. Such efforts on our behalf were seen by me as my professional and ethical obligation as an educator—a responsibility that I take very seriously.

Besides attempting to revise the course curriculum in order to share power between the students and ourselves, we worked to share power between each other as the graduate assistant and the instructor. We met weekly to discuss issues arising from the course. I (JG) sought out ER's feedback on curriculum design before the course started, we worked through the graduate assistant manual to determine shared expectations of grading (Foxe, 2011), I shared students' reflective writing with ER to enable her to discern the level at which students were engaging with the course content, ER and I co-facilitated the final course feedback session with the students, and, finally, when the course was finished we discussed at length our assessments of each other and of the course itself. As ER and I had worked together on a research project and Erin had been a student in one of my previous classes, we were familiar with each other and had a clear understanding of our shared values regarding education. At the time, I was also supervising ER's graduate studies, the course in which she was exploring the development of an interprofessional narratives curriculum. Our pre-established relationship was one of the predicates on which the success of the Families and Health course rested.

ER: As a student who was familiar with the distinct power divide that often exists between student and instructor, my interest was sparked by the opportunity to take on the role of a graduate assistant in this unique course. As one of JG's past students, this role excited me as I continued to be inspired by her passion for teaching along with her leadership in innovation and democracy within the classroom. In my role as a graduate assistant, JG shared the power she held, the power that naturally follows the title of instructor. She invitingly shared this power with me in a similar fashion to how power was circulated with students in the classroom.

The course was designed in a collaborative manner, and this gave me the confidence to take initiative in my new, unfamiliar role as a graduate assistant. I was able to contribute to the creation of the course syllabus, exam questions, and assignments, as well as to the presentation we were to make together with our colleagues at the Health Equity conference. From this experience I learned the significance of democracy and equity both inside and outside the classroom. This involved reflecting on strategies to utilize these skills in an environment in which a power differential between health practitioners or health practitioners and clients might otherwise exist. I found myself identifying with the course feedback from students as they expressed their new knowledge of the link between learning equity in the classroom and applying it to practice in health and community care. Additionally, I felt that I could take the lessons learned from this experience and transfer them to my graduate studies project, as I was simultaneously developing an interprofessional narratives course curriculum in collaboration with JG and others.

JG followed a learner-centred approach with the students enrolled in the Families and Health course *and* with me. This challenged me to dig deep and actualize my potential as a creative equal in the teaching team. It taught me not to stay silence or to be afraid to take on leadership, initiative, and responsibility as an entry-level professional where the societal norm might otherwise have been to play a subordinate role. More importantly, it taught me how to implement similar practices in my role as a future educator.

Course Outcomes

> *Investigations into equitable teaching must pay attention to the particular practices of teaching and learning that are enacted in classrooms.* (Boaler, 2002, p. 239)

Responses to this alternative curriculum were gathered throughout the course via written student feedback. Students were assured anonymity in putting forward their comments, since their names were not required. Students were told that the feedback they provided would serve two purposes: (1) it would enhance the course for future offerings, and (2) it would be shared during a presentation by JG and ER during an upcoming conference on health equity. When students were asked, "Do you think the way the course was designed will help you establish a more equitable practice?," 88 percent of them answered yes. Students indicated that the course enabled them to understand the importance of becoming an activist, listening to stories, being open to differences, thinking reflexively, avoiding generalizations and respecting individuals' ideas, opinions, and thoughts.

One student wrote: "The way the course was facilitated allowed for myself and my peers to openly share our opinions rather than a student vs. teacher oriented course where we are told what we learn, how to learn it and how we must use our own knowledge."

Another student wrote, "I felt like my opinions actually meant something and that I could have power in my own education.... [The course material] made me more aware of inequity in our society and identified many obstacles that need to be overcome in order to make healthcare more accessible and inclusive." Another student stated that "[the class] helped me realize every individual's worth which is an important lesson to use in practice."

When asked, "Does the design of FNF 100 (student-driven curriculum, co-facilitating class discussions, making choices about assignments, etc.) allow you to share your power more equitably outside the classroom?," 77 percent of students answered yes. Students spoke of what they learned as the correlation between racialization, socio-economic status, access to health care, and quality of care. One student wrote that the experiences of shared power within the classroom could translate into professional practice: "The professional-client/patient relationship may be more meaningful to both individuals if there is less power imbalance."

Another student explained that because of how the course was designed, "I feel more empowered, like what I think actually matters." Another student stated, "I feel better prepared to play a more activist role in health promotion and professional practice." Another student described her desire for equitable power sharing outside of the class: "This type of curriculum is very different, but also very beneficial to understand perspectives, share common knowledge and new knowledge, and reinforce the notion that no one's opinions should be diminished."

Students who had answered no to the above two questions also provided constructive feedback for the course instructors. Students spoke to the implications of non-traditional course delivery methods by discussing the anxiety they felt about the new experience of obtaining power within the classroom, specifically regarding the student/teacher power structure. One student wrote, "I felt nervous that the course was not covering all that I needed to know." Another spoke to the unfamiliarity with the learner-centred structure: "I feel as if there is little structure in how the course operates and I just wish there was more structure." A few students also touched on the pressure of having responsibility for their own learning within the classroom: "There is too much stress in a student's life to handle such power." Another wrote, "I found having too many choices to be overwhelming."

In future iterations, additional time and attention will be necessary to explore these tensions further with students. As instructors, we recognize that uncertainty can sometimes promote learning, but too much uncertainty can raise anxieties that thwart learning. As was made explicit on multiple occasions throughout the course, and as could have been made more explicit in the course syllabus, appropriate levels of uncertainty are reflective of professional practice. The course was designed to have students engage with that reality as much as can be done in the classroom in preparation for future practice. The students' anxieties mirror clients' anxieties, and an appreciation of that shared experience helps promote compassion, mutual empathy, and trust between the clients and those who are providing health care service (Gingras, 2012). These tensions point to the differences between traditional, more didactic learning spaces and what we endeavoured to create. What might it mean to hear a student indicate in the end-of-term feedback that the classroom was too equitable?

Reflexive Critique: 'It's Too Equitable'

To our surprise, one student remarked in her course feedback, "Maybe having a course set up like this gave us too many choices. It's too equitable!" This comment lingered with us for a long time. At first we chuckled about it, attributing her comment to her being unused to having the authority to make decisions about her own learning experience, and we supposed that given more time, her perspective might change. But when we began to reflect on the deeper meaning contained in the comment, we wondered if there was such a thing as a classroom being "too equitable" and if this was more significant a comment than we initially thought. We turned to the literature on education for democracy and social justice to buttress our understanding of the comment and how we might integrate our deepened understanding to make the course better.

Ellsworth (1989, 1997) and hooks (1994) state that students have the capacity for holding power in the classroom—they are agentive—but that the expression of that power is typically maladroitly wielded, given that students' deeply ingrained subjective positions exist as recipients of knowledge and not as co-constructors of knowing. A social democracy requires the active engagement of its citizens (Rebick, 2012). Lakey and colleagues (1995) describe social justice as the "intentional steps that move society in the direction of equality, support for diversity, economic justice, participatory democracy, environmental harmony, and resolution of conflicts nonviolently" (p. 5). It follows that in applying democracy in health care, future professionals must become adept at identifying and sharing power. This familiarity can likely be accomplished through practice, making mistakes, learning humility, and repairing relationships in the classroom. For those who prefer a more arm's-length engagement with the emotional curriculum in higher education, we recommend simulation as a means to provide these opportunities for practice in learning equity. Although it might seem that simulation offers high engagement with the emotional landscape of teaching and learning, it is done within a very specific and unique context. The simulation context is well structured by simulator "scripts" along with modifiable levels of affect that the simulator assumes. Feedback that can be provided during simulation is typically much different than similar feedback provided to a student or students in the course of a didactic classroom setting.

Simulation offers an optimal environment for teaching the human dimension of health and social care practice without the high stakes of working as actual health care practitioners. Simulations can also be built upon developmentally throughout the course to deepen the students' understanding of working in equitable teams, addressing conflict among peers and supervisors, and designing and implementing socially just health promotion programs within a community context. The Interpersonal Skills Teaching Centre at Ryerson University is a world-famous resource with expertly trained simulators and an enviable list of simulation topics to use as is or to have adapted for more specific use (www.ryerson.ca/istc).

Though the class began on a very positive first note, that energy was not sustained. The initial anticipation gave way to the challenges inherent in having to make decisions about the course that were typically left to the instructor. While this taught the students to be accountable for their decisions, it was not a role they were familiar with. As in McCallister (2002), our shifting the manner in which power circulated in the course created new and different opportunities for students to think and act as teachers, although students didn't wear their new authority with complete ease. In McCallister's (2002) article, one student aptly remarked, "There was a little confusion about how we were supposed to 'act'" (p. 297). This was one of the most endearing discoveries from the Families and Health course: that some previous experience and familiarity with a real democratic educational space was necessary for power in that space to be authentically contested and shared. Over time (from first year to graduation), students require genuine opportunities to choose the direction of their learning and enjoy the consequences of those choices both as individuals and as collaboratives.

In retrospect, the designed course did meet the planned course objectives as weekly modules, assignments, and discussion questions were carefully set up for students to meet such objectives. Although students co-designed the course, expectations from the previously implemented course were sustained through the manner in which facilitators guided students throughout the course to ensure that similar goals were met. For example, although the students chose the types of assignments they completed, the intended learning objectives for assignments were similar for all students. In terms of course facilitation, there are some aspects of the course that we would have handled differently, including having ER do more facilitation instead of primarily marking. This would have helped ER develop her own democratic facilitation style in a safe and constructive environment. Additionally, JG would have preferred to have the students learn to do more peer feedback of writing content and style. At times, JG observed that the same small subset of students was responding to questions posed in class. JG continually found herself needing to engage more students in this process, since it teaches students to formulate thoughts into words, it allows a more diverse series of perspectives to be heard, and it enables students to learn how to respond when someone shares something with which they don't agree. JG didn't believe that everyone needed to speak during class time, but it was problematic when five out of 80 were the only voices heard. By the midway point of the course, the instructor corrected this dynamic by integrating several of the ideas she had learned from the LTO workshop on promoting broader student participation in large classes. She facilitated "think–pair–share" activities when posing questions; she also invited students to write their responses to questions before calling on individuals to share out loud. She arranged more small group activities where different perspectives could be verbalized and discussed and then shared with the larger group to build on the ideas of a select few. These changes helped promote more participation from a more diverse group of students in the class, which also promoted the community feel the instructor was seeking.

In one class discussion during week 11, when students were expressing some disillusionment about the contingent nature of the course (i.e., being able to decide how something is done, trying it out, and determining that it might have been done better otherwise), an intrepid student said, "Is this class some kind of experiment or something?" Unlike another time when JG didn't have a great response to such an unexpected comment (Gingras, 2008), she responded, "Yes, it is an experiment and it should always be an experiment because I am a professional educator working and reworking the absolute best way to promote learning; yours and my own; we are in this together. It is a very difficult process and it never ends. And it is exactly what I want you to do as future health professionals every single day of your career. It is your ethical obligation to try, retry, measure, assess, share, debate, and question every aspect of your professional practice, whatever that might be." It was an impassioned response and one that reflected an appropriate role for a co-learner in this course—sharing personal and professional experiences as a means to enhance the learning environment. After her response, the students were initially silent, possibly considering how their classroom experiences were so closely mirroring their future practice, but after a break, when the students started working on concept maps of the course to outline the many influences on family health, the students returned to their highly engaged manner of participation and the classroom was re-energized. We were also invigorated. It was the reminder we needed as to the original intent of the course, our enthusiasm for what we anticipated on day one, and the hope we had for our futures. It was exhilarating, but not always easy.

Implications and Conclusions

These outcomes provide a curricular map for promoting social action among budding health care professionals. Student feedback was used to gain insight into students' experiences and learnings from the course as well as to gauge the effectiveness of educating for social action. Students were not explicitly informed at the beginning of the course that the intended goal was to learn social action, for this would likely have created biases with the feedback obtained; however, the feedback allowed us to discover whether students were able to learn, embody, and practise health equity both inside and outside the classroom. This ultimately allowed us to measure whether we had achieved the intended goal for the course. It also allowed us to acknowledge the various interpretations of the course as well as the existing learning gaps. Obtaining constructive criticism was significant in planning for future classes. In the future, we may choose to explore with students some of the challenges, awkwardnesses, and discomforts that may come with non-traditional methods of teaching and learning. We may also choose to further explore the significance of social action and advocacy in health and community care practice within the classroom. Future inquiry would include asking graduates if the course outcomes were translated into practice, what enablers/barriers they experienced in practice, and whether course enhancements could be made retrospectively. The contribution this course makes to the scholarship of teaching relates to transformative learning and actively involves "the educator in the question of just how to teach difference in an educational context" (O'Sullivan, 1999, p. 162). To wit, Dei states that "difference must be taught in a way that allows people to acquire the strength to work for transformative change" (Dei, 1996, as quoted in O'Sullivan, 1999, p. 162). This emphasis on difference as an ethical resource establishes a learning community where power is more equitably distributed. In such spaces, social equity blooms. Our work in this chapter emphasizes that the possibility for equity is tied indelibly to fairness and shared decision making in the classroom. The spaces between the classroom and society are not disparate.

Ongoing support is necessary for instructors who wish to implement this approach in their own classrooms as teaching can position instructors in ways that make sharing power difficult. As Hewett (2003) reminds us in her work with pre-service teachers, "focusing on the learner, planning for student success, creating an inviting environment, and providing appropriate feedback offer an approach for preservice teachers' experience that will prepare them as professional educators" (p. 24). Additionally, Hyman and colleagues (2001–2) emphasize the application of knowledge by extending and applying knowledge to address significant societal problems and to improve quality of life. Certainly, there are ways to prepare health care professionals of the future that do not entail ensuring their compliance with social conventions of thought and behaviour (Foucault, 1980). Learning and teaching offices within higher education often provide the faculty development for the transformation of outdated teaching scripts.

Deciding to go forward with such a curriculum is a bold decision—one that requires facilitator, graduate/teaching assistant, and student buy-in.

Instructors, graduate assistants, and students may need some encouragement in attempting such an alternative structure, given their unfamiliarity with this type of classroom culture, but when the rationale is presented as a means to enhance future health and community care practice, buy-in may be strong. Although the title of this chapter alludes to "educating for social action," the action that was observed was only within the confines of the course itself. Plans are under way to contact students and invite them to consider how their participation in the course influenced their professional socialization and, if enough time has passed, how this course has influenced their health and community care practice. As of this writing, most of the students enrolled in the Fall 2010 Families and Health course will be preparing to enter their fourth year of their undergraduate program, making recruitment to the proposed study (assessing the long-term effects of taking the course) most appropriate in January 2014. By then these students will have graduated from the program and possibly be employed or completing a dietetic internship. Such a study would also seek to know what other courses, extracurricular activities, and other initiatives had added to the students' theoretical understanding and experiential knowing about health equity and social action.

The course as presented here can be adapted for smaller groups, different courses, higher levels, and varying degrees of facilitator experience. It does help to have students who are familiar with some aspect of the course content. This was achieved with Families and Health since students can bring their various family experiences to bear and are familiar with the social determinants of health, having taken a first-year course during which this topic was discussed. Also, since there is more information and content to address about Canadian families and health than one course could contain, it represented a unique opportunity to turn to students to determine what would be addressed and how the learning outcomes would be accomplished. Overwhelmingly, we would do it again. Advocating on behalf of those who live in poverty, who experience violence, who suffer from others' perceptions of their mental health, or who struggle to survive other oppressive conditions is a role of health care practitioners. The curricular map provided here is a means for promoting early awareness of and familiarity with discussions of power, agency, and transformation. Our success as health profession educators in teaching experientially will undoubtedly be revealed in the health of the families we serve. It already does. How can we do better?

APPENDIX ONE

Excerpt from WSI Teaching Assistant Manual: Monthly Activities

Your Team:

1. _____
2. _____
3. _____
4. _____

Theme One:

_____
_____
_____
_____

Which learning objective(s) does this theme address? (circle as many as apply):

1. Critically examine most recent demographic changes in Canadian families.
2. Describe the implications of Canadian demographic changes for health professionals.
3. Apply the social dimensions of health framework to health and illness.

What resource or resources are you suggesting for the class to assist in learning about this theme?

1. _____
2. _____

Theme Two:

_____
_____
_____
_____

Which learning objective(s) does this theme address? (circle as many as apply):

1. Critically examine most recent demographic changes in Canadian families.
2. Describe the implications of Canadian demographic changes for health professionals.
3. Apply the social dimensions of health framework to health and illness.

What resource or resources are you suggesting for the class to assist in learning about this theme?

1. _____

2. _____

Please submit this worksheet to the instructor at the end of class.

APPENDIX TWO

Weekly Themes and Peer Prepping Activity

A. Thirteen-Week Structure

Week #	Date	Theme
Week 1	Sept. 7	Course Development
Week 2	Sept. 14	Theoretical Perspectives
Week 3 to 12	Sept. 21 to Nov. 23	Top Ten Team Themes
Week 13	Nov. 30	Review and Closing

B. Ten Weekly Student-Determined Themes

Week #	Date	Theme
3	Sept. 21	Family Structure I
4	Sept. 28	Family Structure II
5	Oct. 5	Conflicting Values in the Family
6	Oct. 12	Leaving the Nest
7	Oct. 18	Family Illness and Death
8	Oct. 25	Diversity and Culture
9	Nov. 2	Immigration and Adaptation
10	Nov. 9	Access to Health (Social Determinants)
11	Nov. 16	Promoting Family Health (Living Well)
12	Nov. 23	Media and Family Health

C. "Peer Prepping" Activity Guidelines

In pairs of teams (eight students total) from week 1 (Appendix Two), you will identify a brief (not more than 10 pages, please), interesting, informative, and relevant <u>course reading</u> (peer-reviewed journal article, book chapter, or report) that corresponds to theme you identified as educational consultants during the first class (listed above).

You will provide an electronic copy of the resource to the instructor to put on the FNF 100 Bb course site AT LEAST one week prior to the week in which the theme will be discussed.

In class on the week preceding that theme, members of your team will <u>introduce</u> the reading to the class and provide a clear and appropriate

<u>guiding question</u> that students can answer after reading the resource. This peer prepping should take no more than 10 minutes of class time. The guiding question will form the basis of the class discussion during the week following your team's introduction.

In addition to a verbal introduction, members of your team will provide an <u>annotation</u> (half-page, double-spaced, and including the APA citation) of the resource that will be included with the resource on the FNF 100 Bb course site. Any terms that you feel need to be defined for the class will be included in a course <u>glossary</u>. The glossary is available under [Tools] on the FNF 100 Bb course site.

Please distribute these team activities equally, i.e., identification of resource, crafting guiding question, development of 10-minute presentation, annotation of resource, and definition of terms. Each member of the team will be required to complete a <u>self and peer evaluation</u> to be handed in confidentially the week after you present. The peer prepping activity in its entirety will be worth 15% of your final mark.

APPENDIX THREE

Course Deliverables

All students must complete Assignments #1 and #5 as well as submit their choices for Assignments #2, 3, and 4 in writing by Sept. 21. Students wishing the instructor to consider other assignment options must present those for consideration by email between Sept. 14 and Sept. 20 in order for a final decision to be made by Sept. 21.

1. Team-Identified Resource & Peer Prepping   15%

- Each team will identify a brief (not more than 10 pages, please), interesting, and relevant course reading (peer-reviewed journal article, book chapter, or report) that corresponds to one of the 10 course themes identified during week 1.
- A week before the corresponding theme is discussed in class, the team will introduce the reading and provide a discussion question for students to answer in preparation for the next class.
- The team will annotate (summarize in one page) the reading and email that to the instructor Tues. evening after the reading is introduced.
- The instructor (or team leader) will post the annotation on Bb along with the resource.
- The team will also define any difficult terms from the reading and post those on the Bb glossary (under Tools).

2. Choose one of two:

a) Learning Logs   20%

- Three–four learning logs of eight pages total will be submitted on Tues., Oct. 12.
- Each learning log will consist of a student's response to a discussion question, her/his partner's input from the in-class discussion, and the student's reflection on how this topic relates to her/his daily experiences of families and health.
- Entries will be graded on their completeness, level of insight (thoughtfulness), support provided for the reflections (descriptive experiences), and the extent the relevant course content (from readings) is integrated into the entries.

b) *Book Chapter/Journal Article/Film Review*   20%
- An eight-page review (double-spaced) will be submitted on Tues., Oct. 12.
- The paper will address how the reviewed item intersects with families and health.
- The review will be graded on its completeness (positive and negative elements critiqued), level of insight (thoughtfulness), support provided for your review (descriptive experiences), and the extent the relevant course content (from readings) is integrated into the review (out of 20 marks).

1. Choose one of two:

a) *Mid-term Exam*   20%
- Student will complete an in-class mid-term exam on Oct. 26.
- The mid-term format will be multiple choice and short answer. The time for the exam will be 50 minutes.

b) *Team Presentation + Paper*   20%
- This assignment is intended to emphasize the important relationships between health and social environments. Teams of 4–6 students will present in class on a topic related to families and health such as early childhood experiences and poverty, social support and chronic illness, or issues of addiction and impact on family relationships.
- Each class presentation will be 15 minutes long and will be accompanied by an eight-page paper on the topic of the team's choice submitted to the instructor immediately following the presentation. A one-page summary handout or brochure will be provided to the class just prior to the presentation.
- Provide the hard copy of the summary handout/brochure to the instructor a week prior to the presentation in order for copies to be made for the entire class.
- Each student will complete a self and peer evaluation to be handed in confidentially the week following the presentation.
- The paper will be graded on its completeness, persuasiveness, style, and the extent the relevant course content (from readings and other material) is integrated into the paper to support the argument.
- Presentations will be scheduled during November classes. A sign-up sheet will be provided for those that are choosing this option.

1. Choose one of two:

a) Mid-term Study Team   20%

- To successfully complete this assignment, students must be a member of a 4–6-person study team that jointly prepares for the mid-term exam. After taking the exam individually, the team will convene and complete a team exam. Team exam scoring options will be described in more detail below. This assignment also includes an individually prepared five-page double-spaced paper that analyzes what happened in the study team in terms of (1) what the team did/didn't do that contributed to its success or lack of it and (2) what the individual team member did that contributed to the team's success or lack of it. THIS PAPER MUST BE COMPLETED IF EXAM BONUS POINTS ARE AWARDED.
- After students individually write the mid-term exam, students will gather in their study teams to complete one collaborative response sheet representing the answers from the same exam. The team-based mid-term will be finished by 6:00 p.m. on Oct. 26. Students will be required to stay in the classroom to write both the individual and the team version of the mid-term.
- Marks for the individual and the group mid-term exams will be provided on Nov. 9. The individual paper for this assignment will be due on Nov. 16 at the beginning of class.
- The individual and team exams will be marked and compared. If the individual exam mark is HIGHER than the team exam mark, the student will receive her/his individual mark. If the team exam mark is higher than the individual exam mark, the individual will have the difference added to her/his individual exam score.
- The multiple-choice exam will be out of 40 points. I will grade the individual exams first and calculate an average score for team members. Then I will grade the group exam. If the group score is higher than the individual average, that difference gets added to each individual exam score. The maximum number of bonus points a student can receive is five.

b) Participation   20%

- This assignment includes an individually prepared five-page typed participation analysis paper; submitted in three instalments.
- Instalment #1: One page which includes your evaluation of the discussion board conversation [Classroom Culture and Participation Guidelines] and your individual participation goals for the term. Due Sept. 28.

- Instalment #2: Three pages, one of which is a letter to designated partner giving feedback on her/his participation as you have observed it and two pages consisting of a mid-course progress report on your participation. Due Oct. 19.
- Instalment #3: One page that contains the final assessment of your participation in the course. Due Nov. 30.
- Bonus Points: On five unannounced days, attendance will be taken. Those present will receive 1% bonus points.

Team Final Exam Essay   25%

FNF 100—Final Exam Essay: Reflecting on Family-in-Relation
- With a partner, share how your personal family has experienced or addressed two of the overarching themes presented in this course. An hour will be provided for this process in class on Nov. 23.
- After each person has shared, spend 10–15 minutes writing notes about what you heard from your partner about her/his family experiences. Include in your notes the aspects of your partner's story that resonated for you, that reminded you of your family experiences, and/or that was completely new to you. After writing your notes, write a question to your partner that you are left wondering about and then share the writing passage (including the question) with her/him.
- Each partner then incorporates writing in her/his final paper (1500–1800 words).
- The structure of the paper (in order) includes a (very good) title, an introductory paragraph with the question your partner posed as the thesis statement for your essay, your response to that question including specific reference to three to five course readings and the associated themes, a reflective statement (three to five paragraphs) of how this course has prepared you for your future professional work, and a closing statement (two to three paragraphs) that includes a promise or intention or plan describing what you believe is required future learning for you in the area of families and health.
- Include also in your reflective statement specific examples of course content that have been particularly meaningful to you, have given you pause (caused you to examine more closely your family-in-relation), have interrupted your commonly held assumptions about family and health, and/or have been influenced by the stories from a classmate.
- The final exam will be worth 25% of your final grade. You must pass the final exam to pass the course.
- Out of 25 possible marks for this final exam, 1 mark will be based on the title, two marks will be based on the question you posed to your

partner, two marks on structure outlined in (d) above, five marks on organization, five marks on integration of course themes, five marks on flow, and five marks on writing style including grammar, spelling, sentence structure.
- Although the paper is written independently, you must indicate your partner's name under yours in the top right-hand corner of your paper. All papers are to be submitted electronically to me by 4:00 p.m. on Dec. 7, 2010. Late papers will be reduced by two marks for each day past the deadline, including weekends.

APPENDIX FOUR

Assignment Two Rubrics

A. Book Chapter/Journal Article/Film Review (20 marks)

- An <u>eight-page</u> review (double-spaced) will be submitted on Tuesday, Oct. 12.
- The paper will address how the reviewed item intersects with families and health.
- The review will be graded on its <u>completeness</u> (positive and negative elements critiqued), level of <u>insight</u> (thoughtfulness), <u>experiential</u> support provided for your review (descriptive experiences of the author), and the extent the relevant course content (from readings) is <u>integrated</u> into the review.

Grammar, structure, form, spelling, length, organization, flow, APA referencing	4 marks
Completeness	4 marks
Insight	4 marks
Personal experiences/reflections	4 marks
Integrated course content	4 marks
Total	/20

B. Learning Logs (20 marks)

- Three-four learning logs of <u>eight-pages</u> total will be submitted on Tuesday, Oct. 12.
- Each learning log will consist of a (1) student's response to a discussion question, (2) her/his partner's input from the in-class discussion, and (3) the student's reflection on how this topic relates to her/his daily experiences of families and health.
- Entries will be graded on their <u>completeness</u>, level of <u>insight</u> (thoughtfulness), support provided for the <u>reflections</u> (descriptive experiences), and the extent the relevant course content (from readings) is <u>integrated</u> into the entries.

Grammar, structure, form, spelling, length, organization, flow, APA referencing	4 marks
Completeness of three-part structure	4 marks
Insight	4 marks

Personal experiences/reflections   4 marks
Integrated course content   4 marks
Total   /20

References

Beattie, K., & James, R. (1997). Flexible coursework delivery to Australian postgraduates: How effective is the teaching and learning? *Higher Education, 33*, 177–194.

Boaler, J. (2002). Learning from teaching: exploring the relationship between reform curriculum and equity. *Journal for Research in Mathematics Education, 33*(4), 239–258.

Bonner, S. E. (1999). Choosing teaching methods based on learning objectives: An integrative framework. *Issues in Accounting Education, 14*, 11–39.

Cory-Wright, J. (2011). Learner-centric design. *Training Journal,* 47–50. [Available: http://ezproxy.lib.ryerson.ca/login?url=http://search.proquest.com/docview/849267376?accountid=13631]

Ellsworth, E. (1989). Why doesn't this feel empowering? Working through the repressive myths of critical pedagogy. *Harvard Educational Review, 59*(3), 297–324.

Ellsworth, E. (1997). *Teaching positions: Difference, pedagogy, and the power of address.* New York, NY: Teachers College Press.

Foucault, M. (1980). *Power/knowledge: Selected interviews and other writings, 1972–1977.* New York, NY: Pantheon Books.

Foxe, J. P. (2011). *Best practices when working with TAs and GAs: A manual for course instructors.* Learning and Teaching Office, Ryerson University, Toronto, ON.

Friere, P. (1970). *Pedagogy of the oppressed.* New York, NY: Seabury Press.

Gingras, J. (2012). Embracing vulnerability: Completing the auto-fictive circle in health profession education. *Journal of Transformative Education, 10*(2), 67–89.

Gingras, J. (2008). Sacra conversazione—a tender dialectic invoking an arts practice-based autoethnography to bridge language and silence in dietetics. *Educational Insights, 12*(2). [Available: http://www.ccfi.educ.ubc.ca/publication/insights/v12n02/articles/gingras/index.html]

Hewett, C. M. (2003). Learner-centered teacher preparation: A mastery of skills. *Education, 124*(1), 24–30.

hooks, b. (1994). *Teaching to transgress: Education as the practice of freedom.* New York, NY: Routledge.

Hutchings, P., Taylor Huber, M., & Ciccone, A. (2011). *The scholarship of teaching and learning reconsidered: Institutional integration and impact.* San Francisco, CA: Jossey-Bass.

Hyman, D., et al. (2001–2). Beyond Boyer: The UniSCOPE model of scholarship for the 21st century. *Journal of Higher Education Outreach and Engagement, 7*(1–2), 41–65.

Lakey, B., Lakey, G., Napier, R., & Robinson, J. (1995). *Grassroots and nonprofit leadership: A guide for organizations in changing times.* Philadelphia, PA: New Society. [Available: http://www.trainingforchange.org/grassroots_and_nonprofit_leadership]

McCallister, C. (2002). Learning to let them learn: Yielding power to students in a literacy methods course. *English Education, 34*(4), 281–301.

McCombs, B. L., & Whisler, J. S. (1997). *The learner-centered classroom and school*. San Francisco, CA: Jossey-Bass.

McKinney, K. (2007). *Enhancing learning through the scholarship of teaching and learning: The challenges and joys of juggling*. Boulton, MA: Anker Publishing.

Mosston, M., & Ashworth, S. (2002). *Teaching physical education*. San Francisco, CA: Benjamin Cummings.

O'Sullivan, E. (1999). *Transformative learning: Educational vision for the 21st century*. Toronto, ON: University of Toronto Press.

Pinar, W. F., Irwin, R. L., & Aoki, T. T. (2005). *Curriculum in a new key: The collected works of Ted T. Aoki*. New York and London: Routledge.

Ramsden, P. (1988). *Improving learning: New perspectives*. London, UK: Kogan Page.

Rebick, J. (2012). Occupy this! [ebook]. Toronto: Penguin Canada.

Simplicio, J. S. (2000). Teaching classroom educators how to be more effective and creative teachers. *Education, 120*(4), 675–680.

Warren, K. (1998). Educating students for social justice in service learning. *Journal of Experiential Education, 21*(3), 134–139.

Weimer, M. (2002). *Learner-centered teaching: Five key changes to practice*. New York, NY: John Wiley and Sons.

Zhou, M. (2011). Learning styles and teaching styles in college English teaching. *International Education Studies, 4*, 73–77.

8

Narrative Reflective Process: A Creative Experiential Path to Personal Knowing in Teaching–Learning Situations

Jasna Krmpotić Schwind

Most curricula persuasively address the cognitive and the psychomotor aspects of student education, while allowing the affective domain to remain elusively outside the academic boundaries (Schwind, 2008). This is significant in the curricula of applied professions, where teaching–learning needs to address and engage the whole student for meaningful and holistic learning to occur (Miller, 1996, 1990; Miller, Cassie, & Drake, 1990), with particular focus on personal knowing (Chinn & Kramer, 2008). This approach requires authentic and genuine self-expression involving deep reflection, openness to experience, and meaningful interactions with others. By developing personal knowing, future practitioners authenticate themselves, thereby creating the possibility for respectful and "response-able" relationships with those in their care. To engage learners as whole persons in such meaningful teaching–learning situations, I implement Narrative Reflective process (NRP), a creative self-expression tool, which incorporates stories, metaphors, drawing, letter-writing, and creative writing, among other strategies (Fraser & Schwind, 2011; Schwind, 2004, 2008, 2009; Schwind, Beanlands, et al., 2014; Schwind, Cameron, Coffey, Morrison, & Mildonet, 2012). This tool grows out of Narrative Inquiry (Connelly & Clandinin, 1990, 2006), a qualitative research framework that works with reconstruction of experience through storytelling, critical reflection, and co-construction of knowledge. Using NRP, students creatively explore their own personal knowing and so learn about the possibility of person-centred care in education and practice (McCormack & McCance, 2006; Coffey,

Morrison, & Mildonet, 2014). Research literature on humanistic practices in healthcare calls for different tools, approaches, and frameworks that place the person in the centre of our care (Ferrari, 2006; Hill, 2003; Irwin & Richardson, 2006; Kleiman, 2007; Lown, Rosen, & Marttila, 2011; Peek et al., 2007; Picard & Henneman, 2007; Ruddick, 2010; Sawatzky, Enns, Ashcroft, Davis, & Harder, 2009). As an educator working with future caregivers, I utilize NRP to provide students with a tool box of strategies that will not only help them promote more holistic care for patients, but also develop personal knowing in the process (Kelly, 1998; Schwind, Santa Mina, Metersky & Patterson, 2015). Through creative self-expression activities, the notion of *humanness of care* (Schwind, 2008) is lived and inquired into in an educational space so as to be transferable to practice contexts. In this way, the scholarship of teaching–learning and the scholarship of discovery intersect within experiential teaching–learning contexts.

This chapter demonstrates how engaging students in meaningful experiential holistic learning, using NRP, enriches their personal and professional lives and in so doing the lives of those in their care. The chapter opens with my teaching–learning philosophy. I then situate NRP within the Narrative Inquiry research framework. Following, I provide examples of practical applications, including the general steps of NRP, with different populations within educational settings. I conclude the chapter by reflecting on how NRP affects our evolution toward wholeness and consider implications for teaching–learning scholarship.

My Teaching–Learning Philosophy

Key narrative threads that embody my teaching–learning philosophy are: experience, metaphors, self-awareness, reflection, relationship, knowledge co-construction, person-centred, humanness of care, healing, and wholeness. The Latin adage *omnea mea mecum porte*, loosely translated as *everything I am, I carry with me*, encapsulates the premise with which I encounter life and, more specifically, my *teaching–learning* relationships. I link the terms *teaching* and *learning* because I view them as interconnected and reciprocal. My teaching–learning philosophy is grounded in Dewey's (1938/1963) assertion that "every experience enacted and undergone modifies the one who acts and undergoes, while this modification affects, whether we wish it or not, the quality of subsequent experiences" (p. 35). My belief that all life events contribute to who we are in the process of becoming, as we live storied lives within the personal–social contexts over time and space (Connelly & Clandinin, 1990, 2006), further underpins my view of teaching–learning scholarship. Additionally, I agree with

Dewey's declaration (1938/1963) that "without some reconstruction, some remaking" of our life experiences there is no intellectual evolution (p. 64). Thus, my assumption is that people's relationships with self and with others can be augmented by engaging in focused experiential reflection for the purposes of recognizing and accessing the unique humanness that is within each of us.

Exploration and reconstruction of my life experiences through regular reflective practice increases my awareness of the stories I live by and thus bring into my teaching–learning situations. By honouring that aspect of myself, I provide the necessary time and space for my students to do the same. To that end I implement NRP as an experiential teaching–learning strategy. Through these creative self-expressive modes, my learners and I co-construct knowledge and our professional ways of being, thus expanding our consciousness, "finding greater meaning in life [and] reaching new heights of connectedness with other people" (Newman, 2008, p. 6), all the while evolving as persons and professionals over time and in a safe environment. In other words, these experiential teaching–learning tools augment meaningful learning within professional relationships, thus opening possibilities for both the teacher and the learner to evolve toward wholeness.

I believe that, in order to provide this holistic way of teaching–learning (Miller, 1990), we as teachers need to develop the self-awareness and openness for ourselves before we can guide our students to do the same. As I role-model this narrative self-inquiry (Clandinin & Connelly, 2004) with my colleagues and students, my hope is that they will do the same for those in their care, thus creating person-centred contexts where it is safe to heal, learn, and grow.

Furthermore, I believe that a teaching–learning relationship is one of mutual respect between the teacher and the learner, where the "I–thou" (Buber, 1970/1996) philosophy is lived and the whole person, mind–body–soul, is honoured for both. This kind of interconnectedness allows care and respect to flourish beyond the teaching–learning relationship so that it impacts future ways of being for the teacher, the learner, and those we encounter in our personal and professional lives.

Finally, I see teaching–learning as a dynamic and enriching relationship between two human beings whose storied lives intertwine with the program curriculum to give it life and meaning, on both personal and social levels. Through the encounter, the teacher and the learner co-create learning and growth, and the curriculum, as a result, evolves and changes reflexively, generating potential futures for new generations, thus impacting the evolutionary path of education, practice, and research.

Narrative Reflective Process

NRP is a guided experiential reflection that uses creative self-expressive means to access and explore personal and professional life experiences, with the intent to augment personal knowing and insight, which are significant attributes of education, practice, and research. More specifically, NRP engages our deep reflection and, through creative self-expression, accesses tacit knowing (Polanyi, 1966/2009), which, although lying unseen within, impacts how we are in the world. The two key components of NRP, metaphors and drawing, are "known to elicit the depths of our being unreachable by words" (Schwind, 2003, p. 25). Thus, when seeking to access tacit knowing, NRP can be used both as a data collection strategy in research and as an intervention instrument in education and practice. When used in education and practice, it brings about deeper self-awareness and personal knowing; this in turn draws out qualities inherent in *humanness of care*, a core aspect of person-centred practices. For the purposes of this chapter, I focus specifically on the use of NRP in educational contexts.

NRP grew out of my original narrative inquiry research into how nurse-teachers' experiences of personal serious illness impacted their teaching–learning scholarship (Schwind 2003, 2004). The key knowing that came out of this research is the patient's need to be seen and treated as a human being. In other words, patients felt cared for when caregivers connected with them on a "human" level. As a result, I became interested in exploring the phenomenon of *humanness of care*. Because the concept *humanness of care* is nebulous, I often use metaphors to delve deeper into its meaning and to teach it to my students. The following is my developing definition of this concept:

> *Humanness of care* is a concept that expresses itself in all person-to-person interactions, whether in healthcare or education or any professional and/or personal encounters. It includes mindful-awareness, self-knowing, creativity, intentionality, goodwill and respect for self and for others. It means person-centred care, in any human-to-human interaction, and especially so when there is a perceived power differential as it is in teaching–learning, as well as in caregiving–*carereceiving* relationships. *Humanness of care* is an ergonomically sound energy within which the person is responseable to whatever stimulus s/he encounters inside these contexts. As a teacher of future nurses, I work with students and fellow-teachers to help them bring forth various aspects of their own *humanness of care*. (Schwind & Mantas, 2012)

Following the initial study with ill nurse-teachers, I quickly recognized that *humanness of care* needs to be taught holistically: entwining the theories of care frameworks (Newman, 2008; Watson, 1999) with the embodied personal knowing. With this in mind, I formalized the initial narrative inquiry data collection strategies I used with ill nurse-teachers and created NRP to implement with my senior nursing students for the purpose of helping them develop their personal knowing (Schwind, 2008). By engaging directly in NRP, students were invited into their own stories of experience, and through metaphors, drawings, and creative writing, to expand their personal knowing of who they are as caregivers and what they bring into each and every interaction with persons in their care. My belief is that when caregivers value their own stories in this way, they are more likely to provide similar opportunities for their patients, thus helping them make sense of their illness experience. One student, Glenda, who engaged in the experiential teaching–learning strategy of NRP, observed:

> I realized the essence of nursing is to care [for] the whole patient. The nurse actually uses her whole "self" (not only the needles or pumps) to heal the patient. Obviously, my metaphor of life will shape not only my learning process but also my interactions with my patients. (Schwind, 2008, p. 88)

Over the years, I have received much feedback from my former students on how the creative activity of NRP has helped them in their professional practice. The biggest impact on their care seems to be their chosen metaphor, the heart of NRP. One former student participant, whom I met recently, four years after engaging in NRP, told me that as a registered nurse in pediatrics, when she is faced with an issue in practice, she asks herself, *What would an elephant do in this situation?* Her chosen caregiver metaphor was an *elephant*, whose characteristics she had described as *intelligent with a good memory, part of a group, family oriented and caring toward its young*. She revealed that her metaphor was a tool that not only guides her practice but also helps her make sense of its nuanced complexities.

Since the "human dimension of being cannot be taught as an extrinsic object" (Schwind, 2008, p. 89), I decided to engage fellow teachers in NRP (Schwind, Cameron, Franks, Graham, & Robinson, 2012). By experiencing first-hand this reflective process, the teachers not only increase their own self-awareness and personal knowing but are then able to role-model this process for their students and thoughtfully guide them through it. The experiential nature of NRP leads to personal knowing, which, along with critical thinking, supports a holistic approach to person-centred education and care, thus augmenting the scholarship of teaching–learning. Using the metaphor of "self as instrument of care," I invited a group of nurse-teachers to engage in NRP (Schwind et al., 2012), which they then implemented with their respective student groups, with positive outcomes. Four of the group members taught in the undergraduate community nursing courses. The following are excerpts of their experiences using NRP with their own student groups:

> Metaphor drawings and sharing within the classroom enabled students to describe their practice experiences in greater depth, as well as find personal meaning in their journey through community nursing. It also helped to establish trust within the group, creating a climate where they were able to support each other.
>
> Enhancing students' awareness of how reflection supported their personal transition process helped bring them to the point where they could identify situations and apply a reflective process to assist their clients to successfully complete the needed transitions.
>
> In some ways, instruments are metaphors for our voice…giving us a new language for understanding ourselves and our students.
>
> Metaphors help students by creating safe space, and providing them with words to help them express themselves.
> (Schwind et al., 2012, pp. 9–10)

Although this experiential process has been implemented by particular teachers with their respective student groups, it is transferrable and adaptable to other contexts where personal knowing within relationships is of significance. In fact, the goal is to develop capacity of teachers to use NRP through professional development workshops in order to more fully role-model *humanness of care* to their students. These future caregivers would then engage in NRP to access their own *humanness of care*. Based on Dewey's (1938/1963) notion that each experience informs every subsequent experience, these individuals would then be able to express their embodied learning in practice, thus impacting the quality of person-centred care.

Having defined NRP and contextualized it within the narrative inquiry research framework, we can see from the above examples how it was used with students and teachers in nursing education, and its potential for transferability to other disciplines. Although I recognize that other scholars are exploring and using various reflective processes to assist the professional development of future practitioners (Clandinin, Cave, & Cave, 2011; Fraser & Schwind, 2011; Freese, 2006; Johns, 2009; Kent, 2008; Moss, Springer, & Dehr, 2008; Russell, 2005), in this chapter I describe how I developed and use NRP within my scholarship of teaching–learning. What follows is a general guideline on how NRP could be used in teaching–learning situations.

General Approach to Narrative Reflective Process

As I have situated the theoretical and the practical background of NRP, as well as articulated my own philosophical approach to teaching–learning scholarship, what follows is the general approach for this creative experiential process. In teaching–learning contexts, the purpose of NRP is to:

- engage students in meaningful learning that will enrich their personal and professional lives and, by extension, the lives of others;
- increase students' personal knowing and thereby increase appreciation of, and respect for, self and for others;
- role-model, through this experiential teaching–learning approach, person-centred care in education, which students then take with them into their practice contexts;
- contribute to teaching the whole student, with the specific focus on personal knowing.

Following are some general steps and suggestions for using NRP in teaching–learning contexts. Examples of the exact steps may be found in the following appendices: Appendix One is a step-by-step process that may be implemented within a larger theoretical course. The topic I used in this example is "leadership and followership." Appendix Two is the NRP on the concept of caring that I implement with smaller numbers of students, such as clinical or seminar groups.

Although it is impossible to guarantee, it is extremely important to strive to provide "a safe and supportive environment for the process of self-reflection to occur" (Picard & Jones, 2005, p. 183). Participants in NRP are informed of this at the outset, as well as throughout the process. Consequently, the NRP sessions are always an invitation, and the pace is responsive to the participants' needs. In the same way that forcing a bud to open would damage the emerging flower, so too a forceful directive would not yield a rich potential of personal knowing and insight for the participants. This is personal development work, and therefore there are no "right" or "wrong" responses. Also, because this is personal work, I advise the students to "let the unexpected emerge without censorship or judgement" (Chinn & Kramer, 2008, p. 143). I also remind the learners that none of this work is graded, nor is it handed in for scrutiny.

NRP begins with writing down in provided journals personal and professional life stories. This is followed by metaphors, sharing of "safe stories" (two to three minutes each) in small groups (usually of three), and drawing of metaphoric images, with creative and reflective writing throughout the process. Once the stories are written, I invite the students to choose a metaphor (Schwind, 2009) by saying, "Choose a symbolic image or a picture that best represents your [whatever concept is being explored] for you." For those who may find this request challenging, I provide further guidance: "Try to complete the following statement, 'My life is like a...'"

In terms of sharing a "safe story," I counsel the learners that "some of their stories may be intensely personal and emotionally charged, while others may simply be events that stood out in their minds, and for this reason to choose wisely what part of themselves they felt *safe* to expose" (Schwind, 2008, p. 85). After the NRP exercise, during the debriefing, the usual responses from the students about this stage of the process focus on their initial discomfort with being the centre of attention when telling their stories. This, however, is followed by relaxing into the provided time-space, where they report feeling heard and listened to. When they were doing the listening, students expressed frustration at not being able to respond verbally. However, once the initial discomfort had passed, they focused on the speaker's body language and speech, thus more fully hearing the speaker. At this time I explain why I ask them to engage in this attentive listening exercise. I tell them that when patients come in to seek health care services, they often have less than half a minute to tell their story without being interrupted. By experiencing uninterrupted time to tell their story or to hear another's, learners become aware of the importance of doing the same for those in their care.

As a narrativist, I recognize that when we hear one another's stories we are moved into our own inquiry and are therefore able, through our responses to the presented story, to move forward both ours and the storyteller's thinking, thus expanding consciousness towards wholeness. As the poet and writer Ben Okri (1996) notes, "it is in the creation of story, the lifting of the story into the realms of art, it is in this that the higher realms of creativity reside" (pp. 31–32). It is through creative self-expression that our own tacit knowing brims to the surface, where we encounter aspects of ourselves otherwise obscured. In a similar vein, we also experience the space provided for us by our listeners, as they listen with their ears, eyes, and heart, without interruption. Significantly, as per Narrative Inquiry, the telling of our stories to another person brings forward personal–social (relational) knowing that is temporally contextualized (over a period of time) in a situated space (classroom), where we co-construct our (caregiver) identity (Chan & Schwind, 2006; Lindsay, 2006). In other words, students tell stories of their life experiences and reflect on these stories through NRP: the use of metaphors and creative self-expression modalities, such as letter-writing, creative writing, construction of short stories, poems, and prose as the storied experience, reveals itself for scrutiny. The letter-writing can include response letters to other members of the group who just told their story. Learners are invited to respond by considering how the narrative threads inherent in the told story intersect with their own and, if not, then to imagine why that is or to consider how it could come about. Another letter-writing exercise involves the letter students write to themselves *from* their chosen metaphor, thus further stretching their creativity and imagination. Both are significant qualities that help us engage in "deliberative, ethical considerations that make possible new perceptions" (Lyons & Kubler LaBoskey, 2002, p. 14).

Students are then invited to review their personal and professional stories, metaphors, and writing, seeking out key narrative threads, while accessing scholarly literature as their exploration deepens. This activity brings students closer together, strengthening their relationships, as they begin to see one another as persons (fellow human beings). This living out of the *humanness of care* supports my belief that when we connect at that level with others, and especially with those in our care, be it in professional relationships (teacher–learner) or therapeutic ones (caregiver–*carereceiver*), we individually and collectively expand our consciousness of being and becoming, moving forward toward interconnectedness.

Over the years, I have been asked why doing NRP work is important. To that inquiry I respond with a metaphor of a hiker carrying a backpack. I usually share the following story:

> *When the hiker comes down from the mountain into the village gift shop and she is aware of the big backpack on her back, she has a choice: to either take it off and leave it at the door, or to keep it on, but then to mindfully move through the gift shop, so as not to break any fragile merchandise. If the hiker enters the gift shop and is unaware of her backpack, then there is the potential for inadvertently causing a lot of damage by that backpack. In other words, if we know who we are and what we bring into each and every relationship (personal knowing), especially with those in our care, be it in education or practice, then we have a greater chance of creating spaces that foster learning and healing, respectively.*

Implications for Scholarship of Teaching–Learning

NRP, as an experiential teaching–learning approach, has the potential to augment meaningful learning within professional relationships, thus opening possibilities for both the teacher and the student to use their narratives to "understand and re-think [their] practice" (Chan, 2005; Lyons & Kubler LaBoskey, 2002, p. 13). In other words, through this creative self-expressive process the teacher and the learners are able to co-construct their professional ways of being, as they evolve as persons and professionals over time and in a supportive environment. Furthermore, NRP offers a creative way to enhance student experience, not only in the classroom but also in practice placements. It supports the scholarship of teaching–learning excellence by increasing teachers' ability to more holistically support their students, thereby role-modelling *humanness of care*. Students then have the opportunity to take these learned strategies into their practice as new graduates, not only to engender person-centred care, but also to support their own transition into the professional caregiver role. By including the affective domain through this creative experiential approach, the students engage holistically in their learning, and practice.

Over the past number of years I have successfully implemented NRP, as part of my experiential teaching–learning approaches, with my undergraduate and graduate nursing students. Based on the received feedback, students expressed increased personal and professional self-awareness and knowing, which has enhanced the quality of their education and practice experiences. In course feedback received at the end of each semester, learners conveyed an increased appreciation for their peers, thereby expanding their capacity for compassion, tolerance, and respect, not only for themselves but for others as well. The possibility of "I–thou" interactions with others was thus potentiated. However, having said that, it is important to also acknowledge some possible challenges to broader integration of such experiential activities in education. For one, the prolonged time commitment for implementing this process in the classroom might become a barrier. Also, the ability of faculty to skilfully engage their students in NRP could pose a challenge, as some individuals who are not prepared to closely examine their inner worlds through creative experiential reflection could resist taking part. For these reasons, broader integration of NRP would entail intensive and systematic faculty professional development on how to effectively introduce NRP into their course curricula so that it fits into their timelines and so that the learners are appropriately guided and supported in the process.

I have effectively used NRP as an experiential teaching–learning strategy in nursing education. The process is easily transferable and adaptable to other contexts where practitioners' personal knowing within professional therapeutic relationships is of significance. For example, recently I taught a graduate course on advanced therapeutic communication from an inter-professional perspective; subsequently, several social work students reported they had successfully used aspects of NRP with their clients in clinical practice.

Based on the Narrative Inquiry framework, research and teaching–learning are mutually informative, entwining the scholarship of teaching–learning with the scholarship of discovery. NRP, supported by the Narrative Inquiry qualitative research method, has the potential for a long-term impact on program curricula, as well as on research and practice across all disciplines. To that end, I look toward possible futures for the NRP experiential teaching–learning approach, where creative self-expression is fodder for further self-inquiry for both teachers and students. Discoveries and insights conveyed in the creative self-expression of stories and metaphors "give others in the discipline an opportunity for reflection and response, which in turn enriches and deepens the personal knowing potential of others in [and across] the discipline[s]" (Chinn & Kramer, 2008, p. 145). In this way, we collectively gain the potential to move toward wholeness.

Where to from Here?

As suggested earlier, NRP can help students not only to develop personal knowing—a quality deemed essential in caring practices—but also to transition into their professional roles. For that reason, the next step of scholarship could be to explore with new graduates how engagement in NRP impacted their transition from student to professional. If the outcome of this inquiry proved to be positive, it could support the broader implementation of NRP.

APPENDIX ONE

Please note:
There are no right or wrong answers. The process serves to increase self-awareness/self-knowledge and how that may impact your personal/professional self.

You will get out of this narrative reflective process as much as you put into it.

1. Take a moment to think back on the occasions, in your personal and professional life, when you took on a Leadership role.

2. Choose three of these occasions and write a short story about each. (What was the occasion, who was present, what did you do?)

3. Now think back on three occasions where you assumed the role of a Follower.

4. Write a story about each of these situations. (What was the occasion, who was present, what did you do?)

5. Review the two sets of your stories and note narrative threads or themes that flow throughout each set of your stories. Write these down on paper.

6. Now, based on your stories and key narrative threads think of a metaphoric image that best represents you as a:
   a. Leader—Draw that metaphoric image—In point form, describe the characteristics of this image.
   b. Follower—Draw that metaphoric image—In point form, describe the characteristics of this image.

7. Consider which image descriptors, for Leader and Follower, best describe you as a person and a professional.

8. In your small group of three, introduce yourself as your metaphoric image of self as either a Leader or a Follower. In your introduction use the descriptors you used to depict your metaphor characteristics.

9. Consider, in your small group: How will your awareness of yourself as Leader and Follower inform how you are in professional therapeutic relationships? How will it frame your nursing practice?

10. Homework: Reread your stories, review both of your metaphoric images, and then write a reflection on what you learned about yourself as a Leader and a Follower, and explore ways in which you can further expand and/or refine these roles. Introduce scholarly literature into your reflection in order to deepen your reflective activity.

APPENDIX TWO

There are no right or wrong answers. The process serves to increase self-awareness/self-knowledge and how that may impact your personal/professional self.

You will get out of this reflective process as much as you put into it.

1. Take a moment to think back on the occasions, in your personal and professional life, when you felt cared for.
    Choose three of these occasions and write a short story about each. (What was the occasion, who was present, what did you do?)

2. In a small group of three, take three minutes each to share a safe story of when you felt cared for. While one person shares her/his story, the others actively listen without commenting/interrupting/interjecting.

3. Now think back on three occasions in your personal and professional life, when you felt you expressed caring.
    Choose three of these occasions and write a short story about each. (What was the occasion, who was present, what did you do?)

4. In a small group of three, take three minutes each to share a *safe* story of when you felt you expressed caring. While one person shares her/his story, the others actively listen without commenting/interrupting/interjecting.

5. Review your stories and note narrative threads or themes that flow through each set of stories. Write these down on paper.
    Note whether the threads are the same/similar OR are they different between the two sets of stories.

6. Now, based on your stories and key narrative threads, think of a metaphoric image that best represents for you the concept of Caring, i.e., what caring means to you; how you experience caring.
    There is no right or wrong way of drawing this image. It is whatever you choose it to be!
    Draw that metaphoric image. In point form, describe the characteristics of this image.

If being cared for and giving care were different for you, then draw two different metaphoric images.

Write down what caring looks like to you—how it would express itself in lived experience.

7. Within your small group of three, take a few minutes each to describe your Caring metaphor image to your group mates. While one person shares her/his story, the others actively listen without commenting/interrupting/interjecting.

8. Have your Caring metaphor write you, as a Nurse, a letter. What would it say to you? What message would it give you? [Choose a piece of stationery.]

9. Reread your six stories and all the writing you have done thus far; review both of your metaphoric image(s), and then reflect on paper what you learned about yourself as a person and a professional.

    Consider how your awareness of the way you experience and express caring will inform how you are in professional therapeutic relationships. How will it frame your nursing practice?

    Explore ways in which you can further expand and/or refine these caring qualities in your personal and professional life. Introduce scholarly literature into your reflection in order to deepen your reflective activity, expanding your understanding of the layered complexity of the Caring concept.

10. Now, using key narrative threads from your writing/stories, write a poem or poetic prose that best encapsulates for you the concept of Caring.

References

Buber, M. (1996). *I and thou* (W. Kaufmann, Trans.). New York, NY: Touchstone. (Original work published 1970.)
Chan, E. A. (2005). Narrative research trail: Values of ambiguity and relationships. *Nurse Researcher, 13*(1), 43–55.
Chan, E. A., & Schwind, J. K. (2006). Two nurse-teachers reflect on acquiring their nursing identity. *Reflective Practice, 7*(4), 303–314.
Chinn, P. L., & Kramer, M. K. (2008). *Integrated theory and knowledge development in nursing* (7th ed). St. Louis, MO: Mosby Elsevier.
Clandinin, D. J., Cave, M. T., & Cave, A. (2011). Narrative reflective practice in medical education for residents: Composing shifting identities. *Advances in Medical Education and Practice, 2*, 1–7.
Clandinin, D. J., & Connelly, F. M. (2004). Knowledge, narrative and self-study. In J. Loughran, M. L. Hamilton, V. LaBoskey, & T. Russell (Eds.), *International handbook of self study of teaching and teacher education practices* (pp. 575–600). Dordrecht, Netherlands: Kluwer Academic.
Connelly, F. M., & Clandinin, D. J. (2006). Narrative inquiry. In J. L. Green, G. Camilli, & P. B. Elmore (Eds.), *Handbook of complementary methods in education research* (pp. 477–487). Washington, DC: Lawrence Erlbaum.
Connelly, F. M., & Clandinin, D. J. (1990). Stories of experience and narrative inquiry. *Educational Researcher, 19*(5), 2–14.
Dewey, J. (1963). *Experience and education*. New York: Macmillan. (Original work published 1938.)
Ferrari, E. (2006). Academic education's contribution to the nurse–patient relationship. *Nursing Standard, 21*(10), 35–40.
Fraser, R. A., & Schwind, J. K. (2011). Advancement of guided creative and critical reflection in the professional development of enterprising individuals in business and nursing. *Reflective Practice, 12*(5), 645–661.
Freese, A. R. (2006). Transformation through self-study: The voice of preservice teachers. In C. Kosnik, C. Beck, A. R. Freece, & A. P. Smaras (Eds.), *Making a difference in teacher education through self-study* (pp. 65–79). Dordrecht, Netherlands: Springer.
Irwin, R. S., & Richardson, N. D. (2006). Patient-focused care: Using the right tools. *Chest, 130*(1), 73S–82S.
Johns, C. (2009). *Becoming a reflective practitioner*. Oxford, UK: Wiley-Blackwell.
Kelly, B. (1998). Preserving moral integrity: A follow-up study with new graduate nurses. *Journal of Advanced Nursing, 28*, 1134–1145. doi:10.1046/j.1365-2648, 1998.00810.x
Kent, R. D. (2008). An inquiry into mindful caring: A narrative account of my experience in day surgery. In J. K. Schwind & G. M. Lindsay (Eds.), *From experience to relationships: Reconstructing ourselves in education and healthcare* (pp. 39–59). Charlotte, NC: Information Age Publishing.
Kleiman, S. (2007). Revitalizing the humanistic imperative in nursing education. *Nursing Education Perspectives, 28*(4), 209–213.

Lindsay, G. (2006). Constructing a nursing identity: Reflecting on and reconstructing experience. *Reflective Practice, 7*(1), 59–72.

Lown, B. A., Rosen, J., & Marttila, J. (2011). An agenda for improving compassionate care: A survey shows about half of patients say such caring is missing. *Health Affairs, 30*(9), 1772–1778. doi:10.1377/hlthaff.2011.0539

Lyons, N., & Kubler LaBoskey, V. (2002). Why narrative inquiry or exemplars for a scholarship of teaching? In N. Lyons & V. Kubler LaBoskey (Eds.), *Narrative inquiry in practice: Advancing the knowledge of teaching.* (pp. 11–30). New York, NY: Teachers College Press.

McCormack, B., & McCance, T. V. (2006). Development of a framework for person-centred nursing. *Journal of Advanced Nursing, 56*(5), 472–479.

Miller, J. P. (1996). *The holistic curriculum.* Toronto, ON: OISE Press.

Miller, J. P. (1990). *Holistic learning: A teacher's guide to integrated studies.* Toronto, ON: OISE Press.

Miller, J., Cassie, B. J. R., & Drake, S. M. (1990). *Holistic learning: A teacher's guide to integrated studies.* Toronto, ON: Ontario Institute for Studies in Education.

Moss, G., Springer, T., & Dehr, K. (2008). Guided reflection protocol as narrative inquiry and teacher professional development. *Reflective Practice, 9*(4), 497–508.

Newman, M. A. (2008). *Transforming presence: The difference that nursing makes.* Philadelphia: F.A. Davies.

Okri, B. (1996). *Birds of heaven.* London, UK: Phoenix.

Peek, C., Higgins, Il, Milson-Hawke, S., McMillan, M., & Harper, D. (2007). Towards innovation: The development of a person-centered model of care for older people in acute care. *Contemporary Nurse, 26*(2), 164–176.

Picard, C., & Henneman, E. A. (2007). Theory-guided evidence-based reflective practice: An orientation to education for quality care. *Nursing Science Quarterly, 20*(1), 39–42. doi:10.1177/0894318406296783

Picard, C., & Jones, D. (2005). *Giving voice to what we know: Margaret Newman's theory of health as expanding consciousness in nursing practice, research and education.* Sudbury, MA: Jones and Bartlett.

Polanyi, M. (2009). *The tacit dimension.* Chicago, IL: University of Chicago Press. (Original work published 1966.)

Ruddick, F. (2010). Person-centred mental health care: Myth or reality? *Mental Health Practice, 13*(9), 24–28.

Russell, T. (2005). Can reflective practice be taught? *Reflective Practice, 6*(2), 199–204.

Sawatzky, J. V., Enns, C. L., Ashcroft, T. J., Davis, P. L., & Harder, B. N. (2009). Teaching excellence in nursing education: A caring framework. *Journal of Professional Nursing, 25*(5), 260–266. doi:10.1016/j.profnurs.2009.01.017

Schwind, J. K. (2009). Metaphor-reflection in my healthcare experience. *Aporia* (www.aporiajournal.com), *1*(1), 15–21.

Schwind, J. K. (2008). Accessing humanness: From experience to research, from classroom to praxis. In J. K. Schwind & G. M. Lindsay (Eds.), *From experience to relationships: Reconstructing ourselves in education and healthcare* (pp. 77–94). Charlotte, NC: Information Age Publishing.

Schwind, J. K. (2004).*When nurse-teachers become ill: A narrative inquiry into the personal illness experience of three nurse-teachers.* Unpublished PhD diss., OISE/University of Toronto.

Schwind, J. K. (2003). Reflective process in the study of illness stories as experienced by three nurse-teachers. *Reflective Practice, 4*(1), 19–32.

Schwind, J., Beanlands, H., Lapum, J., Romaniuk, D., Fredericks, S., LeGrow, K., Edwards, S., McCay, E., & Crosby, J. (2014). Fostering person-centred care among nursing students: Creative pedagogical approaches to developing personal knowing. *Journal of Nursing Education, 53*(6), 343–347. doi:10.3928/01484834-20140520-01

Schwind, J. K., Cameron, D., Franks, J., Graham, C., & Robinson, T. (2012). Engaging in narrative reflective process to fine tune *Self-as-Instrument-of-Care. Reflective Practice, 13*(2), 223–235. doi:10.1080/14623943.2011.626030. 1-13, iFirst Artcle.

Schwind, J. K., Lindsay, G., Coffey, S., Morrison, D., & Mildon, B. (2014). Opening the black-box of person-centred care: An arts-informed narrative inquiry into mental health education and practice. *Nurse Education Today, Special Issue NET 2013, 34*(8), 1167–1171. doi:10.1016/j.nedt.2014.04.010

Schwind, J. K., & Mantas, K. (2012) Co-constructing holistic knowing through reflective dialogues on a co-creative *artmaking* experience. *International Journal of Holistic Education, 1*(1), 9–22.

Schwind, J. K., Santa Mina, E., Metersky, K., & Patterson, E. (2015). Using the Narrative Reflective Process to explore how students learn about caring in their nursing program: An arts-informed Narrative Inquiry. *Reflective Practice: International and Multidisciplinary Perspectives.* doi:10.1080/14623943.2015.1052385.

Watson, J. (1999). *Postmodern nursing and beyond.* London, UK: Churchill Livingstone.

9

Introducing Art into the Social Work Classroom: Tensions and Possibilities

Samantha Wehbi, Susan Preston, and Ken Moffatt

This chapter discusses various ways of introducing art into the classroom. Building on the principles of transformative education in social work (Bozalek & Biersteker, 2010; Coulshed, 1993; Jones, 2009), we argue that creative arts could play a significant role in enhancing course delivery, curriculum content, and assessments of student learning in community service courses such as those in social work. Throughout the discussion, we rely on our own experiences and teaching practice, with classroom examples to illustrate our main ideas and arguments. This chapter introduces readers to some of the principles and uses of creative arts in community services learning and teaching, and engages in critical reflexivity about the challenges and tensions that arise when we introduce art into the classroom. Throughout this discussion, we examine our roles as educators and how these may be impacted by the introduction of creative arts into our teaching practice. In doing so, we highlight a process of critical engagement with the scholarship of teaching and learning, specifically in terms of "integration of knowledge," where the impetus is for the creation of interdisciplinary linkages (Hyman et al., 2001–2).

The scholarship of teaching provides examples of the uses of art in community services education in various fields. For example, Casey (2009) reports on undergraduate nursing curriculum that included art-based inquiry. The author notes that such inquiry allows the educator to emphasize to students "caring and expressive aspects which are also essential to effective practice" (p. 70) but that have been marginalized in practice contexts, in which science has dominated. These observations are echoed by Davies (2008) in a discussion of the uses of poetry in midwifery education; the author argues that the introduction of expressive art challenges the medicalization of midwifery education and promotes a more holistic approach to practice. Similarly, Fox (2009) describes a pedagogical approach where students were asked to analyze an artwork or to create one of their own in a graduate nutrition program; as with the previously cited studies from nursing and midwifery, the author notes how the inclusion of art allowed students to think critically about the place of science and art in professional practice. Importantly, the authors cited here all note that we have "only scratched the surface" (Davies, 2008, p. 19) in terms of understanding the potential uses and impacts of including art in professional education.

While it is beyond the scope of this chapter to explore these disciplines, it is important to note that our work is embedded in a rich and expanding scholarship on the integration of art in community services education. Indeed, the existence of this scholarship inspires us to add our voices to those attempting to bring art into the classroom and to scratch through the surface to uncover the potential of including art in our teaching practice. Within social work, the attention being paid to this integration of art and education is beginning to grow even though the discipline is still "almost entirely fixed on talk and text in seeking to develop and express its understanding of itself" (Walton, 2012, p. 725). So it is important to sustain this inquiry, especially since "imagination is something which is not usually encouraged in social work practice" even though "employing techniques in social work education that mobilise imagination and creativity through artistic expression has transformative potential for learning" (Letchfield, Leonard, & Couchman, 2012, p. 684).

The available social work scholarship highlights the intersections between social work and creative arts not only in terms of positive impacts for service users, practitioners, and social work students but also in terms of fulfilling the broader aims of social justice, social transformation, and resistance to oppression (Barndt, 2006; Reed, 2005). Specifically, the scholarship notes that these intersections can help build inclusive social networks, empower clients and communities, improve practitioners' problem-solving skills, and reimagine service provision and practices (Boehm, 2007; Harrison, 2009; Huss, 2009; Maidment & Macfarlane, 2011; McCoy & McKay, 2006; Tower, 2000). Chamberlayne and Smith (2007), in their discussion of social work practice, assert "the power of art to promote the imagining of how things might be different—personally, socially, and in research" (p. 265). Indeed, Chambon (2008) urges social work to rely on art to inform its practices, for we must seek alternative and innovative ways of providing services in these times of economic uncertainty and neoliberal state restructuring, both of which are impacting the profession and its practice.

The importance of art to social work has led authors such as Lymberry (2003) to call for the development of more systematic educational practices in social work to enhance the creativity of practitioners. Yet despite the recognition of the potential and actual contributions of creative arts to social work, there is currently a dearth in the teaching scholarship (Chamberlayne & Smith, 2007). The scant scholarship includes some explorations of the use of creative arts in social work practice (e.g., Boehm, 2007; Cadell et al., 2005; Harrison, 2009; Tower, 2000). The scholarship notes that creating art can give rise to new thinking about social issues, as well as to new connections and new understandings and knowledges (Dewhurst, 2010) to inform our practices. Harrison (2009), in referring to her own experiences and those of Lehman (2006), notes the transformative potential of deep reflection through storytelling. Huss (2009) observes how artwork can be transformative in the lives of women negotiating cultural transition. Similarly, we have witnessed how, in becoming engaged with arts-based assignments, our students open up to a "different type of conversation" (p. 599) with themselves, their placement instructors, and their client communities, as well as with us their professors, as we discuss below.

Introducing Art into the Classroom: Some Examples

In writing this chapter, we found the process of discussing our teaching practices to be invigorating. We began with a discussion of what we meant by art practice and agreed that we were using the term to refer to the classroom use of creative arts such as music, photography, film, and performance. In this discussion, we draw on Huss's (2009) definition of art "as a metaphorical or transitional space, which can be visual, verbal as in poetry or popular songs, or can be metaphors and proverbs used within verbal interaction" (p. 612). Among the three of us, we had engaged students in creating artwork and in analyzing existing art practices. In what follows, we provide examples of these practices and the learning opportunities they provided, as well as the challenges we faced in introducing art into the classroom. We end with reflections on the implications for practice and future research directions.

Samantha: Engaging with Photography and Social Justice

I began using art in my classroom as an extension of my long-standing involvement in photographic practice. From the early days of social work, when reformers like Jane Addams worked with photographers like Lewis Hine to document social conditions touching immigrants or children, photography has played a role in social work practice (Huff, 1998; Szro, 2008). This role is often forgotten and infrequently acknowledged in the scholarship

(Chambon, 2008; Huff, 1998). In my own social work classrooms, I have introduced photography in at least three ways: creation of photo books, creation of photo collages, and photograph analysis.

One assignment that captivated my students involved developing a social work awareness-raising tool. I have used this assignment in first-year and upper-year classes, with much interest from students. Students produce an artwork that aims to raise awareness either of a social issue or, optionally, of social work practice itself. Along with the artwork, students produce a supporting paper that discusses the theoretical and conceptual bases of the artwork. The paper requires students to reflect on the social issue or aspect of practice they selected and to rationalize the contribution that art can make to addressing it. Repeatedly, students have chosen to create photo books that illustrate the issue. An example is a photo book by first-year students that addressed the various roles social workers play. In illustrating the book, students had to be familiar with the theoretical aspects of social work practice; they also, by virtue of shifting their focus to visual representations produced to educate others, needed to think about how best to "portray" these roles. They can talk about issues, but can they *show* others what they mean? Huss (2012) argues that the process of illustrating professional ideas, feelings, and experiences through imagery allows us to communicate and problem-solve in new ways that reach a diversity of audiences.

In creating photo collages, students had to reflect on how to portray a particular message to others. This improved their understanding of the issues as well as their creative communication skills. Certainly, the idea of combining images to form photomontages or collages is embedded in a long history of creating such works as critical social commentary—for example, in the use of "documentarist photomontage" to support social reform or political propaganda (Schnapp, 2002). I have used photo collages in various classes, but the example that comes most readily to mind is the creation of photo collages in the international social work course open to upper-level social work students.

I typically end my lecture on the Global South's debt with a discussion of Polack's (2004) edict that social work students need to be educated about the history of that debt as well as its current manifestations, for it is a global social justice issue that deeply concerns social work. I then ask my students to create photo collages that reflect one message about debt that they would like to convey to other social workers (thereby raising awareness and understanding of this issue). I begin the activity by introducing students to the work of Martha Rosler (http://www.martharosler.net/) and Sammy Baloji (http://jhbwtc.blogspot.com/2010/03/beyond-biennial-bamako-at

INTRODUCING ART INTO THE SOCIAL WORK CLASSROOM   159

FIGURE 9.1
Two posters on global debt created by students

-15-years_26.html), both of whom have created photo collages, the first about war and the second about colonialism. I then provide students with scissors, glue, and images previously cut from magazines. Armed with these tools, the lecture, the required readings, and their imaginations, they create a public awareness campaign about debt. Their creations are then posted in a central location at the school of social work for others to see (see Figure 9.1 for two poster examples).

The third example of my engagement with photography in the classroom involves photo analysis. Photo analysis has long been embedded in social sciences such as anthropology and sociology (Knowles & Sweetman, 2004; Pink, Kürti, & Afonso, 2004). Speaking specifically about social work, Marshall, Craun, and Theriot (2009, p. 317) note the importance of photography to "alter society's thinking about topics," as demonstrated in their own study of the use of photographic images to raise awareness about issues related to adult day care services. In my classroom, I rely on photo analysis to engage students in a critical deciphering of the latent meanings and discourses embedded in development work. So for discussions about international development, I expose students to images from the reports of development NGOs to begin the discussion about discourses surrounding foreign aid. For example, images of black children surrounding a white development worker lead to discussions about discourses related to race, helping, and colonialism. Students have found this exercise challenging because when they are confronted with such images, they must reflect not only on what is contained in development reports, but also on the broader media and on their own photo albums of trips past, especially if they have previously engaged in social tourism or international field placements.

Seeing and analyzing many images at the same time pushes students to reflect on the ideas they had taken for granted in terms of media portrayals of the relationship between North and South, which saturate newspapers, magazines, television, and electronic media. In short, as noted by Marshall and colleagues (2008, p. 318), "photography might be an especially powerful way to add the emotional component necessary to communicate the pivotal role of social work in society and to foster an even deeper public awareness of today's social problems." Speaking specifically of the use of visual arts in social work education, Walton (2012) proposes that such methods require students to push beyond regurgitating textbook examples to understanding practice realities on an emotional level. This is especially relevant in the current climate of practice, where so much emphasis is placed on competencies and skills at the expense of a more holistic understanding of our professional roles.

Susan: Engaging Art Forms to Challenge Traditional Knowledge and Practices

Before examining the use of art in my teaching, I must step further back in history. Many art forms were part of my practice as a social work practitioner. Music, poetry, sculpting, drawing, and photography often served as a medium for me to build relationships and encourage dialogue between myself and clients. This was not an intended or preplanned part of my practice—it simply began one day with some crayons and construction paper in a group I was facilitating for children whose fathers were incarcerated. The activity, meant to be a brief interlude in the group's work, was to create Father's Day cards, which we would then send to their fathers. The resulting images conveyed more to all of us than words had ever accomplished, and that experience has remained with me to this day. So as my practice continued largely with clients who had been forced, through state and/or family sanctions, to seek social work intervention and intrusion in their lives, I often returned to some art form when building relationships seemed tenuous or dialoguing failed.

My teaching has only been in social work and only in schools with curricula committed to social justice and equity, within the lens of anti-oppressive social work practice. Some people doubt whether art, social justice, and education can coalesce (Dewhurst, 2010). In my first two years of teaching undergraduate social work, I very much followed the traditional mainstream pedagogical practice of lectures and small group discussions; when I was a student, that is how I had been taught. Since then, I have become increasingly open to engaging art in my classrooms, recognizing how art can transcend standards of logic and rationality (Kokkos, 2010) in the learning process, which in itself is important student learning for future social work practice.

In some courses, I have turned to art forms when developing assignments, as a means to achieve the learning objective of exploring and expressing critical self-reflection about social work practice (through student field education experiences), and as a means to develop critical analysis skills within core social work knowledge learning outcomes in specific content areas (e.g., group work). In both circumstances, I have provided arts-based assignments as alternatives to more traditional assignments; that is, students can choose either form of assignment. I realize that art may be too "outside the norm" of social work education for some students to engage in it. Cadell and colleagues (2005) note a similar approach, but add that over time, arts-based assignments became required assignments without alternative options, and that all students fully engaged with and successfully completed them.

Critical self-reflection is a foundation of social work practice (Fook & Gardner, 2007). Its focus is on intentional consciousness and seeking meaning in the work we do as social workers. As part of critical self-reflection assignments, I have asked students to create posters or poetry regarding their field education experiences. I purposely leave the structure of the assignment open, noting only that the art should emerge from a critical moment in their practice—from a storytelling moment that made them stop and take stock of themselves, the situation, and their practices—to push their learning deeper than surface understandings of practice. Furthermore, the "art" assignment is the sole venue for students to present their work; in other words, no accompanying paper is required. This is intentional, so that the story the student is conveying is done through the art, not with the art as an add-on to an essay. In this way, students are expressing themselves somewhat "outside" the confines of traditional academic assignments. In comparing these completed assignments to those of students using more traditional forms (e.g., essays or process recordings), I have been aware of the depth and complexity of learning that blossoms through arts-based assignments, perhaps echoing Harrison's (2009) experience of students looking at their world and learning about themselves in a different way. As a learning outcome, the level of "meaning making" from within a lived experience comes through strongly, often reaching insights well beyond the expectations of the assignment's objectives, wherein the web of feeling and thinking becomes richer (Kokkos, 2010). This is key to critical self-reflection, a subjective skill that can be difficult to develop and measure. This reflective assignment seemed to fit well with an arts option, for it draws from beyond an intellectualizing of an experience; it reaches into the art and heart of social work. This sense of going outside the "science" of social work is equally relevant to specific substantive content in an anti-oppression-focused social work curriculum, including in social group work courses (Steinberg, 2006).

In the social group work course, I have offered an alternative assignment where students select and observe a feature film that involves a group, not necessarily a social work group but any group with some coherence of members and purpose (e.g., *Alive, Gladiator, Space Jam*). The assignment requires a critical analysis of the group in the film, using group work theoretical concepts such as group development, ethics, and membership. I did this first as an individual assignment and, based on positive feedback, expanded it to create a group assignment for class presentation. The depth of knowledge reflected in these presentations was outstanding, showing a high level of clarity and comprehensiveness in understanding key conceptualizations of group work practice. As a learning outcome, students completing this assignment demonstrated the application of group work theory to social work practice, bridging the gap between knowing and doing much like I saw in the reflective assignment.

In both these assignments, I saw an opening up of students to multiple forms of expression and thus multiple ways of knowing. Seeing beyond the obvious, linking theory to lived experiences, discovering a variety of possible explanations for situations and circumstances—these learning objectives emerged through these assignments. I see these as core to effective social work practice from an anti-oppression perspective, wherein we challenge the status quo and resist generalized assumptions in knowledge about people and their lives. The act of engaging with art seemed to provide an avenue for students to move past more traditional forms of knowing, and this will be important in their future practice as social workers. As Eisner (2008) notes, these "multiple forms of knowing" (p. 5) are possible once we move beyond a sole emphasis on words to convey experience.

I also have used art, mostly photographs, as a pedagogical tool in classroom learning. While I initially simply used pictures to reinforce course content, I soon began using pictures as a means for students to experience course content, as active rather than passive learners. Two strategies seemed particularly effective: making the visible invisible and visible again, and juxtaposing opposite or contradictory images. In the first strategy, I would show only parts of a photograph to garner initial reactions; these were usually group shots somehow "devoid" of their physical setting (e.g., on the grass). I would then show the rest of the photograph (e.g., on the grass of a prison yard), and discuss with students how their initial reactions shifted once the rest of the picture became visible. This is somewhat contrary to the strategy of using images that posit "others" in environments similar to our own (Phillips & Bellinger, 2010); however, this visible/invisible approach has been an equally powerful experience for learning. On an initial basis, some students recognize how their perceptions shift based on context, and how becoming aware of that shift helps attune them to values and "truths" they hold about people in certain groupings or settings. Perhaps students became more open to learning this way, as the initial silent absorption of the photographs allowed students to move beyond defensive reactions to historical injustices in which they might be implicated. Second, again drawing on Huss (2009), some students have an experiential awakening of the connection between the person/subject and the political/context. Both of these experiences clearly connect to their future capacity as critically reflective practitioners who resist dominant norms of "making sense" of people's lives. Perhaps in the fluidity of art, students as practitioners may become open to understandings of people's lives from outside traditional views, similar to drawing multiple meanings from the aesthetic experience (Johnson, 2002; Kokkos, 2010).

In the second strategy, I would put images side by side that reflected particular social values and/or lived experiences. Two images were particularly effective. When discussing colonization and the role of social workers as colonizers with Canada's indigenous peoples, I often projected an image of a young Aboriginal boy before and after his arrival at a residential school. The stark contrast between a proud young boy in his own clothing and hairstyle and a sad young boy in a sailor-suit school uniform with cropped hair spoke louder than any words from a textbook or from me. Students sometimes would audibly gasp in the classroom as the images appeared—a vivid reflection of the practice and impact of colonizing. Voices of students who had surmised the positive value of residential schooling soon quieted, while others found voice in the public image of their dishonouring. Phillips and Bellinger (2010) note the potential for both manifest (content) and latent (context) understandings to emerge from images. Combined with the first example of contextualizing images, perhaps new learning came alive in students' engagement with that image, through the embodied experience of seeing the image of a person change in a new context. The response from students in the class as noted above, plus students asking questions about the images (either during class or after class), suggests to me that the images had an impact. These and other images provoked a different kind of classroom discussion—somehow the image represented a truth that was sometimes questioned when read in a textbook or heard in a lecture. Using images is also a way to respond to multiple learning styles in the classroom, outside the norms of text-based learning. While here I solely reflect on my observations of the impact in class, future research could seek student feedback about the exercise, thus enriching our understanding of the learning experience.

A second image was one showing change over time, one of many stock photographs of a young woman or a young man in the bloom of youthful health, beside a photograph of them ravaged by drug use. However, I would shift the labels above the photographs, and impose "this is what capitalism can do to your child" or "this is what unlivable wages can do to your youth." I was not transparent with students about the sources of the images, which for many students looked oddly familiar but out of place. This was intentional on my part, for it allowed me to use the images in a new way, so that students would respond to the image and the "new" text instead of recalling the images and text in their original form. We would discuss the power of juxtaposed images to convey a message, and the combination of text and images conveying a particular message. Among other intentions, the purpose here was to engage students with course content about how our social world order impacts people's lives, and to consider how images and texts could be used in social work public campaigns and protests seeking social justice. Huss (2009) notes how the art of clients allowed social workers to empathize with their pain, and a similar experience could evolve from the purposeful use of art in social protest. Additionally, student engagement with images reinforced the sense of themselves, as future practitioners, as viewers of the social world of clients, recognizing how, much as with photographs, the image and the viewer are produced simultaneously in their encounter together (Phillips & Bellinger, 2010).

Cadell and colleagues (2005) note the impact of arts-based assignments on students, in terms of deepening their critical engagement, reflection, and analysis with course content as well as their future practice as social workers. I would add that the impact on me, as faculty, was equally strong. I became more comfortable sharing with students and faculty my own engagement with arts; and somehow, in stepping outside the traditions of mainstream classrooms, my own teaching style became more flexible, open, and dynamic—somehow the freeing of my mind through art allowed the freeing of my spirit as a teacher. I imagine that this experience is similar to what a student describes wherein music "reaches places in me that I am often hesitant to expose or examine" (Cadell et al., 143). Here I am referring to my own experience as a faculty member and how engaging with art in the classroom opened me up. While as noted earlier it is important to examine student experiences and potential for learning through the introduction of art into the classroom, it is also important for future explorations to examine the potential impacts for the development of educators.

Ken: The Emotional Life of the Queer Self
I have taught a queer theories course at the undergraduate level and a course focused on gender and sexual variance in the Master of Social Work program. It is within these courses that I have had the most success introducing art to the classroom. The success with integrating art in my pedagogy is partly due to a sometimes vocal and often small contingent of lesbian, gay, bisexual, transgendered, transexual, queer (LGBTTQ) students in the classroom. The creation of images is particularly important for these students from marginalized communities, who often have the image of themselves as being colonized by dominant social forces (Esteban Muñoz, 2009). The LGBTTQ community, for example, is often represented in mainstream media in ways that are stereotypical, and/or they continue to be objects of denigrating imagery and text. Also, silence and invisibility have been politics of exclusion for gay persons so that visibility and representation are key politics for the community (Kinsmen, 1995; Warner, 2002). Discussions of performance and visual art and the presence of LGBTTQ art images in the classroom help disrupt heteronormative and cisgendered assumptions about the classroom and therefore may make the LGBTTQ students feel more comfortable to take risks. Ultimately, this disruption allows us to discuss queer emotional life and queer cultures.

Art takes on an important political role of taking back the concept of the LGBTTQ self. When art is shown that has been created by LGBTTQ persons, the students who self-identify with this community are offered imagery that is more dignified and relevant than mainstream depictions of LGBTTQ persons. Also, since art by its nature is thoughtful and at times provocative, art imagery illustrates a politic of agency for the students to illustrate how one makes oneself present politically. Finally, these images open the discourse, allowing multiple forms of expression in the classroom (Irving & Moffatt, 2002), including discourse that makes the LGBTTQ identity central to the classroom discussion. As well, teaching from the point of view of art allows discourses to be incomplete, ambivalent, and confused in a manner that challenges the taken for granted of sexuality and gender orientation. The possibilities for queer students and other

FIGURE 9.2
Daryl Vocat, *Who Are You!* 2012
Cut aluminum, 43"x30". Image courtesy of the artist

students for self-expression and self-understanding become more varied when images of performance and visual art are introduced.

Also, artwork in the classroom is a vehicle to discuss emotions as well as family and community processes, all of which are concerns of social work that are usually discussed from the point of view of the social and psychological sciences. In fact, some of the most influential theorizing around the emotional lives of queer persons has been through writing associated with the arts and humanities (Munt, 2007; Sedgwick, 2009). In addition, the arts are so enmeshed in local queer cultures that one must include local culture and the arts to completely understand queer communities (Moffatt, 2006). Finally, art, an expression not constrained by text or social sciences, helps students understand that emotions such as love and anger are created in a social context that for marginalized persons is highly politicized. Emotions are not simply the interiority or psychological preconditions to interactions; rather, they are constructed within interpersonal and social relations (Eribon, 2004; Moffatt, 2012).

In my classroom I introduce the art of local queer artists. I use these images to discuss gender, emotions, and marginalization. I use the work of artists such as R. M. Vaughan, Will Munro, Johnson Ngo, and Daryl Vocat. All of these artists include images of themselves in provocative postures to challenge taken-for-granted notions of gender and sexuality. In Figure 9.2, by Toronto artist Daryl Vocat, we see how the simplest of images offering the simplest of gestures suggests difference by gender and sexuality. He manipulates images of Boy Scouts, often in the most playful of ways, to suggest queer desire, gender, and emotional life. His artwork intentionally disrupts the taken for granted in terms of received images, particularly in reference to masculinity.

Shame, an emotional state constituted both through the psyche and through social process, is closely associated with queer communities (Kristeva, 1982; Munt, 2007; Sedgwick, 2009). The reaction of shame is so constant and pervasive for marginalized queer men and for women that it has led me to begin to reimagine, with the aid of art, the importance of teaching gender and sexuality from the point of view of affect of shame (Moffatt, 2004, 2012). Edie Kofovsky Sedgwick (2009) argues that shame is learned at the moment you offer a smile of recognition to another person who, by refusing to acknowledge you, leaves you in social isolation. In other words, we learn that what we said/did is shameful when another person refuses to respond to us. The loss of feedback leaves one caught in the need for relief from the condition of shame and humiliation. Munt (2007) argues that shame is quite specific in its affect but can also be felt as a cloud of emotions. For her, shame is an exclusionary social process as well as an emotional state that marks marginal groups through sexuality, gender, race, and class.

Each of these queer artists exposes the shamed body in some fashion and at times revels in shame as part of their identity. For example, R. M. Vaughan, a Toronto artist, writer, and critic living in Berlin, created a series of photographs called "Am I Becoming My Father?" (Figure 9.3) after his father's death. In this series of self-portraits he stands rigidly with his arms straight down the sides of his body and his fists partially clenched. He is posed in his father's clothing in the hunting cabin his father would retreat to in the summer. Vaughan's rigid posture belies a "not quite fitting in." He seems uncomfortable in the clothes, with the act of recording through photography, and with the environment. He does not fit the commemorative space of his dead father, nor does he fit the alienating wilderness in which he grew up. No matter where he is located, whether on a deck with the forest behind or in a room under renovation, the stance is the same. As the artist explains, he is transfixed by father–son transference,

FIGURE 10.3
R. M. Vaughan, *Am I Becoming My Father?*
Colour photo taken with Instamatic camera. Image courtesy of the artist

memory, grief, and the "cold wild," as well as with the process of record making. He is a "deer in headlights" who is bent and disoriented. The lack of clear audience, the lack of resolution of relationship suggested in this image, is akin to the refusal of both his father and the viewers to recognize him, which leaves him in a state of unresolved shame and humiliation.

As well, his extreme discomfort with the trappings of manliness reflected in his rigid stance suggests that he is an outsider both feeling shame and marked socially by shame. This is a radical reconceptualization of psyche so that it is completely immersed in and constructed through familial structure, gender expectations, and social relations (Eribon, 2004; Moffatt, 2004, 2012; Schulman, 2009). Although the illustration and the lesson are both situated quite specifically within a queer community with specific social and personal consequences, it is a profound lesson for all people to rethink psyche, self, and emotions.

The introduction of simple images such as those above in the social work classroom is a safe starting point for the students to discuss their own emotional responses as well as the social construction of emotions. It invites students to consider their personal experiences of alienation within family and community. They can imagine family and community from the point of view of the marginalized person within the family instead of imposing the ideal family and community on their understandings of social processes. In addition, I draw on a many images from a variety of artists who are either women or queer so that the social dynamic is intentionally complicated by the treatment of persons by gender, sexuality, race, class, and ability. The artwork that is voluntarily offered up to the public is a means to face down the same kind of tremendous discomfort and the same painful processes that social work students need to face when working with marginalized communities. But just as important, artwork offers the opportunity to exalt in outsider status and to relish one's own difference. In the process that Tomkins (1995) characterizes as existential agency, the artists themselves expose their shamed bodies, knowing full well that doing so will create discomfort for others. I take advantage of this posture of some artists to help students think through their relationship to their self as well as to others. In this way, students start to imagine images that best fit their own sense of agency when it comes to gender and sexuality.

The students in these courses are then offered the opportunity to do a multimedia presentation that includes text, performance stills, photography, visual imagery such as a painting, recorded music, and music videos as a means to discuss some aspect of marginalization as well as resilience to that marginalization. They are invited to use both "low art" or pop culture and "high art." They are also invited to use their own images and autobiographies, especially if it advances understanding of the queer community. These presentations involve the students in critical engagement and give them a sense of agency when considering symbol creation. At this point, students may be involved in deep reflection that helps reconstitute the psyche, leading to a sense of worth. The students are required to submit a copy of their multimedia presentation for grading. The elaboration of student voice and the construction of an academic argument through the use of multiple modes of media is a complex task. Although there is no requirement to submit an accompanying essay with the presentation, the presentation is graded according to principles often used to grade academic papers, such as coherence, analysis, and demonstrated knowledge of concepts and theory. The hope is that the students will use an articulate and sensitive argument about queer community and social relationships to advance their literacy not only in text but also in images.

Concluding thoughts: Challenges and implications

In this chapter we explored the possibility of integrating art into the social work classroom. We provided examples from our teaching experiences and noted the multiple learnings that art methods or content can bring to students as future practitioners. These examples focused on the uses of art in classroom activities, such as photo analysis and creating photo collages, as well as on providing students with the opportunity to integrate art with their assignments. Examples of these assignments include developing multimedia presentations and creating photo books to illustrate a social issue. In addition to these examples, we discussed our learnings, including how art can introduce students to new ways of knowing and provide the space to explore sensitive or contentious issues.

We also noted the role that art has played in allowing us as educators to develop more open, self-reflexive, and flexible teaching styles. We contend that this learning merits further exploration within the scholarship of teaching, in which the primary focus, understandably, has been on student experience. We believe that future scholarship could shift its focus to the role of educators, while maintaining the importance of examining student experiences. We believe that an emphasis on the educator would allow us to centre an understanding of teaching as scholarship. As Hyman and colleagues (2001-2) note, thinking of teaching in this way allows us not only to engage in teaching practice but also to share our "discoveries" with other educators who are interested in enhancing their teaching as well as learning outcomes for students. The role of the educator becomes not only about a limited conception of "imparting knowledge"—for example, through the use of art in the classroom—but also about observing, engaging, and sharing new findings from one's own teaching practice, through, for example, discussions such as the one offered in this chapter. Put differently, thinking of teaching as scholarship allows us as educators to think of ourselves as part of the educational process as learners, as opposed to detached "knowers" who share their expertise with students. This is consistent with how we have discussed art as allowing new ways of knowledge production to emerge; it is also in keeping with our understanding of our role as educators to contribute to social transformation (Jones, 2009).

In addition to all this, we have found it important to reflect critically on the challenges we have faced when introducing art into the classroom. One such challenge has been dealing with the question posed by both graduate and undergraduate students: "How is this method/content relevant to social work?" At times, the integration of art content or methods into the classroom is seen as the instructor's own personal interest, and students struggle to see its applicability to the curriculum. Indeed, as Walton (2012) notes in her discussion of the use of visual methods in social work education, "artistic activity could easily be made to appear frivolous, trivializing or eccentric" (pp. 724–725). This type of questioning has challenged us to reflect on the ways we can clarify the relevance of art to social work in our classrooms.

We have also reflected on where this questioning may be emanating from. We believe it to be partly due to social work being tied too narrowly to social science and positivist paradigms of knowledge production and communication. As Eisner (2008) argues, art has been seen as having "little to do with matters of knowledge" (p. 3). Specifically related to community services, Hafford-Letchfield, Leonard, and Couchman (2012) note in their discussion of the potential for the integration of art into social work, health, and social care education that "the current education climate with its emphasis on targets, standards, predetermined objectives and outcomes, favours a cognitive, rational style of learning, more dependent upon linguistic or logical intelligences" (p. 689) and that this can be disempowering. In such a climate, we endeavour to deconstruct these positivist paradigms early in the course in order to help students become more receptive to the learnings such as those we have noted throughout this chapter that can be garnered from the introduction of art content or methods.

Another challenge we have faced concerns the integration of arts-based or arts-informed assignments such as those we describe in this chapter. We have generally found that resistance to these types of assignments is usually tied to worry about grades. There is an assumption that grading will be unfair or subjective (more so than for essays). We have dealt with this issue by making these assignments optional and by providing concrete criteria for evaluation tied directly to course objectives and learning outcomes. For example, for some graded art-based assignments, students are expected to submit an accompanying support paper situating the piece within the overall theoretical frameworks and scholarship covered in the course. Students are then expected to provide a scholarly background to the artwork they are submitting in a format in which they are used to being evaluated (i.e., academic essay writing). Typically, students are provided with guidelines such as critical questions, format considerations, and so on to help them write the accompanying papers. A similar method is utilized by Walton (2012), who describes the integration of visual arts methods in a social work assignment. Following development of an artwork reflecting on an encounter with a service user, students are required to write a theory paper that focuses on some of the themes that emerged from the encounter. Discussing the anxiety about grading criteria, Walton notes that it is important to emphasize to students that as with other assignments, the criteria are "effort, depth and detail, reflection and criticality, and definitely not artistic ability" (p. 738).

Keeping in mind the above-mentioned challenges and our teaching experiences, our learnings to date suggest that art, through classroom activities or assignments, creates opportunities for ways of thinking outside the traditional learning approach. This has several implications for practice and suggests future research directions.

A key implication is the need to allow for the potential role that art can play in creating a space for learning that might have otherwise been shut down. Huss (2009) notes that "a symbol or a metaphor, as an indirect way of saying something, is less threatening or confrontational" (p. 613), while Hafford-Letchfield, Leonard, and Couchman (2012) note the role art can play in opening dialogue among various types of learners. In short, art in the classroom can enhance the learning experience, allowing that a more ample and complex exploration of how this is accomplished is needed in the scholarship (Phillips, MacGiollaRi, & Callaghan, 2012; Walton, 2012). So a future research direction could involve critical inquiry into and theorization of the impacts of art on community service educators and students alike. Future research could engage more directly with this exact question of ensuring that students understand the relevance of art specifically through explorations of the links between art and knowledge production. Building on Eisner's (2008) ideas about art allowing new forms of knowledge production, future research could explore how this link is understood by and conveyed to students specifically in ways that allow them to see its potential for community practice and for their future roles as service providers or community practitioners.

On a related note, as we reflect on our experience, we realize that another key implication is the need to recognize the powerful role that art can play *outside* the classroom. Put differently, it is important to explore the role that integrating art into the classroom plays, but it is also important to move this inquiry toward understanding the impact of such integrated education on social work practice and potentially for others in community service practice. Indeed, Walton (2012) notes that "in the light of practice realities [...] arts approaches readily invoke the complexity and sensory tone of practice situations, giving analysis a 'lived edge'" (p. 739). The author notes that when students are asked to begin their understanding of social problems and of communication with clients from an arts-based inquiry, they are able to push beyond received notions of practice (e.g., from textbooks) toward a deeper, more creative and personal understanding of issues facing service users, social workers, and the profession. To further solidify our understanding of these impacts, we call for future research that focuses specifically on how the learning gained in arts-based or informed education is or can be transferred to practice settings. Concretely, future research could explore not only how students could understand the relevance of art to their learning and future practice, as we noted earlier, but also the potential impacts of infusing art into community service education on actual practice in the field. Here, the focus of inquiry shifts from the classroom to the practice setting, for example, through exploring the experiences of students on field placements, or the work of students engaged in community activism. Put differently, future research could ask: How does the learning gained in the classroom through the integration of arts-informed approaches reflect and reinforce new ways of knowing and practising in the community?

Finally, our experiences have led us to the understanding that for social work practice to be further enriched, we need to continually infuse our teaching with resources from the humanities. While the historical push has been to distance our profession from these disciplines in order to gain recognition in an educational climate that favours positivism and evidence-based inquiry, we believe an important implication to be the need to break through these disciplinary boundaries and to forge interdisciplinary linkages with arts-based disciplines. Not only can we stand to learn from the creative arts' historical engagement with social issues and social transformation, but we could also impart some of our theoretical knowledge and understanding of practice realities to colleagues from these disciplines who may be interested in enhancing their practice with communities. A related future research direction concerns the process and outcomes of building such interdisciplinary linkages and what we can learn from one another along the way. In other words, if our ultimate goal is social transformation for communities, service users, and students, we must allow no stone to remain unturned in our quest for deeper and more meaningful learning and teaching experiences.

References

Barndt, D. (2006). Introduction. In D. Barndt (Ed.), *Wild fire: Art as activism* (pp. 13–22). Toronto: Sumach Press.

Boehm, A. 2007. Integrating media and community practice: A case of television report production. *Social Work Education, 23*(4), 417–434.

Bozalek, V., & Biersteker, L. (2010). Exploring power and privilege using participatory learning and action techniques. *Social Work Education, 29*(5), 551–572.

Cadell, S., Fletcher, M., Makkappallil-Knowles, E., Cladwell, S., Wong, L., Bodurtha, D., ... Shoblom, W. (2005). The use of the arts and strength perspective: The example of a course assignment. *Social Work Education, 24*(1), 137–146.

Casey, B. (2009). Arts-based inquiry in nursing education. *Contemporary Nurse, 32*(1–2), 69–82.

Chamberlayne, P., & Smith, M. (2007). Editorial to the Special Issue on Social Work Practice and Creative Arts. *Journal of Social Work Practice, 21*(3), 263–270.

Chambon, A. (2008). Social work and the arts: Critical imagination. In J. G. Knowles & A. L. Cole (Eds.), *Handbook of the arts in qualitative research* (pp. 591–602). Thousand Oaks, CA: Sage.

Coulshed, V. (1993). Adult learning: Implications for teaching in social work education. *British Journal of Social Work, 23*, 1–13.

Davies, L. (2008). Rhyme and reason—the use and value of poetry in midwifery practice and education. *New Zealand College of Midwives Journal, 38*, 17–19.

Dewhurst, M. (2010). An inevitable question: Exploring the defining features of social justice art education. *Art Education, 63*(5), 6–13.

Eisner, E. (2008). Art and knowledge. In J. G. Knowles & A. L. Cole (Eds.), *Handbook of the arts in qualitative research* (pp. 3–11). Thousand Oaks, CA: Sage.

Eribon, D. (2004). *Insult and the making of the gay self.* Durham, NC: Duke University Press.

Esteban Muñoz, José. 2009. *Cruising utopia: The then and there of queer futurity.* New York, NY: NYU Press.

Fook, J., & Gardner, F. (2007). *Practicing critical reflection: A resource handbook.* Berkshire, UK: Open University Press.

Fox, A. L. (2009). Evaluation of a pilot arts and health module in a graduate community nutrition program. *Canadian Journal of Dietetic Practice and Research, 70*(2), 81–86.

Hafford-Letchfield, T., Leonard, K., & Couchman, W. (2012). "Arts and extremely dangerous": Critical commentary on the arts in social work education. *Social Work Education, 31*(6), 683–690.

Harrison, L. (2009). "Listen: This really happened": Making sense of social work through story-telling. *Social Work Education, 28*(7), 750–764.

Huff, D. D. (1998). Every picture tells a story. *Social Work, 43*(6), 576–583.

Huss, E. (2012). Utilizing an image to evaluate stress and coping for social workers. *Social Work Education, 31*(6), 691–702.

Huss, E. (2009). A case study of Bedouin women's art in social work: A model of social arts intervention with "traditional" women negotiating Western cultures. *Social Work Education, 28*(6), 598–616.

Hyman, D., et al. (2001–2). Beyond Boyer: The UniSCOPE model of scholarship for the 21st Century. *Journal of Higher Education Outreach and Engagement, 7*(1–2), 41–65.

Irving, A., & Moffatt, K. (2002). Intoxicated midnights and carnival classrooms: The professor as poet, *Radical Pedagogy, 4*(1) [Available: http://www.icaap.org/iuicode 2.4.1.5]

Johnson, L. (2002). Art-centered approach to diversity education in teaching and learning. *Multicultural Education, 9*(4), 18–21.

Jones, P. (2009). Teaching for change in social work: A discipline-based argument for the use of transformative approaches to teaching and learning. *Journal of Transformative Education, 7*(1), 8–25.

Knowles, C., & Sweetman, P. (Eds.). (2004). *Picturing the social landscape: Visual methods and the sociological imagination*. New York, NY: Routledge.

Kokkos, A. (2010). Transformative learning through aesthetic experience: Towards a comprehensive method. *Journal of Transformative Education, 8*(3), 155–177.

Kristeva, J. (1982). *Powers of horror: An essay on abjection* (L. S. Roudiez, Trans.). New York, NY: Columbia University Press.

Lymberry, E. F. (2003). Negotiating the contradictions between competence and creativity in social work education. *Journal of Social Work, 3*(1), 99–117.

Maidment, J., & Macfarlane, S. (2011). Older women and craft: Extending educational horizons in considering wellbeing. *Social Work Education, 30*(6), 700–711.

Marshall, H. L., Craun, S. W., & Theriot, M. T. (2009). The big picture: How social work can effectively utilize photographs. *Social Work, 54*(4), 317–325.

McCoy, H., & McKay, C. (2006). Preparing social workers to identify and integrate culturally affirming bibliotherapy into treatment. *Social Work Education, 25*(7), 680–693.

Moffatt K. (Summer 2012). Shame and men: A queer perspective on masculinity. *C Magazine, 114, International Contemporary Art*, 5–8.

Moffatt K. (2006). Dancing without a floor: The artists' politic of queer club space. *Canadian Online Journal of Queer Studies in Education, 2*(1). [Available: http://jqstudies.oise.utoronto.ca/journal/viewarticles.php?id=12]

Moffatt, K. (2004). Beyond male denial and female shame: Learning about gender in a sociocultural concepts class. *Smith College Studies in Social Work: Special Issue on Teaching, 74*(2), 243–256.

Munt, S. (2007). *Queer attachments: The cultural politics of shame*. Aldershot, UK: Ashgate.

Phillips, C., & Bellinger, A. (2010). Feeling the cut: Exposing the use of photography in social work education. *Qualitative Social Work, 10*(1), 86–105.

Phillips, J., MacGiollaRi, D., & Callaghan, S. (2012). Encouraging research in social work: Narrative as the thread integrating education and research in social work. *Social Work Education, 31*(6), 785–793.

Pink, S., Kürti, L., & Afonso, A. I. (eds.). (2004). *Working images: visual research and representation in ethnography*. New York, NY: Routledge.

Polack, R. J. (2004). Social justice and the global economy: New challenges for social work in the 21st Century. *Social Work, 49*(2), 281–290.

Reed, T. V. (2005). *The art of protest: Culture and activism from the civil rights movement to the streets of Seattle*. Minneapolis, MN: University of Minnesota Press.

Schnapp, J. T. (2002). The mass panorama. *Modernism/Modernity, 9*, 243–281.

Schulman, S. (2009). *Ties that bind, familial homophobia and its consequences.* New York, NY: New Press.

Sedgwick, E. K. (2009). Shame, theatricality, and queer performativity. In D. Halperin & V. Traub (Eds.), *Gay shame* (pp. 49–62). Chicago, IL: University of Chicago Press.

Steinberg, D. (2006). The art, science, heart and ethics of social group work: Lessons from a great teacher. *Social Work with Groups, 29*(2–3), 33–45.

Szro, P. (2008). Documentary photography in American social welfare history: 1897–1943. *Journal of Sociology & Social Welfare, 35*(2), 91–110.

Tomkins, S. (1995). *Shame and its sisters: A Silvan Tomkins reader.* E. K. Sedgwick & A. Frank (Eds.). Durham, NC: Duke University Press.

Tower, K. (2000). In our own image: Shaping attitudes about social work through television production. *Journal of Social Work Education, 36*(3), 575–585.

Walton, P. (2012). Beyond talk and text: An expressive visual arts method for social work education. *Social Work Education, 31*(6), 724–741.

Warner, T. (2002). *Never going back: A history of queer activism in Canada.* Toronto, ON: University of Toronto Press.

Conclusion

Usha George

This book is about the scholarship of teaching, which aims to generate new knowledge about engaging students within the classroom and outside it. The authors of the various chapters have attempted to capture our imagination and attention to energize teaching and learning to produce the best learning outcomes for our students.

A review of the broader environment of higher education in Canada is important in this context. Voices from far and near alert us to impending drastic and dramatic changes in higher education. Predictions about the changing landscape are prompted by a number of factors such as budgetary constraints, the rising costs of higher education, graduate unemployment, and the technological revolution.

Facing severe budgetary constraints, provincial governments in Canada have been trying to rein in the increasing costs of higher education by capping budgetary allocations. Without alternative access to financial resources, universities are being forced to increase student fees. Although within the government-stipulated ranges, this fee increase has prompted debates about the cost of higher education and the burden of debt incurred by graduates, particularly those completing their first degree. In addition, growing dissatisfaction about the job-readiness of graduates has triggered questions about the return on investment in higher education and alternative ways of providing university education to the rising numbers of applicants.

Enter technology with the promise of unprecedented opportunities to control runaway costs of higher education by delivering courses for a fraction of the cost. In addition to technology-based interventions such as online courses, massively open online courses (MOOCS) are promoted as a viable alternative to the "sage on the stage" model, which is expensive besides being exclusive to those who manage to get into post-secondary institutions. The term was coined in 2008 by David Cormier at the

University of Manitoba for a course designed by George Siemens and Stephen Downes. The original MOOC was built on connectivist principles of education, which embrace the idea that learning is not so much about acquiring content as about working collaboratively and building networks that allow knowledge to circulate, to be used, and to grow (Bady, 2013, p. 18). It was a socially inspired experiment in which the participants shared their enthusiasm for exploration and creativity. Bady argues that the MOOCs that emerged in 2012, introduced by Silicon Valley start-ups, are radically different in principles and intent as they "transfer course content from expert to student—only to do so massively more cheaply and on a much larger scale" (p. 18). Naturally there is a great deal of interest in MOOCs. Some consider MOOCs to be the long overdue disruptive innovation in higher education.

In spite of the enthusiasm surrounding the online and cost-free availability of courses from premier institutions of higher education such as Harvard and MIT and the possibility of unlimited numbers of students accessing these courses to enhance their knowledge and skills, there is still solid support for classroom learning. What is emerging is a strong voice that supports a combination of online learning and teacher-led classroom experience (Friedman, 2013). Friedman summarizes his takeaway message after attending a conference on online learning organized by MIT and Harvard University: we need to move to a model "in which students are asked and empowered to master more basic material online at their own pace, and the classroom becomes a place where the application of that knowledge can be honed through lab experiments and discussions with the professor" (2013, p. A23). A number of experts have added their voices to this call. The classroom interactions that are fundamental to undergraduate education cannot be transmitted online (Millar, 2013). For example, in the 2013 Canadian University Report by *The Globe and Mail*, political science Professor Clifford Orwin and Nobel Prize–winning physicist Carl Weiman are quoted as endorsing the blended model. Orwin maintains that the classroom experience is at the core of university education and that "the electricity that crackles through a successful classroom can't be transmitted electronically" (quoted in Millar, 2013, p. 19). While acknowledging the positive difference that digital education can make, David Naylor argues that "in-person education—and the competencies fostered by interpersonal exchanges—will be irreplaceable on our hot and crowded planet for a very long time" (2013, p. 4).

Students seem to endorse the idea of the blended model or the hybrid form of instruction. In a 2011 report by Higher Education Strategy Associates, four out of five respondents said they preferred to attend in-person lectures as opposed to watching online lectures. On the whole, there is endorsement of the idea that instead of replacing the face-to-face classroom experience with online education, e-learning should be employed to supplement face-to-face education.

Concepts such as "effortful study," "inverted classroom," and "flipped classroom" are being introduced to describe the new method of instruction. These are based on the belief that true learning happens when students actively engage with the content and create "their own understanding through a process of mentally building on their prior thinking through effortful study" (Wieman, quoted in Millar, 2013, p. 20). In what the University of Toronto calls the "inverted classroom," lectures involving large classes are taped and made available to students ahead of time and class time is used for small group discussions, hands-on experience, and community-based projects. The idea of flipped classrooms—homework in class and classwork at home—is gaining ground (Mazar, 2013).

In this context, it is interesting to review some of the current metaphors about the new model of higher education. Gaffield (in Calamai, 2006) suggests a transformation from the pyramid model to an hourglass model, in which students pass from a broad general base of knowledge through a narrow specialization, expanding outward again into interdisciplinary and multidisciplinary learning and experience. Many educators and employers are embracing the notion of T-style education, which combines substantial breadth in a wide range of areas with deep knowledge and understanding in a special area, enhanced by technology, innovation, and creativity. This, according to Naylor, means more multidisciplinary and experiential learning and lots of opportunities for interactive problem solving inside and outside the classroom (*Globe and Mail*, 2012).

So what are the essential components of the new model of higher education? I would like to summarize them as follows: rich and varied in-class and outside-class experiences that offer opportunities for "effortful study"; experiential opportunities; and interdisciplinary and multidisciplinary engagement, with a solid grasp of appropriate technology. These characteristics speak to the core of teaching—and, in fact, innovative teaching, which is the tagline of all the chapters in this book.

A great deal of evidence from the literature supports the notion that faculty support and interaction are essential to student success at the postsecondary level. It has been demonstrated that in-class engagement as well as outside-classroom engagement are equally important to achieve the best educational outcomes for students. In a literature review on "faculty–student interaction," Michelle Schwartz (2012) suggests a holistic approach, one that includes institutional factors, student factors, and faculty factors.

Faculty factors point to faculty attitude and commitment toward student engagement inside and outside the classroom, suggesting that those who value faculty–student interaction create opportunities to engage students. Most of the chapters in this book provide new insights into innovative processes of engaging students within the classroom. For example, Kennedy and Jancar's chapter on the writing skills initiative describes writing skills development as one creative intervention for engaging first-year students. Church articulates how she provides opportunities for "effortful study" to engage students, most of whom come from the disability practice field. Schwind addresses the gap in our curricula and teaching—a gap that privileges the cognitive and psychomotor aspects of student education. In introducing the narrative reflexive process, she focuses on the student's affective domain to engage the whole student as a personal knowing learner—an important skill for practitioners in the caring professions. Friedman and Poole reimagine "[teaching as] a form of connection and caregiving and a site of intimacy" and "nurturing as pedagogy"; this is relevant especially to the teaching of helping professions. Gingras and Rudolph's approach to student engagement in the classroom is to create a democratic learning space by engaging students as co-instructors. By examining their own experience of introducing art in the classroom, Wehbi, Preston, and Moffatt argue that "creative arts could potentially have a significant role to play in enhancing course delivery, curriculum content and assessment of student learning."

Experiential learning is student-centred learning that focuses on individual learning processes. Various models of experiential learning are found in the literature. Common to all of these are action, reflection, conceptualization, and application. Experiential opportunities enable students to become engaged in the real world outside the classroom and the university and help them develop much-needed skills for the world of work. While most of the chapters mentioned above have an experiential dimension, Ali and Bailey and colleagues specifically address learning beyond the classroom. Ali argues that students in the caring professions have to learn the "ethics of care" or "a sense of moral obligation associated with specific professional roles" and that the best way to learn the ethics of care is to listen to the lived experiences of the families they serve and to document their stories. For Bailey and colleagues, engaging students in scholarly research and creative activities outside the classroom enhances their ability to think critically as well as their intellectual development.

Interdisciplinary and multidisciplinary opportunities are at the heart of a progressive post-secondary curriculum and education. Most academics, as well as leaders in business and government, agree on the importance of research and teaching that transcends traditional disciplinary boundaries.

Whether we embrace interdisciplinarity (where a core discipline works with others in complementary roles) or multidisciplinarity (where disciplines work together as equal partners), "boundary busting" (Calamai, 2006) is what post-secondary education should aim for. Of course, one has to recognize and work with both institutional and individual-level challenges in working toward this goal. Hart and Kaas-Mason's chapter on IPE in this book examines our attempt at "boundary busting" and collaborative learning.

Technology is integral to current post-secondary education in two ways. As discussed earlier, technology is an essential tool for enhancing the quality of educational experience. Important also is to note that technological literacy is a necessary skill that modern graduates are keen to have as they face the labour market. As Diana Lawrence observes, "Generation Y—those born between 1981 and 2000—is walking into an unpredictable job market, one that is for the most part, driven by technology" (Canadian University Report, *Globe and Mail*, 2013). Most of our authors use various forms of technology in their teaching.

What does the university of the future look like? Alex Usher was asked to look ahead and describe the anticipated trends in university education in 2034. He states: "The most successful institutions were the ones that managed to control their financial base, made difficult choices about areas of expertise and were out-ward looking, risk-taking, technology smart and quality-focussed. For them a new world of opportunity waited at the other end" (Usher, 2009, p. 33). That is where we want to be within the next decade.

Notwithstanding the predictions and uncertainties regarding the shape of higher education in the coming years, one trend is clear: we need to be attentive to relevance, excellence, and innovation. While we may feel confident that classroom learning will still be in demand, the classroom teaching of today will undergo tremendous transformations in the direction of the trends mentioned above. By introducing novel ideas for learning and teaching, this book rekindles our enthusiasm for enhanced learning outcomes for our students.

References

Bady, A. (2013, May). The MOOC bubble and the attack on public education. *Academic Matters*, 18. Retrieved online from http://www.academicmatters.ca/2013/05/the-mooc-bubble-and-the-attack-on-public-education/

Calamai, P. (2006, 26 November). At Universities, time for re-examination. *Toronto Star*, p. D3.

Friedman, T. L. (2013, 5 March). The professors' big stage. *New York Times*. Retrieved from http://www.nytimes.com/2013/03/06/opinion/friedman-the-professors-big-stage.html?_r=0

Lawrence, D. (2013). Man and Machine. *Canadian University Report, Globe and Mail*. Retrieved from http://www.theglobeandmail.com/news/national/education/canadian-university-report/man-and-machine-gen-y-combines-creativity-and-passion-with-technology/article4620507/

Mazar, R. (2013). Goodbye class lectures: How to flip your classroom. *Academic Matters*, 80. Retrieved from http://www.universityaffairs.ca/career-advice/career-advice-article/how-to-flip-your-classroom

Millar, E. (2013). Classroom of 2020: The future is very different than you think. *Canadian University Report, Globe and Mail*. Retrieved from http://www.theglobeandmail.com/news/national/education/canadian-university-report/classroom-of-2020-the-future-is-very-different-than-you-think/article4620458

Millar, E. (2012, 4 April). U of T president counters "self-taught" innovator genius myth. *Globe and Mail*.

Naylor, D. (n.d.). Digital synergy for higher education. *U of T Magazine, 40*(4), 4.

Schwartz, M. (2012, 22 March). The Learning & Teaching Office—Ryerson University [Available: http://www.ryerson.ca/lt]

Usher, A. (2009, November). Back to the future. *University Affairs*, 30–35.

About the Contributors

Mehrunnisa Ahmad Ali is the Director of the Graduate Program in Early Childhood Studies at Ryerson University. She teaches in the interdisciplinary graduate programs in Policy Studies and Immigration and Settlement. Her research interests include newcomer children, youth and families, parent–teacher relations, and preparation of teachers and other professionals to work with diverse populations. She is currently writing a book on how the history of colonialism has shaped immigrant integration in Canada.

Annette Bailey is an Assistant Professor in the Daphne Cockwell School of Nursing at Ryerson University. She holds a PhD in Public Health Science and has worked in both public health and clinical settings. Her research focuses on understanding the grief and trauma experiences of survivors of violence. She has conducted research on traumatic stress and resilience among survivors of gun violence. She has published in this area of scholarship as well as in the scholarship of teaching and learning and of health promotion.

Kathryn Church is Director and Associate Professor in the School of Disability Studies at Ryerson University in Toronto. An arts-informed ethnographer, Kathryn is the author of *Forbidden Narratives: Critical Autobiography as Social Science*, curator of the exhibit *Fabrications: Stitching Ourselves Together*, and co-curator of *Out from Under: Disability, History and Things to Remember*, which is now in the permanent collection of the Canadian Human Rights Museum. The recipient of an Ontario Confederation of Faculty Association's Woman of Distinction Award and a David C. Onley Award for Leadership in Accessibility, she is a foundational contributor to the emerging field of Mad Studies.

Linda Cooper is a Professor in the Daphne Cockwell School of Nursing. She has provided educational leadership in the DCSON in the roles of Associate Director of the Ryerson, Centennial, George Brown Collaborative Nursing Degree Program and as Lead Faculty for nursing courses in the Collaborative

Program. She is the recipient of internal and external teaching awards. Her scholarly foci include exposure to violence, creative strategies in the classroom, and student–faculty mentorship. She is involved in the FCS Centre for the Advancement of the Scholarship of Teaching and Learning.

May Friedman blends social work, teaching, research, writing, and parenting. Her passions include social justice and reality TV (she is firmly in favour of living with contradiction). Recent publications include work on digital media transnationalism, gender fluidity, and *Here Comes Honey Boo Boo*. A faculty member in the Ryerson University School of Social Work and Ryerson/York graduate program in Communication and Culture, May lives in downtown Toronto with her partner and four young children.

Usha George is Professor and Dean of the Faculty of Community Services, Ryerson University. Her scholarship focuses on social work with diverse communities, and her research interests are in the areas of newcomer settlement, settlement services, community work with marginalized communities, and international social work. She has completed research projects on the settlement and adaptation issues of newcomer communities in Ontario. Dr. George has extensive academic and administrative experience in India, Ethiopia, Nigeria, and the US. She works with several community agencies on research and knowledge-transfer activities.

Jacqui Gingras, PhD, is an Associate Professor in the Department of Sociology at Ryerson University. She has a particular interest in how health profession students' and professionals' subjectivities are constituted by power and discourse to inform advocacy, policy, and pedagogy. Her research engages feminist autoethnographic, narrative, and arts-informed methods as means to understanding health theory, education, and practice. She has written journal articles and co-authored chapters in *Critical Perspectives in Food Studies* (2012) and *Historical and Critical Perspectives of Obesity in Canada* (forthcoming). She is the recipient of Ryerson University's Research (2010) and Teaching (2009) Awards and is Founding Editor of the online *Journal of Critical Dietetics*.

Corinne Hart is an associate professor in the Daphne Cockwell School of Nursing at Ryerson University, where she teaches community health nursing and practice. Her research examines links between power, status, and professional identity in interdisciplinary health care work as well as professional identity in client-centred care. Her doctoral work used the lens of emotion management to examine the work of personal support workers; she is looking now at how emotion management can be used to investigate concepts such as worker agency, professional identity, and professional power and status. Corinne is also a collaborator in a CIHR-funded project that uses discourse analysis to unpack the history and rhetoric of inter-professional discourse across multiple professions.

A graduate of the Ryerson University School of Nursing, **Aafreen Hassan** is currently focused on program development and health promotion for a diabetes-prevention program at Flemingdon Health Centre. She believes that investing in disease prevention and health promotion can ease the burden on the health care system and help create informed consumers of the health system. Aafreen also has a long-standing passion for pediatric nursing, and works as a floor nurse for children living with disabilities at the Holland Bloorview Kids Rehabilitation Hospital.

Sonya Jancar, RN, BScN, M(HL&M), CRA, CCRP, has been working as a research coordinator in cardiology for five years and is employed at Toronto General Hospital in the Peter Munk Cardiac Centre. Concurrently, she works at Ryerson University as a project coordinator on research projects in the Faculty of Community Services Dean's office. Sonya has for four years been a board member of Sigma Theta Tau International, Lambda Pi Chapter. She has also been active on the RNFOO board as a gala committee member as well as a Co-chair of the IEN committee.

Sanne Kaas-Mason is from Denmark and has an MA from Brock University. Sanne is interested in intergroup prejudice reduction and how individual identification with a group's values informs perceptions of other groups. As project manager for RU Inter-professional at Ryerson University, she works to increase access to education resources and experiential learning opportunities in the Faculty of Community Services—opportunities in the traditional health care sector and in community service locations, to reflect the community lens of schools within the Faculty and the core value of social justice and equity that underlies FCS programs.

V. Logan Kennedy is an alumnus of the Daphne Cockwell School of Nursing at Ryerson University and teaches in the undergraduate program as a sessional instructor. Her teaching focuses on community health and professional development. She has an active research career that focuses on her clinical area of expertise. While pursuing her master's in Nursing, she was from 2009 to 2012 the coordinator of the Writing Skills Initiative.

ABOUT THE CONTRIBUTORS

Ken Moffatt is a Professor in the School of Social Work, Ryerson University, and Adjunct Professor with the School of Social Work, McMaster University. He is interested in cultural studies, postmodern theory, reflective practice, and gender studies as well as symbol creation and meaning making in the context of global neo-liberalism. He is the editor of *Troubled Masculinities: Reimaging Urban Men* (University of Toronto Press, 2012) and is at work on a book for Columbia University Press on reflective postmodern teaching in the helping professions.

Gordon Pon, MSW, PhD, is an Associate Professor in the School of Social Work at Ryerson University. His research interests include anti-racism, anti-colonialism, child welfare, and Asian Canadian Studies.

Jennifer M. Poole is an Associate Professor in the School of Social Work at Ryerson. She is interested in Mad Studies, grief, "mental health," the body, oppression and discrimination, social theory, qualitative research, and all her students past and present. She is currently Director of the MSW program and working on projects on anti-Black sanism, grief, precarious employment, reporting, heart transplantation, and end of life.

Susan Preston has practised social work in child protection and criminal justice systems and with homeless youth. Through critical inquiry that deconstructs neoliberalism and its influence on social work, her research examines government and institutional policies that affect service users, social workers, and students. Susan takes a critical/interpretive stance concerned with interrogating assumptions, practices of power, and social relations enacted through capital. Her prior social work practice included creative arts as part of both clinical practice and social action. Drawing on this experience, Susan incorporates photographs, texts, and graphics into her teaching and research.

Pamela Robinson, PhD, MCIP, RPP, is the Associate Dean, Graduate Studies and Special Projects, in the Faculty of Community Services and an associate professor in the School of Urban and Regional Planning, Ryerson. She is also a registered professional planner. Pamela's research and practice focus on urban sustainability issues with a focus on cities and climate change and the use of civic technology in civic engagement. She serves on the board of directors the Metcalf Foundation and has participated in four Metrolinx Community Advisory Committees. Pamela is an editor of *Urban Sustainability: Reconnecting Space and Place* (University of Toronto Press, 2013) and is a columnist for *Spacing* magazine.

Erin Rudolph, MHSc, RD, is a registered dietitian who has been practising since 2012. She completed her Bachelor of Applied Science in Nutrition and Food along with her Master of Health Science in Nutrition Communication at Ryerson University. She completed her dietetic internship at University Health Network in Toronto. Erin is currently employed as a dietitian in the eating disorders program at Toronto General Hospital, where she works with a large inter-professional team of health care providers. Her research interests are in education in health care and inter-professional practice.

Jasna Krmpotić Schwind, RN, PhD, is Associate Professor of nursing. Through Arts-Informed Narrative Inquiry she explores personal and professional self within professional and therapeutic relationships in education and practice. She developed Narrative Reflective Process (NPR), which is both a data-collection tool and a professional development instrument. This creative self-expression method includes storytelling, metaphors, drawing, creative writing, and reflective dialogue. In her scholarship of teaching-learning, Dr. Schwind utilizes NRP to mentor and support students and peers.

Divine Velasco is a former Bachelor of Science in Nursing student of Annette Bailey. After achieving her Registered Nurse licence in 2012, she worked in Complex Continuing Care at Brampton Civic Hospital for two and a half years caring for patients with medically complex and chronic health conditions. Currently, Divine is pursuing her master's in Nursing at Ryerson University. Her thesis work centres on the trauma experiences of marginalized youth who lost a loved one to gun violence. She is also working at Ryerson University as a Research Assistant for qualitative research projects.

Janice Waddell is an associate dean in the Faculty of Community Services and an Associate Professor in the Daphne Cockwell School of Nursing, Ryerson University. Her teaching and curriculum development experience has centred on nursing education, leadership, and violence against women and children, and her research interests have focused on curriculum-based career planning and development on student and new graduate nurse career resilience, faculty mentorship, student engagement, curriculum design, and transition experiences for nursing students. Her career planning and development work with students was adopted as a national strategy for the Canadian Nurses Student Association (CNSA) for six years. She has won several awards for her contributions to education and the profession.

Samantha Wehbi has an interest in critical perspectives on international social work and activism on a variety of social issues. Her work has included community practice on queer issues, disability rights, and feminist organizing. She has worked as a social development consultant, a program manager, a director of services, and in other positions in community organizations in Canada and in Lebanon, her country of origin. With her background in critical documentary media, Samantha has developed and taught courses in social work practice infused, through social justice and anti-colonial lenses, with creative arts. Her recent photography has focused on neocolonial visual tropes and created alternative visual discourses related to topics of displacement and translocality.

Karline Wilson-Mitchell, RN, RM, CNM, MSN, DNP(C), has practised midwifery since 1992 and has been on the Midwifery Education Program Faculty at Ryerson University since 2008. She has taught at two US universities and practised in three states and two provinces, including an Inuit community in Quebec. Karline has used intellectual partnerships to teach clinical students in placements and tutorials and has supervised student-researchers exploring advocacy for vulnerable populations. Areas of research include perinatal outcomes of refugee and migrant women and newborns, perinatal loss, cultural health beliefs, mental health issues facing newcomer women, psychosocial factors affecting pregnant Jamaican adolescents, and respectful maternity care.

Margareth Zanchetta is a senior educator and researcher with undergraduate and post-graduate university education in the disciplines of Nursing and Education. Both areas of education support her understanding of theoretical aspects of learning. Throughout her career as a clinician nurse in the field of Oncology Nursing, Cardiology and Intensive Care, she had many opportunities to apply her knowledge of Paulo Freire's popular education for self-care, which was a precursor of her interest in issues of health literacy. Her main research interest relies in individual and family health literacy as well as health professionals' awareness of this issue as lived by linguistic minorities. Working with faculty and front-line professionals in several countries, she has experience in issues of global health, health promotion, as well as global cancer education.

Index

Page references followed by *fig* indicate a figure.

Accreditation of Interprofessional Health Education (AIPHE), 10
Addams, Jane, 157
Ali, Mehrunissa Ahmad, 180
"Am I Becoming My Father?" (Vaughan), 167, 168*fig*
art: in classroom, introduction of, 157, 166, 170–71; in community services education, 156; definition of, 157; as form of knowledge production, 171, 172; future research on impact of, 172, 173; impact on learning experience, 172; as method of expression, 156; in midwifery education, 155–56; in multimedia presentations, 169; in nutrition program, 156; as pedagogical tool, 162–64; in personal experience, role of, 160; of queer artists, 167; in queer theories course, 165; in social work classroom, 155, 162, 170; in social work practice, role of, 156, 157, 171, 172–73; in student assignments, 158, 161–65, 171–72; in student posters, 159*fig*; in teaching, scholarship on use of, 155–56; as vehicle to discuss emotions, 166

Bailey, Annette, 6, 180
Baloji, Sammy, 158
Baskin, Cyndy, 91, 97
Beattie, K., 110
Belcher, J., 91
Bellinger, A., 163
Bonner, S. E., 108
Britnell, Judy, 7
Brooker, L., 45

Cadell, S., 161, 164
Canada's population profile, 43–44
Canadian Interprofessional Health Collaborative (CIHC), 16
Canadian Leaders group, 49
Canadian University Report, 178
caregiver: metaphor of, 141
caring: concept of, 151; pedagogy, 94, 103; practices, 101–2
Carr, D., 47
Casey, B., 155
Centre for the Advancement of the Scholarship of Teaching and Learning (CASTL), 2–3
Chamberlayne, P., 156
Chambon, A., 156
Chandler, Mielle, 94
Charon, Rita, 1
Church, Kathryn, 91, 180
Clandinin, D. J., 46, 48
classroom learning: benefits of, 178
Collins, Patricia Hill, 95
Colquhoun, D., 14
community mothering, 94–95
competency framework, 16, 17

Confessions (Saint Augustine), 46–47
Connelly, M., 46, 48
conscientization: idea of, 11–12
Cormier, David, 177
Couchman, W., 171, 172
Coulter, I., 14
critical development: educational approaches to, 59–60; ode to, 59
critical pedagogy: characteristics of, 11–12, 62; idea of conscientization in, 11–12, 19; intellectual partnership within, 64; interprofessional education and, 19; potential of, 19–20
critical thinking, 59, 60
curriculum development: students involvement in, 107–8, 116; Weimer's model for, 107

Dahlberg, G., 45
Davies, L., 155
Dewey, J., 138, 139, 142
dialogue: as academic narrative, 77
Diamond, Timothy, 85n1
Disability Studies, 75–76, 78
Downes, Stephen, 178

education: banking model of, 90; changes in, 3; colonial, 97; ideas of Enlightenment and, 90; neglect of workplace in traditional, 79–80; practices of neoliberal, 91; role of educators, 170; traditional pedagogies in, 95
Eisner, E., 162, 171, 172
Ellsworth, E., 118
emotions, 166, 167
ethic of care: importance of listening, 45; in public service, model of, 55; strategy for learning, 43; studies of, 44–45
experience, 138, 139
experiential learning, 180

experiential teaching–learning tools, 139

Faculty of Community Services (FCS): "caring" professions programs, 43; interdisciplinary education, 11; mandate of, 1–2; schools and programs, 10; writing skill development initiative, 23
faculty–student interaction: importance of, 179–80
Families and Health course: assignments, 112, 127–28, 129; book chapter/journal article/film review, 127, 132; class discussions, 120; contribution to scholarship, 121; course facilitation, 119; critique of equitability of, 117–18; deliverables of, 127–31; description of, 110–11; exams, 128, 129; final exam essay, 130–31; impact on students, 112, 119, 122; implications of, 121–22; learning logs, 127–28, 132–33; objectives, 111, 119, 123–24; outcomes, 116–17, 120–21; papers evaluation, 128, 129; participation, 113–14, 129–30; "peer prepping" activity, 127; resources, 111, 123; responsibilities of instructors, 113; student feedback, 116–17, 120; students' role in development of, 111–12, 113; teaching assistant manual, 123–24; team-based midterm, 129; teams activity, 111, 112, 125–26, 128; theme selection, 112, 125
family narrative documentation project: combination of research and practice, 55; confidentiality aspect, 53–54; goal of, 53; learning curve of family support workers, 49–52, 53; learning curve of project leaders, 52–53; participating families,

50–51, 53; positive impact of, 54, 55; potential risks for practitioners, 55; practice of "receptive attention," 51; time-consuming tasks of, 52
family narratives, 43, 47, 48–49
Fenwick, Tara: academic status of, 85n5; on contemporary workplace, 81; conversations with, 78, 84; expression of gratitude to, 85n1; on knowledge, 80; on neglect of workplace in education, 79–80; on problem of training, 78; vision of learning, 76–77
Fiese, B. H., 46
Foucault, Michel, 63, 90, 96, 101
Fox, A. L., 156
Frazee, Catherine, 85n2
Freeman, Richard, 75
Freidson, E., 14
Freire, Paulo, 11, 60, 62, 66, 67–68
Friedman, May: on caring pedagogy, 94, 180; as educator, 99; motherhood experience, 92, 93; scholarly work of, 93; teaching experience of, 98–99, 102; vision of learning, 178
Friere, Paulo, 90

Gaffield, Chad, 179
Gambrill, E., 48
George, Usha, 7
Gilligan, Carol, 44
Gingras, Jacqui: as course facilitator, 119–20; as instructor, 113, 114; reflection on Families and Health course, 114–15, 120; on student engagement in classroom, 180
Gurm, B., 97, 102

Hafford-Letchfield, T., 171, 172
Hankivsky, O., 44
Harrison, L., 157, 161

Hart, Michael Anthony, 91, 97, 181
Hassan, Aafreen, 71
health care systems: differences across provinces, 51; in Ontario, 10; person-centred approach in, 138
health education, 12, 138
health professions, 14
Hewett, C. M., 121
higher education: budgetary constraints, 177; future trends in, 181; idea of "inverted classroom," 179; in-person vs. online instructions, 178–79; interdisciplinary opportunities, 180–81; massively open online courses (MOOCS), 177; new models of, 179; role of technology in, 177, 181
Hine, Lewis, 157
Hinyard, L., 45
hooks, bell, 118
humanness of care: concept of, 138, 140; holistic teaching of, 141
Huss, E., 157, 163, 164, 172
Hyman, D., 121, 170

images: of indigenous peoples, 163; labels and, 164; as pedagogical tool, 162–63; in teaching, use of, 163–64
intellectual partnership process: acknowledgement of students' ideas, 66–67; components of teacher's work, 66; knowledge development, 67–68; role of critical reflection, 66; schematic representation of, 65*fig*
intellectual partnerships (IPs): benefits of, 61–62, 69; characteristics of, 61; creativity and critical thinking, 68–69; critical development of students, 65*fig*, 67, 68, 71; critical dialogue, 63, 68; critical pedagogy and, 64; definition of, 60–61; impact on students, 62, 64, 69–70, 71;

knowledge creation, 63, 64; power relations in, 63–64; priority of critical self-reflexivity, 64; proposed model of, 65; schematic representation of, 65*fig*; skills development, 61, 70; subjectivities and contradictions of, 63; teacher–student relationships, 60, 71
interprofessional competencies, 16
interprofessional education (IPE): assumptions about, 11, 14; challenges of promotion of, 14–15; focus on health care professions, 11; *vs.* interdisciplinary teaching and learning, 13, 15; literature on, 9, 11; long-term impact, 15; marketing strategy, 17; meaning of, 13–14, 16; principles of critical pedagogy in, 9–10, 17, 18–20; at Ryerson University, 9–10; as teaching strategy, 9, 10–11; workshops, 18

Jackson, Nancy: academic status of, 85n6; on competent actors, 80; on contemporary workplace, 81; conversations with, 80–81, 84; on definition of learning, 76; expression of gratitude to, 85n1, 85n3; personality of, 81
James, R., 110
Jancar, Sonya, 180
Jelly, K., 103
jobs in global economy, 78
Johnston, D. D., 93

Kaas-Mason, Sanne, 181
Kalinowski, C., 101
Kennedy, V. Logan, 180
Knight, C., 91
knowledge: academic *vs.* working, 79; conditions for emergence of, 67–68; as continuous process, 80; ideas of Enlightenment and creation of, 90; in intellectual partnership, 63, 64; nature of, 80; perceptions of, 79; in practice professions, 102–3; in relation to art, 171; as substantive "thing," 79; in teaching, applications of, 121
Kreber, C., 89, 92
Kreuter, M., 45
Kuper, A., 14

Lakey, B., 118
Lavallée, Lynn, 91
Lawrence, Diana, 181
learner-centred approach: definition of, 110
learners, 79, 84
learning: characteristic of optimal, 110; definition and context of, 76, 107; face-to-face interactions in, 84; false conceptualization of, 78; feminists debate about, 82; forms of, 92; quality of, 110; simulation in, 118; in work, 76–77, 80
Learning, Inc., 111
learning-centred teaching model, 103
learning in work: *vs.* learning for work, 80
learning styles, 109*t*
Lee, K. W., 14
Leonard, K., 171, 172
LGBTTQ (lesbian, gay, bisexual, transgendered, transsexual, queer) community, 165–66
Listening to Families: Reframing Services, 49
Lymberry, E. F., 157

Mad studies, 96–97
Marshall, H. L., 160
massively open online courses (MOOCS), 177, 178
maternal pedagogies, 94
McCallister, C., 119

Merleau-Ponty, Maurice, 90, 96
Moffatt, Ken, 180
Moss, P., 45
Mosston's Spectrum, 108
motherhood: career and, 92, 93; modern discourse of, 92–93, 95; myths of good, 93; perception of, 104n1; scholarship on, 94
Munro, Will, 167
Munt, S., 167
Mykitiuk, Roxanne, 96

narrative: critical analysis of, 48; definition of, 45–46; first- and second-order, 47–48; as form of communication, 46, 47; functions of, 46; in medicine, 1; *vs.* story, 46; in teaching and learning, use of, 46–47
Narrative Inquiry, 137
Narrative Reflective process (NRP): in access to tacit knowledge, 140; benefits of, 147; characteristic of, 140; definition of, 137; in educational process, 138, 139, 148–49; as experiential teaching–learning approach, 146–47; general approaches to, 143–45; implications for teaching–learning scholarship, 146–47; importance of, 145; key components of, 140; metaphoric images in, 144, 148, 149, 150–51; in nursing education, 142–43; participants' needs, 143; potential impact on curricula, 147; purpose of, 143; small group exercises, 148–49, 150, 151; story sharing, 144, 148, 150, 151; student engagement in, 141, 146; teacher engagement in, 142–42; in teaching–learning context, 143, 148
National Assembly of Colored Women: motto of, 104n2
National Commission on Writing, 23

National Survey of Student Engagement (NSSE), 25–26
Naylor, David, 178, 179
neoliberal education, 91
Ngo, Johnson, 167
Noddings, N., 94
nursing, 14–15, 141
nurturing: benefits of, 97; definition of, 90; as pedagogical practice, 89, 102

Okri, Ben, 144
Ontario Coalition of Family Support Programs, 48–49
Ontario Institute for Studies in Education (OISE), 85n6
Ontario Leaders group, 48–49, 52–53
Orwin, Clifford, 178
othermothering model, 94–95

Pecukonis, E., 91
pedagogic resonance, 103–4
personal knowing, 137
Phillips, C., 163
photography, 158, 159–60
Poetics (Aristotle), 46
Polack, R. J., 158
Pon, G., 66
Poole, Jennifer: as educator, 99; relations with students, 102; student feedback about, 100–101; on teaching as caregiving, 180; teaching experience of, 90, 97, 100, 101
"post-conventional" thinking, 96
Preston, Susan, 180
professional growth: motherhood and, 92
professions: sociology of, 14
public service: client-centred approach to, 44; ethics of care in, 55; family-centred care model, 45; patient-centred approach to, 45; population change and, 43–44; slow responsiveness to change, 43

queer artists, 167
queer people: emotional life of, 166
queer theories course, 165
Quinney, L., 47

Ramsden, P., 103
Reissman, C. K., 47
researchers: *vs.* teachers, 3
resistance practices, 101
Rinaldi, C., 45
Risser, P., 101
Rogers, Carl, 44
Rosler, Martha, 158
Rudolph, Erin, 113, 115–16, 119, 180
RU Interprofessional: Collaborating for Healthy Communities (RU IP), 10, 16, 17–18
Ryerson's Interpersonal Skills Training Centre (ISTC), 48
Ryerson University: competency framework for, 16; Disability Studies programs, 75–76; environmental scan, 12, 13; Interpersonal Skills Teaching Centre, 118; interprofessional education, 9–10, 12–13; survey of student experience, 26; value of engagement of students in, 70; writing skill development initiative, 23

Salhani, D., 14
scholarship of teaching and learning (SoTL), 1, 2, 4–5, 6, 76
Schwartz, Michelle, 179
Sedgwick, Edie Kofovsky, 167
Sevenhuijsen, S., 45
Shale, S., 103
shame: artistic representation of, 167–68, 169
Shildrick, Margrit, 96
Siemens, George, 178
Silver, Sarabeth, 59
Sinclair, Raven, 91

Smith, Dorothy, 77, 85n1
Smith, M., 156
social justice, 118
social work, 156, 157, 161, 171
social work education, 171
social work practice, 172–73
Spagnola, M., 46
storytelling, 144–45
students: anxieties of, 117; art-based assignments for, 161–62, 164–65; in classroom, power of, 118; creative artwork of, 157; critical development of, 59; in critical dialogue, 68; dislike of large classes, 100; emotional responses of, 169; engagement with photography, 157–60; face-to-face interactions with instructors, 84; family narratives creation, 47; fear of responsibility, 117; feedback on non-traditional course delivery, 116–17; field experience, 54; image analysis, 159–60, 163–64; intellectual partnership with, 60, 62, 65, 69; involvement in scholarly work, 67, 68; letter-writing exercises, 145; multimedia presentations of, 169; Narrative Reflective process and, 138, 141, 144, 146; posters of, 159*fig*; relations with teachers, 62–63, 67; view of academic writing by, 77
Swanson, D. H., 93

teachers: classroom experience, 80; contribution to intellectual partnership, 65; dominant status of, 62; Narrative Reflective process and, 141–42; relations with students, 62–63, 67; *vs.* researchers, 3
teaching: aim of, 103; approaches to, 3–4, 103, 121; conception of, 4–5, 84; evaluation of, 99, 102; ideas of Enlightenment in, 104; incorpora-

tion of experience in, 98; integration art-based assignments in, 171–72; investigations into equitable, 116; meaning of, 90; notion of good, 97; pedagogic resonance of, 103–4; reflection on intimacy in, 89; research grants and, 3; role of educators in, 93, 170; as scholarship, 170; simulation in, 118; as traditional pedagogical practice, 160–61

Teaching as Scholarship (Gingras): acknowledgements, 7; central idea of, 6; planning process, 4; purpose of, 5; relevance to educators, 6–7; significance of title, 3; structure of, 6

teaching assistants (TAs). *See* writing teaching assistants

teaching dossier development, 6

teaching-learning philosophy, 139

teaching styles, 108, 109*t*, 110

Tomkins, S., 169

training: new model of, 84; in North America, obsolete system of, 82; tradition of vocational, 83

Trigwell, K., 103

T-style education, 179

university educators, 91

Usher, Alex, 181

Vardi, I., 25

Vaughan, R. M., 167

Velasco, Divine, 71

Vocat, Daryl, 166*fig*, 167

Wade-Gayles, Gloria, 99

Walton, P., 160, 171

Wehbi, Samantha, 180

Weiman, Carl, 178

Weimer, M., 107, 110, 114

Whitehead, C., 14

Who Are You! (Volat), 166*fig*, 167

Wilson-Mitchell, Karline, 67

Witz, A., 14

Woodhouse, R. A., 103

working knowledge, 79

working practice, 82

workplace, 81–83

workplace learning, 76

writing: as form of inquiry, 77

writing skills, 23, 24, 25, 26

Writing Skills Initiative (WSI): administration of, 31; assessment questionnaires, 32–33; coordinator's role in, 31–32; curricular framework, 27; development of, 26; evaluation of, 32–34; feedback on, 33–34; focus groups sessions, 33, 39; future directions of, 35; as hybrid of three forms of scholarship, 34; integration in academic programs, 26–27; student engagement in, 32, 34–35; as teaching methodology, 34

writing teaching assistants: classroom activities, 37; developmental writing feedback, 28–29; manual monthly activities, 36–38, 123–24; orientation of, 30, 36; preparation duties, 30; professional development activities, 30–31, 37, 38; qualifications of, 28; relationships with students, 35; role in writing skills initiative, 27–28; tasks and responsibilities of, 29*t*

Zanchetta, Margareth, 68, 69

Zwyno, Gosha, 114